associative illusions
of memory

ESSAYS IN COGNITIVE PSYCHOLOGY

North American Editors:
Henry L. Roediger, III, *Washington University in St. Louis*
James R. Pomerantz, *Rice University*

European Editors:
Alan D. Baddeley, *University of York*
Vicki Bruce, *University of Edinburgh*
Jonathan Grainger, *Université de Provence*

Essays in Cognitive Psychology is designed to meet the need for rapid publication of brief volumes in cognitive psychology. Primary topics will include perception, movement and action, attention, memory, mental representation, language, and problem solving. Furthermore, the series seeks to define cognitive psychology in its broadest sense, encompassing all topics either informed by, or informing, the study of mental processes. As such, it covers a wide range of subjects including computational approaches to cognition, cognitive neuroscience, social cognition, and cognitive development, as well as areas more traditionally defined as cognitive psychology. Each volume in the series will make a conceptual contribution to the topic by reviewing and synthesizing the existing research literature, by advancing theory in the area, or by some combination of these missions. The principal aim is that authors will provide an overview of their own highly successful research program in an area. It is also expected that volumes will, to some extent, include an assessment of current knowledge and identification of possible future trends in research. Each book will be a self-contained unit supplying the advanced reader with a well-structured review of the work described and evaluated.

Titles in preparation

Gernsbacher: *Suppression and Enhancement in Language Comprehension*
Park: *Cognition and Aging*
Mulligan: *Implicit Memory*
Surprenant & Neath: *Principles of Memory*
Brown: *Tip-of-the-tongue Phenomenon*

Recently published
Cowan: *Working Memory Capacity*
McNamara: *Semantic Priming*
Brown: *The Déjà Vu Experience*
Coventry & Garrod: *Seeing, Saying, and Acting*
Robertson: *Space, Objects, Minds, & Brains*
Cornoldi & Vecchi: *Visuo-spatial Working Memory and Individual Differences*
Sternberg et al.: *The Creativity Conundrum*
Poletiek: *Hypothesis-testing Behaviour*
Garnham: *Mental Models and the Interpretations of Anaphora*
Engelkamp: *Memory for Actions*

For continually updated information about published and forthcoming titles in the Essays in Cognitive Psychology series, please visit: **www.psypress.com/essays**

associative
illusions of memory

false memory research in DRM and related tasks

DAVID A. GALLO

University of Chicago

Psychology Press
Taylor & Francis Group

NEW YORK AND HOVE

Published in 2006 by
Psychology Press
Taylor & Francis Group
270 Madison Avenue
New York, NY 10016
www.psypress.com

Published in Great Britain by
Psychology Press
Taylor & Francis Group
27 Church Road
Hove, East Sussex BN3 2FA
www.psypress.co.uk

Psychology Press is an imprint of the Taylor & Francis Group, an informa business

Typeset by Macmillan India Ltd, Bangalore, India
Printed and bound in the USA by Sheridan Books, Inc., Ann Arbor, MI, on acid-free paper
Cover design by Lisa Dynan

10 9 8 7 6 5 4 3 2 1

Library of Congress Cataloging-in-Publication Data

Gallo, David A.
    Associative illusions of memory: false memory research in DRM and related tasks /
David A. Gallo.
    p. ; cm. – (Essays in cognitive psychology)
Includes bibliographical references and index.
ISBN-13: 978-1-84169-414-6 (hardback : alk. paper)
ISBN-10: 1-84169-414-2 (hardback : alk. paper) 1. Recovered memory. 2. False memory syndrome.
I. Title. II. Series.
[DNLM: 1. Memory—physiology. 2. Association. 3. Illusions. 4. Psychological Tests. 5. Repression.
WL 102 G176a 2006]
    RC455.2.F35G35 2006
    616.89′14–dc22
                                                    2006016486

ISBN13: 978-1-84169-414-6 (hbk)

ISBN10: 1-84169-414-2 (hbk)

To Dad and Mom... the truth is out there

CONTENTS

Preface

The ability to remember the seemingly infinite episodes of our lives is a miracle of the human mind. But memory is not always accurate, and we sometimes think that an event that never happened actually did. Such false memories can be benign, as when we entertain each other (and our own egos) with exaggerated personal stories that are eventually believed to be truthful. Other times they can have grave implications, as when an eyewitness falsely recognizes an innocent person as a murderer.

Over the past decade or so there has been a boom in the scientific study of certain types of false memories. These are false memories of events that did not occur but are related, via associations and/or similarity, to events that did occur. Hundreds of researchers have contributed to these experiments, using a variety of tools from cognitive psychology, neuropsychology, neuroscience, and personality/social psychology. This essay provides a detailed review of this research enterprise, with implications for contemporary theories of memory, consciousness, and cognition.

Research on associative memory errors has a long and varied history (discussed in Chapter 1), but most of the recent research involves a family of tasks that are all quite similar: Subjects study lists of related stimuli, such as associated words or perceptually similar pictures, and are then given recall or recognition tests. As discussed in Chapter 2, these tasks elicit false memories of nonstudied stimuli, memories that often are subjectively compelling and hard to avoid. This collection of tasks therefore has been adopted as the paradigmatic demonstration of laboratory-based false memories. Chapters 3–6 provide a review of the behavioral findings from those experiments using younger adults (usually college students) as subjects, as well as the major theoretical developments. The content of these chapters is technical, with meticulous attention to basic research methods and results. Chapters 7–10 provide a review of research that has applied these studies of memory distortion in the domains of individual differences, development and aging, brain damage and other special populations, pharmacological agents, and neuroimaging. To many people these are the most interesting topics, and they highlight how basic and applied research can (and should) build upon each other. Chapter 11 provides a general summary and some possible future directions.

I am thankful to Henry (Roddy) Roediger for suggesting this manuscript. As my graduate mentor at Washington University, I owe a great deal of indebtedness to Roddy for guiding my thinking on many of the topics reviewed here, as I do to many other members (past and present) of the powerhouse on human memory research in St. Louis. I am also grateful to Dan Schacter for encouraging this venture during my postdoctoral fellowship, and to Jim Lampinen, Benton Pierce, and Valerie Reyna for their scholarly comments on the first draft. Finally, to bring things full circle, I thank John Seamon for kindling my interest in human memory exactly one decade ago. Hopefully, my collaborations in other areas of psychology will be as rewarding as all of these, forged while studying memory illusions.

David A. Gallo
University of Chicago

BACKGROUND

Associations and Errors through History

From Aristotle's early musings on the mind to computational models of neural networks, the concept of association—or the hypothetical link between mental representations—has reigned supreme in understandings of memory. Of particular relevance to this essay is the role of associations in episodic memory, or the ability to consciously recollect the events or episodes of one's past (Tulving, 1972, 1983). This form of memory evolved to provide us with a link between present thoughts or environmental cues and relevant information from our past, and this linking power often is attributed to mental associations. The classic view of association, as advocated centuries ago by philosophers such as Thomas Hobbes, John Locke, and James Mill, was based on the intuition that one idea or memory tends to meaningfully lead to another during the course of thought. A common assumption was that the mind forms associations between contiguous events (those close in time or space) and between similar events (those with similar meanings or sensory attributes). At a later point in time, thinking of one event could activate the other via the associative link that was stored in memory.

This philosophical doctrine has always influenced psychology. William James' (1890) theory of memory, as outlined in his definitive *Principles of*

Psychology, echoed that of the philosophers before him. For James, memory was based on the associative structure of traces in the brain:

> The machinery of recall is thus the same as the machinery of association, and the machinery of association, as we know, is nothing but the elementary law of habit in the nerve-centres. ... Retention of an experience is, in short, but another name for the possibility of thinking it again, or the tendency to think it again, with its past surroundings. Whatever accidental cue may turn this tendency into actuality, the permanent ground of the tendency itself lies in the organized neural paths by which the cue calls up the experience on the proper occasion, together with its past associates, the sense that the self was there, the belief that it really happened, etc., etc. ... These habit-worn paths of association are a clear rendering of what authors mean by 'predispositions,' 'vestiges,' 'traces,' etc., left in the brain by past experience. Most writers leave the nature of these vestiges vague; few think of explicitly assimilating them to channels of association. (pp. 654–655)

Few modern scientists would deny these general assertions, although they could add that cellular long-term potentiation might forge the associations between "nerve-centres," that specialized brain structures such as the hippocampus seem to associate (or bind together) "experiences" or "past surroundings" that are represented in distributed cortical areas, or that certain regions of prefrontal cortex are involved in making sense of retrieved information, as well as "the sense that the self was there" and "the belief that it really happened."

In addition to specific episodic memories, associations are relevant to memories for more general knowledge about the world. Each of us carries a large corpus of knowledge in our heads, including specific concepts, abstract ideas, language, and relationships between "things" in the universe. Such general knowledge, or semantic memory, is continually accessed as we try to make sense of the events that we experience, and as we encode episodic memories about these events (see Tulving, 1972). According to many theories, this information is organized and accessed through associative connections. The result can be considered an elaborate associative web of general knowledge about the world and about our particular experiences within it.

The brain relies on associations to accomplish great feats of memory, but like all biological systems the brain is not perfect. Even the healthy brain can make computational errors, leading to a variety of perceptual and cognitive illusions (for an overview see Pohl, 2004). In the same way, associations sometimes can lead our memories astray. Most everyone has had the experience of remembering events (or features of events) that did not occur in a context, but that were in some way associated to events that did occur. Students of memory have described such associative illusions of memory for quite some time, although intensive research into their origins is a relatively recent development.

This chapter provides a brief historical background to the research reviewed in the remaining chapters. Broad historical reviews of associationism in memory already exist (e.g., Anderson & Bower, 1973), as do historical reviews of research on memory illusions and distortions (e.g., Roediger, 1996; Schacter, 1995). Of particular relevance here is the intersection of these two areas: How have different thinkers conceptualized memory errors and associations over time? As reviewed by Roediger, McDermott, and Robinson (1998), associative theories of memory have a long history, but only recently have theorists focused on how associations can cause episodic false memories. Nevertheless, historical trends have greatly impacted current research and modern ideas. References to associative memory errors are nearly as old as the field of psychology itself (Kirkpatrick, 1894), and as experimental methods and theories have changed over time so too have the types of memory errors that were studied as well as the role (and definition) of associations in the resulting theories.

□ EARLY ASSOCIATIONISM

In his historical review of memory research, Burnham (1889) devoted an entire section to what he called "paramnesia," referring to "pseudo-reminiscences," "illusions," or "hallucinations" of memory. Burnham traced references to illusory memories as far back as Saint Augustine in medieval times, but mostly focused on observations made by influential 19th century thinkers such as James Sully, John Hughlings Jackson, Théodule-Armand Ribot, and Emil Kraepelin. Of particular relevance here was Kraepelin's idea of "associirende Erinnerungsfälschungen"—or associatively based memory errors—in which "a present perception calls up by association pseudo-reminiscences of something analogous or related in the past" (Burnham, 1889, p. 433). An example might be walking through a park with a friend and mistakenly remembering that one had done so before, when in fact they had been with a different friend. These and other ideas adeptly presaged modern research on topics such as imagination-based errors, déjà vu, source confusions, unconscious attributions, and vague feelings of familiarity. Of course, there were few (if any) experimental studies of these ideas, which were mostly based on introspection, anecdotes, or informal observations of memory abnormalities following brain damage. As Burnham admitted at the outset of his treatise, his examples represented "a class of phenomena long known, yet but little investigated" (p. 431).

In fact, at the time of Burnham's (1889) review, the experimental study of human memory was only a few years in the making. The earliest research on memory, at least by modern standards, often is attributed to Ebbinghaus (1885), who studied the serial learning of lists of nonsense syllables (e.g., DOQ, ZEH, XOT, and so on). Ebbinghaus was primarily interested in the formation and retention of associations, and so he measured how repeated practice (across testing sessions) facilitated the learning of the order of the items in each list. Although his methods had a strong influence on subsequent research, they left little room for the study of pre-existing associations or knowledge on false memories. Indeed, the whole point of using nonsense syllables was to avoid the potential influence of pre-existing associations and meaningfulness on memory performance. (Although, as demonstrated by Glaze (1928) and Hull (1933), even nonwords can be meaningfully processed, so Ebbinghaus' hope of avoiding pre-existing knowledge in memory experiments went unfulfilled.)

The fact that Ebbinghaus did not focus on false memories does not imply that memory errors for such simple stimuli could not occur. In a classic demonstration of errors in immediate serial recall, Conrad (1964) found that subjects who tried to recall a visually presented string of letters (e.g., M-T-S-C-X-V) often would falsely recall letters with similar sounds (M-T-F-C-X-B). No doubt Ebbinghaus encountered analogous errors in his serial recall experiments. Such errors have been explained by acoustic recoding in short-term memory, so that letters with similar sounds would be confused. This phenomenon provides a good example of how pre-existing knowledge associated with incoming stimuli (in this case, their phonemic code) can influence the processing of those stimuli. Even with the simplest stimuli, our brain activates associated information from memory and this process can lead to memory errors.

E. A. Kirkpatrick (1894) published one of the first laboratory demonstrations of memory errors based on meaningful or conceptual associations. In his experiments, Kirkpatrick read a few lists of common objects for subjects to recall. Although his primary interest was in other variables (e.g., age and gender differences on recall), an incidental observation made at the end of his report is of central interest here. He noted that "...when such words as 'spool,' 'thimble,' 'knife' were pronounced [to students] many students at once thought of 'thread,' 'needle,' 'fork,' which are so frequently associated with them. The result was that many gave those words [on the recall test] as belonging to the list" (p. 608). Kirkpatrick's observations nicely presage the associative response later proposed by Underwood (1965), discussed in the next section, and show how studying one word can lead to falsely remembering a nonstudied associate on a recall test. Kirkpatrick did not present any numeric data to support his observations, but we can assume that false recall did not occur very often in his task—at least not in a systematic way. Kirkpatrick used lists of mostly unrelated words, so that associative intrusions ostensibly would have been idiosyncratic to each subject, depending on their individual associations to the study words. In any event, more rigorous research on the sorts of associative memory errors that Kirkpatrick had noticed did not arise until at least half a century later.

Other early experimental investigations of associative processes in memory can be found throughout the famous works of animal learning theorists, such as Ivan Pavlov, Edward Thorndike, and Clark Hull. A review of these research areas is well beyond the present scope, and the types of associations that were studied are very different from those discussed above in the context of recalling letters or words. It is important to realize, though, that the principles developed from animal learning studies motivated the field of behaviorism that dominated experimental psychology, and associative theories of memory, in the United States in the early 1900s. The central tenet of behaviorism (or at least the extreme version initially advocated by John Watson) was that the past influences behavior through an associative link between a stimulus (S) and a learned response (R). Under this doctrine, known as S→R psychology, researchers primarily were interested in specifying the conditions under which various stimuli could lead to a response, and were resistant to proposing theories regarding the mental processes that could potentially mediate this relationship. Correspondingly, the more "mental" quality of associations (e.g., how pre-existing knowledge and meaning influence processing) was mostly left out of the equation.

Like the Ebbinghaus paradigm, this framework left little room for the study of pre-existing associations on false memories, but the importance of meaningful associations could be demonstrated with these methods too. For instance, a well-known phenomenon in the conditioning literature is that of "stimulus-generalization," in which a behavior that was trained to occur in response to an arbitrary stimulus (e.g., salivating on hearing a bell, because the bell would be accompanied with food) was then found to occur in response to a perceptually similar but novel stimulus (a buzzer). Importantly, this sort of generalization also occurs for semantically similar stimuli, such as related words in human conditioning experiments (e.g., Lacey & Smith, 1954). Even new stimuli can elicit learned responses, as long as those stimuli activate the trained stimulus via a pre-existing association. An analogous episodic memory phenomenon is false recognition of a new event or word due to its association or similarity to an old one (this effect is discussed later in this chapter). These are very different phenomena, of course, but the common idea is that similar events or stimuli can be mentally confused, eliciting a learned response in one case, and false memory in the other.

Both the Ebbinghaus tradition and behaviorism had strong influences on early research in human memory (or, more appropriately, human "learning" research). In his seminal book, McGeoch (1942) summarized much of the work in the years after Ebbinghaus (1885), which relied on tasks such as nonsense syllable learning, paired-associate learning, and various perceptual-motor activities (e.g., maze learning). Associations continued to dominate theoretical descriptions of memory, including memory errors. For instance, associatively based interference played a prominent role in early research on the learning of simple skills (e.g., maze completion). Many learning errors were conceptualized as "negative transfer," or the inhibition of new learning by strong associations to an older, irrelevant skill (e.g., the solution to a different maze). The idea of similarity again played an important role, although not necessarily semantic similarity, as the degree of transfer was found to be a function of the perceptual/motor similarity between the two tasks.

The study of "anticipatory errors" is also relevant. Such errors were commonly observed on rote-learning tasks in which the subject would have to master a sequence through repeated learning attempts (e.g., repeated study and serial recall of the same sequence of numbers). Anticipatory errors reflected the fact that subjects sometimes recalled an item earlier in the sequence than it actually had occurred, ostensibly because of an erroneous association formed at an earlier stage in learning. At the time, these types of errors were not considered episodic false memories, but instead were seen as specific instances of the more general principles of learning that equally could apply to motor skills. Errors that more appropriately would be considered as episodic false memories were known, such as those demonstrated by Bartlett (1932). However, such findings did not yet have much influence on mainstream learning and memory research in North America. In McGeoch's (1942) tome, only 6 out of 633 pages were devoted to these sorts of errors, which were readily assimilated into the basic learning principles of motivation and transfer. This state of affairs did not change much even in the revision of McGeoch (1942) that was published a decade later (McGeoch & Irion, 1952).

☐ THE VERBAL LEARNING TRADITION

This strong associative tradition developed into the methods and theories of the so-called verbal learning tradition (for overviews see Hall, 1971 and Kausler, 1974). This area was heavily influenced by S→R theorizing, and much research was aimed at understanding the basic processes in the learning, transfer, and forgetting of various kinds of associations (e.g., forward, backward, contextual, mediating, inter-item, intra-item, and remote). Perhaps the most popular task during this era was the paired-associate learning technique, which was developed by one of William James' most influential students, Mary Calkins (Calkins, 1894). (Of course, serial learning tasks continued to be used, and later on free recall and recognition tasks gained prominence.) In the paired-associate task, which had dozens of variations, subjects would study several lists of word pairs (or other types of stimuli) and then be tested with one word as a recall cue for the other. The main variable of interest was the number of trials that it would take subjects to learn to pair stimuli with responses, or how easily they could relearn these associations following interpolated activity of various sorts.

One relevant finding from the paired-associate literature was that learning one stimulus-response pair (e.g., A-B) could later interfere with the learning of a new response to the same stimulus (e.g., A-C), and such proactive interference was proportional to the similarity between the two response terms. For instance, when trying to learn the pair "willing-unclean," Morgan and Underwood (1950) found that subjects would often recall "dirty" instead of "unclean" if they had previously learned the pairing "willing-dirty." The learning of multiple responses to the same stimulus was thought to cause response competition or blocking at the time of retrieval. These sorts of data were prominent in the development of interference theories of forgetting, which dominated research on human memory from the 1930s to the 1970s (and are still relevant today; see Wixted, 2004). Such intrusion errors closely approximate what we would consider now to be episodic false memories (or source memory errors), although the research methods of the times usually did not measure whether the subject believed that they were retrieving the correct response when they had retrieved the incorrect one. The subjective belief that one is remembering something correctly, when in fact it was incorrect, is the defining feature of an episodic false memory (or "illusion"), but such ideas rarely were explored in the early verbal learning literature. Instead, such intrusions were seen as systematic byproducts of the associative processes, and it was these associative processes that were of central interest.

With more direct relevance to the idea of false memories, Underwood (1965) provided one of the earliest empirical demonstrations of associatively based false recognition. In his seminal study, college students received a list of 100 words, some of which were repeated, and for each word they had to indicate whether they thought it had been previously presented in the list. The critical manipulation was that some unrepeated words (the lures) were associated to words that had been presented earlier (e.g., "rough" was a lure related to the studied word "smooth").

Underwood found that subjects were more likely to falsely recognize related lures than unrelated lures (lures without strong associates on the list). This effect was greatest when the related studied word (e.g., smooth) had been presented three times prior to the presentation of the lure (rough), or when several related words had been studied (e.g., studying "sugar," "bitter," and "candy" caused subjects to later falsely recognize "sweet"). Underwood used the concept of an "implicit associative response" to explain these false recognition effects. The idea was that, on encountering the stimulus word (smooth), associated words were implicitly activated (or mentally generated) as a response (rough). As a result, when the subject later encountered the nonstudied associate (rough), they mistakenly thought that it had been presented in the list.

Underwood's (1965) study inspired dozens of similar investigations of false recognition (e.g., Anisfeld & Knapp, 1968; Cramer & Eagle, 1972; Hall & Kozloff, 1970, 1973; Kausler & Settle, 1973; MacLeod & Nelson, 1976; Paul, 1979; Vogt & Kimble, 1973; Wallace, 1968). Although Underwood's (1965) study focused on pre-existing associations, Wallace (1967) and others (e.g., Saegert, 1971) showed that associations to unrelated words that were recently learned in the laboratory could cause false recognition (using a paired-associates technique). In general, all of these studies probed associative influences on false recognition, such as the strength, type, and direction of the associative connections between studied words and their associated lures. The implicit associative response hypothesis played a central role in these investigations, and this and other ideas clearly harked back to the S→R theories in earlier verbal learning tasks. As an alternative to this associative activation process or to the idea that the nonstudied word literally "pops into mind" during the study phase, some researchers focused on semantic similarity or feature overlap theories. The idea was that different features of a studied word could be encoded (e.g., meaning, orthography, etc.), and that a lure would be falsely recognized if it contained features that overlapped with the features stored in memory (e.g., Anisfeld & Knapp, 1968; Fillenbaum, 1969; Grossman & Eagle, 1970). The debate between these two explanations of false recognition—associative activation versus semantic feature overlap—still rages on today, although some major gains have been made. We will return to this issue in Chapter 3, where the different roles of "similarity" and "association" in specific information processing theories are considered more thoroughly.

Many of the findings from Underwood's (1965) task and other tasks that were popular in the verbal learning era (e.g., paired-associate learning) are still relevant in modern research, although most of that literature is rarely (if ever) cited in much detail anymore. For a variety of reasons, interest in Underwood's (1965) false recognition task eventually waned.

One difficulty with Underwood's task was that the resulting false recognition effects often were quite small—on the order of only 10% above base rate (i.e., false recognition of related lures was 10% greater than that of unrelated lures). These small effect sizes made it difficult to test various theories of the phenomenon. Perhaps a larger reason, though, was that these associative methods imposed constraints that did not lend themselves to the testing and development of more elaborate theories of memory that had begun to dominate the research landscape in the 1970s. As discussed below, other methods of studying false recognition that produced larger effects with more naturalistic materials became more popular (e.g., Bransford, Barclay, & Franks, 1972; Loftus, Miller, & Burns, 1978).

This change in theoretical focus could be seen as a rejection of associative theories of memory, or at least a discontent with the nonmentalistic associative theories that dominated the field. In 1966, many leading researchers on verbal learning and psycholinguistics met at a conference that aimed to facilitate communication between fractionating fields of "verbal behavior" and to move toward acceptance of a "General S→R" theory of behavior. Ironically, the conference signaled the death knell for S→R theories of cognition. Developments in psycholinguistics made it clear that S→R theorizing provided an inadequate framework to understand language acquisition and use, and many of the adherents to the verbal learning tradition were troubled by the state of affairs in their field. Interest in the topics of inquiry had waned, and the concept of association had become sterile. The conference proceedings were published in a series of chapters, and the title of Asch's (1968) contribution summarized the sentiments of some of the more rebellious contributors: "The doctrinal tyranny of associationism: Or what is wrong with rote learning." The basic problem, as noted by Tulving (1968), was that learning theorists (such as McGeoch) had used the concept of association to describe mental phenomena, but that "association" was not a theoretical explanation in and of itself. In McGeoch's (1942) own words:

> The psychology of learning studies the characteristics of such associations among psychological events and the conditions of which their acquisition and retention are a function. Association will be the term most used in this book as a convenient name for the facts described. It carries no theoretical implication beyond the definition given; it commits to no systematic theory of learning. (p. 26)

The issue here was not so much that the concept of association was useless. Rather, by embracing methods that minimized the meaningfulness of materials (as in the Ebbinghaus tradition), and by incorporating these methods into a framework that ignored mental phenomena (as in the behaviorist tradition), the field had ignored many important aspects of memory.

☐ THE COGNITIVE REVOLUTION

In the cognitive revolution that took place in and around the 1960s, giving birth to modern research traditions, memory researchers moved away from the theoretical style of the verbal learning tradition and began to discuss memory phenomena in terms of information processes, stages, and stores (cf. Crowder, 1976). The movement was influenced heavily by research in the areas of perception and attention, and also by analogy to the electronic computer, through which the human mind was viewed as an information processor that stored memories in various systems (see Bower, 2000, and Tulving & Madigan, 1970, for brief historical overviews). Of central importance was the different information processing mechanisms within these systems. Under this new look, mental concepts that mostly were ignored under the verbal learning tradition flourished in memory theories, including concepts such as consciousness, strategies, organization, general knowledge, subjective experience, and imagination. Eventually, even nominal ties to the old school were severed. In 1985, the prominent *Journal of Verbal Learning and Verbal Behavior* (est. 1962) changed its name to the *Journal of Memory and Language*, apparently because the older title did not do justice to the theoretical riches of the new approach.

Amidst this sea change in the methods and theories in memory research, the role of associations in memory theories also changed. In contrast to S→R theories of association, associations were put "back into the head," much as they were in the classic philosophical doctrine, as a way of explaining how unseen mental structures could activate each other during the course of thought. Often these links were embedded within more elaborate theories or models of memory and cognition, which were aimed at explaining a variety of mental phenomena (e.g., Anderson, 1983; Collins & Loftus, 1975; Gillund & Shiffrin, 1984; McClelland & Rumelhart, 1986; Nelson, McKinney, Gee, & Janczura, 1998b). Exactly how associative connections influence various aspects of memory has been questioned from time to time (e.g., Nelson, McEvoy, & Pointer, 2003; Thomson & Tulving, 1970), but appeals to associative processes are nevertheless found throughout the literature. To this day, associatively driven processes are thought to be involved in any number of memory phenomena, including mnemonics, knowledge activation (semantic memory), priming, categorization, and source memory, to name a few.

The cognitive revolution also ushered in a renewed interest in the falli-
bility of memory, but associative influences did not assume as large a role
as they had in the past. For instance, much research was focused on how
pre-existing knowledge could influence the encoding and retrieval of
information, such as the remembering of something that was consistent or
implied with a passage of text but that was not actually in the text itself
(e.g., Bransford et al., 1972; Brewer, 1977; Sulin & Dooling, 1974; see Alba
& Hasher, 1983, for review). These demonstrations revitalized interest in
the idea of memory as a constructive act. Memory is not a simple recording of the past, but is a deliberate "piecing-together" of retrieved information and other relevant information in an effort to make sense of the
past. Neisser's (1967) seminal book *Cognitive Psychology* championed the
notion of mental constructivism, and ideas such as schematic distortion
and generalization in memory (e.g., Bartlett, 1932) came back into vogue.
In much of this work, the emphasis was on higher-order inferential
processes and how they could influence memory, as opposed to the lowly
influence of simple associations.

Elizabeth Loftus and colleagues provided some of the most compelling
demonstrations of laboratory-induced false memories at this time (e.g.,
Loftus et al., 1978; see Loftus, 1991). In what became known as the "misinformation" task, subjects would first study a sequence of events, such as a
car passing through a stop sign and knocking down a pedestrian in a cross-
walk. After this initial study phase, subjects would be exposed to additional information pertaining to the witnessed event, embedded within some
related task (e.g., answering questions about the event). Unbeknown to
subjects, misleading information would be presented at this stage (e.g.,
"Did another car pass the red Datsun when it was stopped at the yield
sign?"). On a final memory test, it was found that subjects were more likely to misremember the original event in a manner that was consistent with
the misinformation (e.g., they would remember a yield sign as opposed to
a stop sign), relative to a control condition where no misinformation was
provided. Another intriguing demonstration was that of "imagination
inflation," or the finding that if a person imagined performing an activity
(i.e., breaking a window with her hand during childhood), she was later
more likely to falsely remember having actually done it (e.g., Garry,
Manning, Loftus, & Sherman, 1996; Hyman, Husband, & Billings, 1995).

☐ MODERN ASSOCIATIONISM

Although the methods and theories were newly formulated, it is important to realize that some of the same processes operating in these newer

tasks also operated in classic interference tasks. In both cases, subjects would be exposed to competing sources of information and errors would result when the inappropriate information was retrieved. Much like the associative explanations that were critical in the earlier research, associative explanations of the newer effects have been proposed. These newer association-based models often are better specified than earlier models or conceptualizations, and tend to be enriched with more elaborate cognitive theorizing. Ayers and Reder (1998) provided one such explanation of the misinformation effect, in which each piece of information (true and misleading) was thought to be stored as a node in an associative memory network (see Figure 1.1). (Several other associative models of memory are listed in Chapter 2.) Memory confusions were hypothesized to arise from activation of the misleading information at retrieval, due to its association to the experimental context, and mistakenly attributing this activation to the original event. Of course, variables other than associative activation also can be involved in the misinformation effect (e.g., social suggestibility and credibility of the information), but the main point here is that associative mechanisms have been proposed to explain even these more naturalistic types of memory errors.

Seen in this light, associative mechanisms could be used to describe any type of false memory occurring via the confusion of the source of an event. For instance, Winograd (1968) demonstrated that, after studying

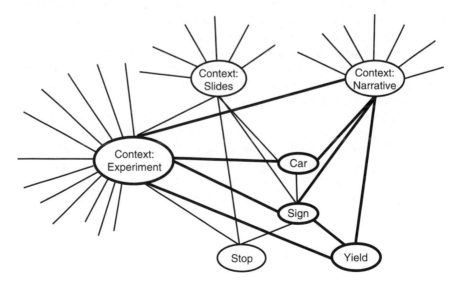

FIGURE 1.1   Associative model of the semantic concepts that are activated in the misinformation task. Adapted from Ayers and Reder (1998).

words in two separate lists, subjects could recognize that a word was studied but confuse the list in which it had earlier been presented. To explain these effects, Winograd appealed to the notion of list differentiation, an idea owing back to earlier work in the paired-associate literature. The idea was that, as words were studied in a list, the subject would form associations between the words and also between each word and the experimental context in which it had been presented. Confusing the source of a word would result from a failure to associate it to the proper list context, and attributing it to the improper context.

Although an associative framework for such source confusion effects is possible, caution needs to be exercised. In the absence of a good explanation as to *why* an event would activate the inappropriate context, these associative theories run the risk of simply redescribing the effect of interest as opposed to explaining it (the same sort of criticisms that were leveled against the older associative theories). In fact, many cognitive theories of source memory errors (and list-confusion errors in particular) have focused very little on associative processes. Jacoby and colleagues used these sorts of errors (and others) to advance the influential dual process framework of recognition memory (e.g., Jacoby, 1991). Under this framework, the recollection of an event—the ability to recall to mind detailed information about an event's prior occurrence, such as its position in a particular study list—is distinguished from the familiarity of an event—a feeling or sense that an event had previously occurred without necessarily recalling specific information (see Yonelinas, 2002, for review). Johnson and colleagues also provided numerous demonstrations of source memory errors, focusing on how differences between sources (e.g., visually presented pictures or imagined pictures) could influence source attributions (e.g., Johnson, Hashtroudi, & Lindsay, 1993; see Mitchell & Johnson, 2000, for review). These and other demonstrations led to the development of the influential source monitoring framework, which emphasizes the use of various decision processes in source attributions. All of these theoretical topics will be discussed more extensively in subsequent chapters. The main point here is that the underlying processes are more complicated than a purely associatively based theory could capture.

Associative descriptions of source confusions also run the risk of overextending the concept of associatively based memory errors. If one assumes that memory is inherently associative in nature (as in the James quote at the outset of this chapter), then any type of memory error will involve associative processes at some level, even if the direct cause of the error is not an active associative process. Take an illustrative example from the associative recognition task (e.g., Rotello, Macmillan, & Van Tassel, 2000; Underwood, 1974). In this task, subjects study several pairs of unrelated words (dragon-pie; lamp-grass) for a subsequent test. A typical finding is that subjects are more likely to falsely recognize new pairs of words when the corresponding words had been previously presented (dragon-grass) than when they had not been presented (ocean-mug). Similarly, when subjects study compound words (blackmail and jailbird), they are more likely to falsely recognize rearranged new words (blackbird) than completely new words (bathroom) (e.g., Jones & Jacoby, 2001; Underwood, Kapelak, & Malmi, 1976). In these cases the familiarity of the new pair is thought to drive the false recognition effect, due to prior presentation of the elements. Associations certainly are involved in the task, but they are not the primary cause of the false recognition effect (indeed, false recognition occurs when one *fails* to retrieve the appropriate associations). The same argument applies to other types of "external" source confusions, such as the list-confusion effects and the misinformation effects described above.

In contrast to confusions about the source or context of a previously presented event, of central interest in this essay are false memories for events that were not previously presented. Can pre-existing associations, stored in our general knowledge about the world, cause us to fabricate a new event and then falsely remember it as having actually been experienced? Source confusions would be involved in this sort of error, but the origin of the generated event would be purely mental (or "internal"). Underwood's (1965) original notion of the implicit associative response is a good example of this sort of associative process, although, as discussed, Underwood's false recognition effect alternatively could be explained by feature-matching or semantic similarity to studied words. These latter processes could fall under the broad umbrella of "types of associations," but importantly they do not involve the active mental generation of an associated event. More definitive evidence for such a process would be the false recall of a nonstudied event that was related to studied events, analogous to the phenomenon reported by Kirkpatrick (1894). Underwood (1965) cited what has since become the best known laboratory demonstration of this sort of phenomenon (Deese, 1959b), but, like Kirkpatrick's observations, Deese's findings had very little impact on the early memory research reviewed in this chapter. The next chapter introduces the false memory effect reported by Deese (1959b), and the rest of this essay reviews the large amount of research that has been conducted in this area in the past decade.

In conclusion, this chapter has highlighted how associations have been used to explain memory errors throughout history, but, equally important, it has shown how the very concept of "association" acts like a chameleon. Its definition changes with respect to the surrounding research environment. This state of affairs makes it pointless to simply say that association causes some memory phenomenon, without further elaboration. Along these lines, the title of this essay—Associative Illusions of Memory—should not be interpreted as an endorsement of associationism, or even an endorsement of an associative explanation for false memory effects. The title is meant to be descriptive, in that it refers to a class of false memory tasks that take advantage of associative relationships among the stimuli. This description does not imply that the associations themselves directly *cause* the false memories. As will be discussed, associative processes do seem to play an important role in these tasks, but the exact nature of these processes is not without question, and there is good evidence that nonassociative processes also play important roles.

CHAPTER

Converging Association Tasks

At any one time a science is simply what its researches yield, and the researches are nothing more than those problems for which effective methods have been found and for which the times are ready. (E. G. Boring, 1950, p. 343)

Deese (1959b) reported one of the most powerful false recall effects ever created in the laboratory. He was interested in the influence of associations on the "extra-list intrusion" (i.e., false recall) of nonpresented words, and to measure these intrusions he presented subjects with several word lists to study and recall. Unbeknown to his subjects, each study list comprised 12 associates to a nonstudied stimulus word, based on previously published free-association norms (Russell & Jenkins, 1954). To create these free-association norms, subjects were given a list of stimulus words (e.g., "sleep") and instructed to report the first word that comes to mind in response to each stimulus word (e.g., "bed"). The responses for each stimulus word were then tabulated across many subjects, and the frequency that a certain response was given to a certain stimulus was considered to be a measure of the strength of the association between those two words. For his own subjects, Deese presented the 12 strongest associates to each stimulus word, but not the stimulus word itself. For example, for the nonstudied word "sleep," subjects heard the words "bed, rest, awake, tired, dream, wake, night, comfort, eat, sound, slumber, snore." Each of these lists was followed by an immediate free recall test (i.e., write down as many of the presented words as possible, in any order).

Deese found that many of the lists often elicited false recall of the non-presented associate (or related lure). For instance, 44% of the subjects falsely recalled the word "sleep" after hearing its list of associates. He further found that the variability among lists to elicit false recall (which ranged from 0 to 44%) was related to the associative strength of each list (as calculated from the free-association norms). The correlation was quite high ($r = +.87$), and the effect had a strong linear tendency (see Figure 2.1). The more likely each of the list words was to elicit the related lure on the free-association test (on average), the more likely that the related lure would be falsely recalled on the recall test. Based on these results, Deese tentatively proposed that associative mechanisms were involved in constructive-memory processes.

In hindsight, Deese's (1959b) results are important for two reasons, although neither of these ideas was discussed much in the original paper. First, they highlighted the power of presenting multiple associates (or associative convergence) on false recall. By presenting 12 associates to the related lure, and by using the strongest associates to that lure, Deese was able to elicit very high levels of false recall in some lists. Second, these results indicate that the mental activation (or generation) of a nonstudied associate can lead to the false recall of that word. Because the related lure was not studied in the list, the subject must have mentally generated the

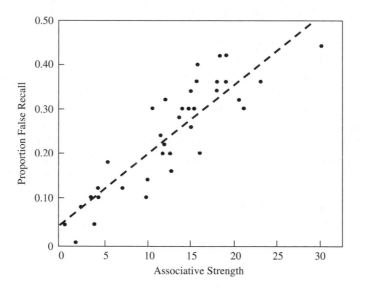

FIGURE 2.1   Relationship between associative strength and false recall observed by Deese (1959b). (Deese, J., On the prediction of occurrence of particular verbal intrusions in immediate recall. *Journal of Experimental Psychology*, *58*, 17–22, 1959, APA, reprinted with permission.)

word in order to falsely recall it. As discussed in Chapter 3, this mental generation can be conceived as spreading activation within a pre-existing associative network (a process dubbed "associative activation"), or alternative theories or metaphors could be used to describe this mental generation process. The main point to be made here is that, no matter what the conceptual scheme, it is clear that the subject thought of the related word in response to the presentation of its associates.

Despite these two important contributions to memory research, Deese's (1959b) paper had only little immediate influence on the field. In a historical analysis of the impact of Deese's article, Bruce and Winograd (1998) noted that by the 1970s Deese's paper on recall intrusions had "gone into eclipse" (p. 615). Although several prominent memory researchers had heard of the effect, and even had used it as a classroom demonstration (e.g., a variant of the effect was published in a teaching manual by Appleby, 1987), Bruce and Winograd (1998) argued that the importance of the effect for understanding false memories was not initially grasped because it did not mesh with the *Zeitgeist*. As discussed in Chapter 1, Deese published his paper at a time when memory researchers were still under the pull of the verbal learning tradition, which had little interest in ideas such as false memories.

All of that would change in three decades time, when Roediger and McDermott (1995) and Read (1996) independently published multiple experiments that replicated and extended Deese's (1959b) findings. Using several of Deese's lists and others that they had created, Roediger and McDermott made several novel contributions. In addition to replicating the recall data (and providing a more thorough analysis), they extended the effect to recognition tests, obtained subjective judgments, and investigated the effects of prior testing on false recognition. Read also made several novel contributions, by obtaining subjective judgments on recall tests and by investigating other variables (e.g., encoding strategies and type of recall test). We will return to the specific findings of each paper within the relevant section of this review. More important here is that both papers made significant theoretical contributions, by couching the results within current memory theories, and emphasizing how this technique provided a simple yet powerful way to create high levels of false memories in the laboratory. For mainly these reasons, research on these types of false memories exploded onto the scene.

This task has had a widespread influence on memory research. This influence is reflected in the frequency of citations of these papers. Figure 2.2 presents a graph of the cumulative citations of four papers: Deese (1959b); Read (1996); Roediger and McDermott (1995); and Shiffrin, Huber, and Marinelli (1995). This last paper was included to provide a comparison to the Roediger and McDermott paper. Shiffrin et al. reported false recognition effects that were analogous to those of Roediger and McDermott, was

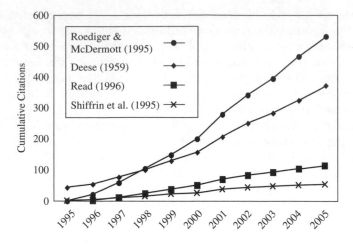

FIGURE 2.2 Cumulative citations (via the Social Science Citation Index) of four research articles that are relevant to associatively based false memories.

published in the same year and in the same journal as Roediger and McDermott, and even was cited by Roediger and McDermott. Two critical differences were that (1) the false recognition effects in Shiffrin et al. were smaller than those of Roediger and McDermott and subjective judgments were not obtained, and (2) the results were couched within an influential model of memory (the search of associative memory, or SAM model), as opposed to false memory research. As can be seen from the figure, the Roediger and McDermott paper clearly has had the largest impact. As of December 2005, this paper had been cited over 500 times. Of all these citations, at least 150 were published research articles that had used the task, with a combined total of at least 350 individual experiments. Considering that not all experiments get published, the actual number of experiments that have been conducted using this task is probably much higher than that—at the very least, we can safely assume a rate of one new experiment every 2 *weeks* over the past 10 years!

The theoretical influence of this and related tasks is evident from the consideration of these effects in different models and frameworks of memory. Such models include CHARM (composite holographic associative recall model; see Dodhia & Metcalfe, 1999), MINERVA2 (see Arndt & Hirshman, 1998), PIER2 (processing implicit and explicit representations 2; McEvoy, Nelson, & Komatsu, 1999), and SAM (Shiffrin et al., 1995). We will not delve into the precise details of these individual models, but it should be noted that many of these and other models (e.g., John Anderson's [1983]

ACT* model) provide more precise (and testable) formulations of associative processes than the general notion of "association" that sometimes is used. Others have couched Deese–Roediger–McDermott (DRM) effects within a broader conceptual framework, such as SCAPE (selective construction and preservation of experience; see Whittlesea, 2002), FTT (fuzzy trace theory; see Payne, Elie, Blackwell, & Neuschatz, 1996), the dual-process framework of recollection and familiarity (e.g., Benjamin, 2001), the activation-monitoring framework (see Roediger & McDermott, 2000), the constructive-memory framework (see Schacter, Norman, & Koutstaal, 1998a), and the source monitoring framework (e.g., Mather, Henkel, & Johnson, 1997). Roediger and McDermott (1995) touched on many of these ideas in their original report, and the key processes will be discussed more throughout this review.

Because of the instrumental role of Roediger and McDermott (1995) in reviving interest in the illusion, and because many subsequent experiments were modeled after Roediger and McDermott's design, the procedure is often dubbed the DRM task, after Deese–Roediger–McDermott. In their historical analysis, Bruce and Winograd (1998) argued that this label appropriately captures the key contributions of both sets of authors—Deese (1959b) for developing these types of lists to look at recall intrusions, and Roediger and McDermott for extending the task to false recognition and pointing out its relevance to false memory research. It is interesting to note that other names have been used, including the "Deese paradigm" (Johnson, Nolde, Mather, Kounios, Schacter, & Curran, 1997), the "false memory paradigm" (Dodhia & Metcalfe, 1999), the "associative memory illusion" (Park, Shobe, & Kihlstrom, 2005), the "prototype-familiarity effect" (Whittlesea, 2002), and the somewhat unwieldy "DRMRS effect" (after Deese–Roediger–McDermott–Read–Solso; McKelvie, 2003). Despite these and other labels, the term "DRM" is by far the most popular and is recognized by most researchers in the field.

☐ THE DRM TASK: BASIC METHOD AND RESULTS

Most of the work reviewed in this essay involved variants of the DRM task, so this section summarizes the basic methods and results of Roediger and McDermott (1995). These methods and results will be referred to as "standard" or "basic" throughout the rest of this review. Their second experiment was a more carefully controlled replication of the first, so only the second experiment will be discussed here. Those instances where subsequent experiments have yielded similar results, or results that should otherwise be discussed at the outset of this review, also are discussed below.

Method

In this study, as well as most of the other studies reviewed in Chapters 1–6, college students participated as subjects. Thirty subjects were presented with 16 lists of words. Each list contained the first 15 associates (e.g., bed, rest, awake, etc.) to a critical nonpresented lure (e.g., sleep). Only those lists that the authors thought would elicit high levels of false memories were included, using Deese's (1959b) results as a guide (some of Deese's lists rarely elicited false memories, a point that will be discussed more in Chapter 3). Table 2.1 presents a sample of the word lists, and a more complete set of lists and normative data can be found in Roediger, Watson, McDermott, and Gallo (2001c). (Similar effects subsequently have been found in other languages, either using translated lists or new lists created from associative norms specific to that language.)

TABLE 2.1   Five DRM Lists that Tend to Elicit False Recall of the Nonstudied Related Lure (in Capitals)

WINDOW	SLEEP	SMELL	DOCTOR	CHAIR
Door	Bed	Nose	Nurse	Table
Glass	Rest	Breathe	Sick	Sit
Pane	Awake	Sniff	Lawyer	Legs
Shade	Tired	Aroma	Medicine	Seat
Ledge	Dream	Hear	Health	Couch
Sill	Wake	See	Hospital	Desk
House	Snooze	Nostril	Dentist	Recliner
Open	Blanket	Whiff	Physician	Sofa
Curtain	Doze	Scent	Ill	Wood
Frame	Slumber	Reek	Patient	Cushion
View	Snore	Stench	Office	Swivel
Breeze	Nap	Fragrance	Stethoscope	Stool
Sash	Peace	Perfume	Surgeon	Sitting
Screen	Yawn	Salts	Clinic	Rocking
Shutter	Drowsy	Rose	Cure	Bench

Note: Lists are taken from Stadler, Roediger, and McDermott (1999).

Associates were arranged in descending order of relatedness to the related lure, based in part on the same word association norms that Deese (1959b) had used. In fact, subsequent studies have found that the order of the associates within each list does not matter that much (e.g., Brainerd, Wright, Reyna, & Mojardin, 2001; McEvoy et al., 1999). Each word was read aloud to the subjects at a rate of approximately 1.5 s per word.

After the last word of each list was presented, subjects were signaled either to recall all of the items in that list or to instead perform mathematics problems (for each subject, half of the lists were recalled and half were followed by math, in an unexpected order, and the order of these tasks was counterbalanced across subjects). They were given 2 min for either task. For the recall task, they were asked to recall the list by writing down as many of the words as they could remember, without guessing, in any order (a single-trial free recall test). For the math task, they performed arithmetic problems instead of recalling the list. This task was included as a control condition, to determine the effects of recall testing on the subsequent recognition memory test. Importantly, subjects were not told that the lists were designed to get them to think of a nonpresented associate, although they did know that this was a test of their memory accuracy. (Note that these immediate recall tests involve short-term or working memory, but because the number of studied words is beyond the working memory span of most subjects the effects discussed here and throughout this review are thought to arise from long-term episodic memory. Consistent with this conceptualization, these sorts of false memory effects have been found to last for weeks and months, as reviewed later.)

After the last recall or math task, subjects were given instructions for a final recognition test. Such instructions typically take 5 min or less. (Many subsequent studies eliminated initial testing of the lists altogether, and measured only final recognition.) This test contained 96 words printed in columns on a test sheet. Half of the test words (48) had been studied in the previous lists (3 words from each of the 16 study lists, drawn from serial position 1, 8, and 10). The other half (48) had not been studied. These were the 16 related lures from each studied list (e.g., sleep), in order to measure false recognition of related lures, as well as 3 list words (from serial positions 1, 8, and 10) and a related lure from 8 nonstudied lists, of the same type that had been studied. From the subjects' perspective, these latter lures would be relatively unrelated to the studied lists, and thus provided a base rate level of false recognition. Whether a particular list was studied or nonstudied was counterbalanced across subjects. Subjects were instructed that the test would contain studied and nonstudied items, although they were not told that some of the lures were critical associates to the list words. They were to circle "old" for the studied words (those presented on the tape player) and "new" for any word that was nonstudied.

Immediately after making each "old" decision, subjects were asked to make a "remember"/"know" judgment (e.g., Rajaram, 1993; Tulving, 1985). A "remember" judgment was to be made if they vividly remembered something specific about the word's occurrence in the study list (i.e., "they remembered something distinctive in the speaker's voice when he said the word, or perhaps they remembered the item presented before or after it, or what they were thinking when they heard the word," Roediger & McDermott, 1995, p. 807). A "know" judgment was to be made if they were sure the word had been presented, but they could not remember a specific detail about the word's presentation (i.e., they just knew that the word was presented, perhaps because it was very familiar). These judgments were designed to measure the subjective experience accompanying recognition judgments. Finally, at the end of the experiment, all subjects were asked whether they "knew what the experiment was about." Only one subject reported that they had realized that the lists were designed to get them to think of a nonpresented word, and the data from this subject were replaced. All of the subjects were then debriefed, and told that the lists were designed to get them to think of nonpresented words.

Recall Results

Results from the recall test are presented in Figure 2.3. A typical serial position curve was obtained, so that words from the beginning of the list were recalled better than words from the middle of the list (the primacy effect),

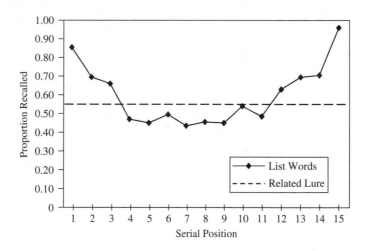

FIGURE 2.3 Recall results from Roediger and McDermott (1995, Experiment 2).

and words at the end of the list also were remembered relatively well (the recency effect). More importantly, false recall of the related lure (represented by the dashed line) was extremely high, at 55%. Even though this word was not presented, it was recalled at about the same rate as words that were presented in the middle of the list. This finding replicates the false recall effect reported by Deese (1959b), although Deese did not report true recall results for comparison. The probability of falsely recalling other words (i.e., noncritical intrusions) was not reported for Roediger and McDermott's (1995) Experiment 2, but these intrusions tend to be quite low—in Roediger and McDermott's first experiment, the intrusion of any nonstudied word (other than the critical word) occurred on only 14% of the lists. These intrusions tend to be other semantically related items that did not occur in the list, or, less frequently, words that were phonologically similar to studied words, perhaps because the subject misheard the studied word (e.g., Gallo, McDermott, Percer, & Roediger, 2001a; Johansson & Stenberg, 2002; McDermott, 1996; Robinson & Roediger, 1997; Watson, Balota, & Sergent-Marshall, 2001). The important point is that false recall of related lures occurred at least as often as true recall of some list words, and more often than false recall of other words (the relative merit of these two comparisons is discussed later, in the context of recognition memory).

Similar to Roediger and McDermott (1995), Read (1996) found high levels of false recall on a free recall test. He also found high levels of false recall on a serial recall test (i.e., recall the words in the order of presentation), indicating that the false recall effect was not simply an artifact of free recall testing. Read further asked subjects to judge the input position of each recalled word. Subjects tended to judge the related lure as having occurred near the middle of the list (i.e., a position of 6 out of 12 items), or earlier. Read argued that these latter results reflected mental activation of the related lure relatively early in the presentation of the study list, although the generality of this last result is limited because Read only used one list.

Another consideration is the recall position (or "output position") of the related lure on free recall tests. Roediger and McDermott (1995, Experiment 1) reported that false recall of the related lure tended to occur toward the end of the recall test—that is, subjects typically recalled this lure only after they had recalled several of the studied words (for similar results, see Balota et al., 1999; McDermott & Watson, 2001; Payne et al., 1996; Watson et al., 2001). Although some have interpreted this as a theoretically meaningful effect (e.g., Payne et al., 1996), these findings are qualified by the fact that there is usually a strong recency effect for studied words (i.e., words at the end of the list are recalled better than those in the middle of the list). In fact, subjects typically tend to recall the last few words of the list early in the recall sequence, apparently because these words are still being rehearsed in short-term memory (see Balota et al., 1999). Out of necessity, this recency effect would tend to displace recall of the related word toward the end of the recall sequence.

McDermott (1996) replicated this recall output phenomenon under conditions similar to those of Roediger and McDermott (1995), but also included a condition where the recall of each list was delayed by 30 s of math problems. Such a procedure interferes with the rehearsal of words in short-term memory, and thus makes it less likely that these words will be the first words that tend to be recalled. Under these conditions, McDermott found that (1) the recency portion of the serial position curve was eliminated (as expected), and (2) there was no systematic output position of the related lure. Similarly, Read (1996) reported that the related lure was recalled, on average, near the middle of the recall sequence (or perhaps a little later), using a recall test that was delayed by 2 min (Experiment 2). Thus, the relatively late recall output of related lures, under standard conditions, might be an artifact caused by the recency effect for list words.

An additional consideration is that differences between lists can influence recall output position of the related lure. In McEvoy et al. (1999), the output position of related lures was influenced by the degree of associative connections between the list words (as measured by free-association norms). Related lures were falsely recalled at later output positions when list words were more strongly associated to each other, relative to lists of words with weaker connections. They argued that the studied words of highly connected lists would be more likely to cue each other on the recall test, as opposed to the related lure, thereby pushing recall of the related lure to a later output position. In terms of output order of all the words, it has been observed that more strongly associated words tend to be clustered together at recall, suggesting that associations guide the recall of these types of lists (e.g., Basden, Basden, Thomas, & Souphasith, 1998; Payne et al., 1996).

Recognition Results

The recognition results from Roediger and McDermott (1995, Experiment 2) are summarized in Table 2.2. Turn first to lists that were not previously tested with recall (top half of the table). True recognition of studied words (i.e., the hit rate, mean = .65) was significantly greater than false recognition of their control words (i.e., the false alarm rate to list words from nonstudied lists, mean = .11). This difference reflects the influence of studying the list on subsequent true recognition of words from that list.

TABLE 2.2   Recognition Results from Roediger and McDermott (1995, Experiment 2)

Condition and item type	"Old"	"Remember"
No prior recall		
List words	.65	.63
Related lures	.72	.53
Prior recall		
List words	.79	.72
Related lures	.81	.72
Control lures		
List words	.11	.18
Related lures	.16	.19

Notes: "Remember" judgments are expressed as a proportion of the overall recognition rate (p "Old"). Control lures were unrelated to the studied lists (list words and related lures from nonstudied lists).

Similarly, false recognition of related lures (.72) was significantly greater than false recognition of their control words (.16), or related lures from nonstudied lists. By the same logic, this difference reflects the influence of studying the list on subsequent false recognition of related lures. As was the case in recall, false recognition of related lures was extremely high— at least as great as true recognition of some list words, and much greater than false recognition of unrelated lures.

Another important finding was that false recognition of the related lure often was accompanied by judgments of actually "remembering" details about the word's presentation, as opposed to judgments of "knowing" (or vague feelings of familiarity). In fact, the rate of "remember" judgments for related lures was similar to that for studied words, and much greater than that for falsely recognized control lures (which were mostly given "know" judgments). These findings suggest that false recognition of the related lures was subjectively compelling, much like a perceptual illusion that feels real. The compelling subjective nature of this false memory effect is one of the reasons why it has become such a popular means of studying false memories. Other relevant findings and theories of this subjective phenomenon are discussed more thoroughly in Chapter 4, where the concept of illusory recollection is treated more thoroughly.

Also notice that previously recalling the list increased true and false recognition relative to lists that were not previously recalled. This difference reflects a testing effect on subsequent memory, so that previously recalling a list word or a related lure led to a subsequent boost in recognition of that word (much like rehearsal can increase remembering). This effect is reviewed more extensively in Chapter 6, in the context of other testing effects. The main point to make here is that prior testing can influence subsequent recognition performance, which introduces theoretical complications. As a result, all recognition results reported in the rest of this review, as part of the "standard" DRM conditions, will only be from conditions that are not confounded by prior testing (unless otherwise noted).

Measurement Issues

Two measurement issues deserve comment. The first is whether the size of the false recognition effect should be gauged by comparison to true recognition of list words or by comparison to false recognition of control words (a similar issue can be raised in the context of true and false recall). Although there is something compelling about conditions in which false memories occur as frequently as true memories, comparisons between true and false memories can be misleading, and will be used sparingly throughout this review. As discussed in Chapters 3 and 4, memory errors do not have to occur as frequently as true memories in order to properly be considered illusory or false, and observable differences between true and false remembering will depend on an infinite number of rather arbitrary task variables such as time of testing, which list words are tested, etc. To give one example, Jou, Matus, Aldridge, Rogers, and Zimmerman (2004) found that true and false recognition were similar when the recognition test was given after several DRM lists were studied (in terms of overall recognition rates, response latencies, and confidence ratings), but differed considerably when the test was given immediately after each list (when memory for list words was strongest). If one had used differences between true and false recognition as the critical dependent variable, then one would have drawn different conclusions based on this seemingly benign methodological difference (i.e., how many lists are presented prior to testing, which is rarely equated across studies in the literature). Direct comparisons between true and false memories also are ambiguous in terms of the theoretical causes of false remembering. True memory and false memory can be influenced by different processes, and can influence each other, so that directly comparing the two (or deriving a composite "accuracy" score from both) is not always theoretically meaningful.

In terms of understanding the processes that influence false recognition, per se, a comparison between false recognition for related and unrelated lures is more interpretable. As discussed next, this difference reflects a systematic relatedness effect on false recognition, which is usually the phenomenon of interest. Analogous relatedness effects on false recall can be computed, but because noncritical intrusions are usually rare, absolute proportions of false recall usually are sufficient. Under standard DRM conditions, false recall and recognition of related lures are always greater than false recall or recognition of more weakly related lures (for quantitative reviews of these relatedness effects, see McKelvie, 2003, 2004).

A related measurement issue is how to correct or adjust true or false recognition for base rate responding. In Table 2.2, notice that false alarms to control items (or list words and related lures from nonstudied lists) were greater for related lures (.16) than for list words (.11). Although the effect was small, it was statistically significant and it has been replicated numerous times in other studies using DRM materials (e.g., Gallo & Roediger, 2002, 2003; Gallo et al., 2001a; Gallo, Roediger, & McDermott, 2001b; McCabe & Smith, 2002; Schacter, Verfaellie, & Pradere 1996c; Seamon, Luo, & Gallo, 1998; Whittlesea, 2002). This base rate effect indicates that there are inherent differences between the related lures and list words that are typically used in this task, and these differences can influence recognition even when the relevant list had not been studied. A careful investigation of the exact causes of this base rate effect has yet to be conducted, but likely culprits are word characteristics such as frequency, associative neighborhood, or orthography. Base rate differences also can occur across different experimental conditions. These differences are often considered to be due to response bias (e.g., a tendency to guess "yes" in the absence of memory), and/or due to idiosyncratic associations or other factors that might enhance the familiarity of new items.

One way around all of these base rate issues is to correct or adjust recognition memory scores using the false alarm rate to unrelated words. The idea is that the hit rate to list words (or the false alarm rate to related lures) is not a pure measure of recognition memory for these words, but also reflects the probability of responding "yes" to these words based on processes other than the retrieval of a "memory signal" (be it true or false). Basic experimental logic can be used to correct for this discrepancy. Because the control lures are similar to targets (or related lures) in all regards, except that the relevant list was not studied, the difference between recognition of targets (or related lures) and their control lures reflects the effect of presenting the relevant study list on true (or false) recognition. Thus, by subtracting responses to control words from those to experimental words (targets or related lures), the effect of studying the relevant list on recognition can be measured. Other correction methods (such as d' or A') involve similar logic, except they make different assumptions about the underlying memory distributions and decision processes (see Snodgrass & Corwin, 1988). There is no general agreement as to which is the best measure for recognition memory, and every method makes questionable (or at least overly simplistic) assumptions. Fortunately, the measures usually agree. The subtraction method is preferred here because it is based on simple experimental logic, and hence its limitations are the easiest to understand, and also because it maintains the same scale as the original recognition scores. Unless otherwise noted, care was taken to evaluate each recognition finding in this review using both raw and corrected data, where possible.

Response Latencies

Although there are over a hundred published experiments measuring false recognition in the DRM task, response latency data are reported relatively rarely (as is the case in many studies of recognition memory). An early exception was a study by Tun, Wingfield, Rosen, and Blanchard (1998). In this study, latencies for correctly recognizing list words were similar to those for false recognition of related lures (each around 1 s, across Experiments 1 and 2). The recognition test was confounded with prior recall tests in this study, but other studies have reported similar patterns even when recognition was not confounded with prior recall (e.g., Düzel, Yonelinas, Mangun, Heinze, & Tulving, 1997; Johnson et al., 1997; Schacter, Buckner, Koutstaal, Dale, & Rosen, 1997a). However, true recognition is sometimes faster than false recognition (Curran, Schacter, Johnson, & Spinks, 2001; Fabiani, Stadler, & Wessels, 2000; Jou et al., 2004; Payne, Nadel, Allen, Thomas, & Jacobs, 2002; see also Brown, Buchanan, & Cabeza, 2000; Westerberg & Marsolek, 2003a). These latter differences likely reflect differences in underlying processes. True recognition can be based on recollection, whereas false alarms are driven more by familiarity-based processes (or illusory recollection). Responding on the basis of familiarity sometimes takes more effortful or time-consuming decision processes than responding on the basis of recollection (such monitoring processes are discussed more in Chapter 5).

Of course, direct comparisons between response latencies for true and false memories are not necessarily important. Conditions can be created where true and false memories differ or where they do not differ, depending on any number of task parameters. Of more theoretical interest is the relatedness effect on false memory, that is, differences in responding to related versus unrelated lures. Latencies to related lures often differ from those to unrelated lures. Fabiani et al. (2000), Johnson et al. (1997), Jou et al. (2004), and Schacter et al. (1997a) all found that false alarms to related lures were faster than false alarms to unrelated lures. Apparently, because related lures are more familiar than unrelated lures, subjects are quicker to falsely recognize related lures. Similarly, Schacter et al. found that correct rejections of unrelated lures were faster than those of related lures (see also Tun et al., 1998). Because unrelated lures are relatively unfamiliar, subjects are quicker to correctly reject them. Another way to look at these latency effects is in terms of relatedness. When the word is related to one of the study lists (studied words or related lures), positive decisions tend to be faster and more frequent than negative decisions. When the word is unrelated to the lists, negative decisions (correct rejections) tend to be faster and more frequent than positive ones (false alarms). Both of these patterns highlight the large influence of associative or relational information in the decision.

□ ENCODING MULTIPLE ASSOCIATES

An important point, if not obvious, is that these powerful false recall and recognition effects arise because the DRM task takes full advantage of associative convergence. Unlike earlier associative tasks (e.g., Underwood, 1965), in which only one or a few associates were studied, many strong associates are studied in the DRM task. Presenting multiple associates leads to high levels of associative and conceptual information that converges on the nonstudied lure, strongly "suggesting" its potential occurrence. This phenomenon is most readily demonstrated by the effect of the number of studied associates on false recall and recognition. Robinson and Roediger (1997) had subjects study several DRM lists for recall testing after each list (delayed by 30 s of math). The length of the lists either was 3, 6, 9, 12, or 15 items (shorter lists were obtained by removing weaker associates from the end of the list). Recall results from their first experiment can be found in Figure 2.4. Not surprisingly, average true recall of list words decreased as a function of list length, indicating that the probability of recalling any individual list word decreased when more list words needed to be recalled (i.e., the list-length effect, Murdock, 1962). More important, false recall of the related lure followed the opposite pattern, steadily increasing as more associates were studied. This pattern was replicated in a second experiment, in which the total list length was held constant by adding unrelated studied words (or filler words) to the shorter lists (e.g., for lists of 3 associates, 12 unrelated words also were studied). Thus, the critical factor for false recall was the total number of associated words that were studied, as opposed to the length of the list per se. The effect of number of studied associates on false recall has been replicated numerous times (e.g., Clancy, McNally, Schacter, Lenzenweger, & Pitman, 2002; Hutchison & Balota, 2005).

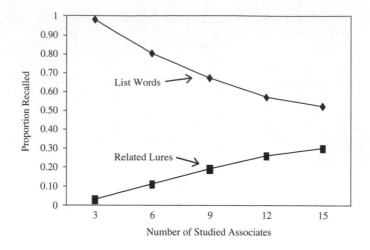

FIGURE 2.4   Effect of number of studied associates on true and false recall in Robinson and Roediger (1997, Experiment 1, approximated from their Figure 1). The mean number of noncritical intrusions, per list, was .02, .09, .08, .10, and .11 for lengths 3, 6, 9, 12, and 15. (Reproduced with permission.)

The number of studied associates also affected false recognition in the predicted direction. When more associates had been studied, the related lure was more likely to be falsely recognized. False recognition was confounded with prior recall in Robinson and Roediger (1997), but the effect of list length was obtained even when they examined only those related lures that were not initially recalled. Many subsequent studies have found the predicted effect of list length on false recognition in the absence of prior recall testing (e.g., Arndt & Hirshman, 1998; Gallo & Roediger, 2003; Hutchison & Balota, 2005; Marsh & Bower, 2005; Mintzer & Griffiths, 2001c; see also Shiffrin et al., 1995). Interestingly, Robinson and Roediger (Experiment 1) found that true recognition of studied associates increased as more associates were studied. An effect of list length on true recognition would not be too surprising if it is assumed that the same associative processes that influence related lures also could influence list words (which also are associated to each other). However, this effect was not replicated in their second experiment, and an effect of list length on true recognition was not always obtained in the other studies cited here. The failure to find consistent effects on list words probably is due to the fact that these words are not as strongly associated to each other as they are to the related lure, and also to the fact that, in addition to associative processes, memory for list words is influenced by the recollection of their actual presentation.

☐ OTHER CONVERGENCE TASKS

Although this review is focused on findings within the DRM task, it is important to realize that other types of convergence also can lead to false remembering. Numerous studies have demonstrated false recall or recognition of nonstudied category exemplars (e.g., robin) after studying related exemplars (e.g., canary, blue jay, cardinal, etc.), as in Dewhurst and Anderson (1999); Hintzman (1988); Seamon, Luo, Schlegel, Greene, and Goldenberg (2000); Smith, Ward, Tindell, Sifonis, and Wilkenfeld (2000); and Tussing and Greene (1999). Other studies have demonstrated that words can be falsely recalled or recognized based on orthographic and/or phonological confusions (e.g., veil, bail, gale, rail, etc.), as in Schacter, Verfaellie, and Anes (1997b); Sommers and Lewis (1999); and Watson, Balota, and Roediger (2003). These false memory effects are similar to those in the DRM task, in that all of the stimuli share some sort of pre-existing mental relationship. Many of the theoretical mechanisms discussed in the context of the DRM task readily extend to these other tasks. Some of the key findings from these other tasks will be discussed in subsequent chapters, as well as potential differences between the tasks.

There also are convergence effects on false recognition that have nothing to do with pre-existing associative relationships. In seminal studies, Posner and Keele (1968, 1970) showed that subjects could correctly classify a nonstudied category exemplar (i.e., a pattern of dots) after studying several other exemplars from that category (i.e., other patterns with similar configurations of dots, which were deviations from a nonstudied prototype). In some instances, subjects were better at categorizing the nonstudied prototype than they were at categorizing exemplars that were studied. Posner and Keele proposed that, during the learning phase, subjects extracted a mental representation of a categorical "prototype," or an abstract representation that captured the basic pattern found across the studied exemplars. Subsequent categorization of new exemplars could then be achieved by matching to the most similar prototype in memory. More critically for present purposes, studying these stimuli also leads to false recognition of the nonstudied prototypes, or nonstudied exemplars that are perceptually similar to studied exemplars. Similar false recognition effects have been uncovered for a whole host of novel but perceptually related stimuli, including nonsense words, abstract figures, shapes, and patterns, as well as novel faces that share common features (e.g., Budson, Desikan, Daffner, & Schacter, 2001; Franks & Bransford, 1971; Homa, Smith, Macak, Johovich, & Osorio, 2001; Koutstaal, Schacter, Verfaellie, Brenner, & Jackson, 1999b; Nosofsky, 1991; Slotnick & Schacter, 2004; Solso & McCarthy, 1981; Zeelenberg, Boot, & Peecher, 2005).

Is the DRM task another instantiation of a prototype effect, as some have suggested (e.g., Whittlesea, 2002)? There certainly are similarities between the two tasks, in the sense that both make use of convergence to elicit false memories of nonstudied stimuli. As discussed in the next chapter, there also is some common theoretical ground between the two classes of phenomena. However, there are some critical differences. In prototype effects the stimuli are novel to the subject (e.g., random dot patterns, new faces), and the resulting false memory effects can be considered a failure of perceptual discrimination from memory. In the DRM task the relationship between the stimuli is mostly semantic or conceptual, based on pre-existing knowledge. Although it is tempting to explain all of these effects through a general principle of "relatedness," the real theoretical distinctions rest in the nature of the relations, and how different types of relationships can cause false remembering through different mental processes. Exactly how these processes are thought to cause false remembering is discussed in the next chapter.

BASIC THEORIES
AND DATA

3
CHAPTER

Processes that Cause False Memory

What causes false memories in converging associates tasks? Researchers have grappled with this question ever since Roediger and McDermott (1995) popularized the DRM technique, and earlier. Some progress has been made in narrowing the set of candidate processes, but within the remaining set there remain some thorny theoretical issues. In fact, Roediger and McDermott touched on several potential causes of the effect that remain viable alternatives today. Three of the major theoretical alternatives are discussed here: *associative activation*, *thematic consistency*, and *feature overlap*. These three theories are all memory-based, in the sense that the subject decides that the nonstudied item was studied based on a memory "signal" for the item, or a subjective experience that it had been presented in the earlier study phase. These memory-based accounts stand in contrast to decision-based accounts, such as *response bias*, *criterion shifts*, and *demand characteristics*. These accounts do not necessarily posit a memory signal for the nonstudied item, but instead propose that subjects endorse this item on the basis of their assumptions about the studied materials or the experiment as a whole. Of course, retrieval processes and decision processes are involved in all memory tasks. These explanations differ critically in terms of what they assume is retrieved and what exactly is decided.

Before delving into the nuances of each theory, some general observations on the construction of DRM lists might be useful. (Exactly how these distinctions apply to other convergence-based false memory tasks is discussed later in this chapter; the focus here is on the DRM task because this has been researched most extensively.) Figure 3.1 presents a diagram of the types of relationships between list words and the related lure, beyond those that would occur for a list of unrelated words. The largest circle represents associations, indicating that all of the words have pre-existing associations to the related lure, by design, and many are associated to each other (to varying degrees). "Association" is used here in the broadest sense, applying to any two words that can be mentally related (e.g., by frequent co-occurrence in language, categorical membership, conceptual or orthographic similarity, etc.). The other solid circle represents semantic similarity, or the idea that a subset of the associated words has similar meanings or shares overlapping semantic features with the related lure (e.g., sleep-rest; sleep-doze), in contrast to other associates that have different meanings (e.g., sleep-bed; sleep-awake). Other types of similarity also occur (orthographic, phonological, concreteness, frequency of usage, etc.), but usually not much more than would be expected from a random set of words. The dashed circle represents the theme or gist of the list that subjects can form (and remember) to summarize or categorize the words (e.g., "actions or items involved in sleep"). It is assumed that the related lure is a central concept in the gist

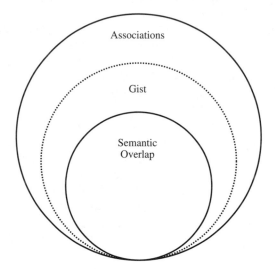

FIGURE 3.1   Schematic of the types of relationships between list words and the related lure in the DRM task. By design, all list words are associated to the related lure. Some or all of these words may be consistent with a theme or gist that mentally summarizes the list, and a subset of the list words are often semantically (or conceptually) similar to the related lure.

representation, and so the gist necessarily encompasses semantically similar words, as well as other words that are consistent with the corresponding theme (e.g., dream; snore). This circle is dashed to emphasize the idea that the contents of the theme will depend on subjective organization, or what the subjects notice and retain about the relations between the words. Some studied associates of the related lure (e.g., peace) might not fit with the gist that is encoded from the list. At least one of these relationships (association, semantic similarity, or theme) plays a role in any theory of DRM false memories.

☐ DECISION-BASED THEORIES

Decision-based theories deserve to be carefully considered from the start because they imply that the memory errors obtained in the convergence-based false memory tasks do not truly reflect illusory memories. These explanations focus on the idea that each list is related to a theme. They argue that subjects accept related lures on memory tests, not because there is a memory signal that these words had occurred at study (i.e., illusory recollection or familiarity), but rather because they fit well within the themes of the list. According to these theories, subjects rely on their knowledge of the study materials to infer that words that they cannot remember, but that are related to words that they can remember, were probably presented too. That is, subjects strategically guess or infer that the related word was studied, based only on its perceived relationship to the list. Subjects might use such a guessing strategy to maximize their test score (because they assume most related words were probably studied), or because they believe this is what the experimenter wants them to do (i.e., demand characteristics). These accounts have been somewhat controversial, and have not been supported by the evidence.

Miller and Wolford (1999) proposed a decision-based argument in terms of a criterion shift in signal detection theory (SDT). According to their formulation, even if related lures failed to evoke a feeling of familiarity or had only a weak memory signal (like unrelated lures), subjects might be more likely to accept related lures because these items are perceived as related to the study list. This decision process would represent the use of a more liberal response criterion when presented with related lures, yielding more "old" responses to these lures than to unrelated lures (see top panel of Figure 3.2). To investigate this idea, Miller and Wolford conducted two experiments in which list items, related lures, and unrelated lures were actually studied in some conditions (so that all three item types would be targets on a recognition test) and nonstudied in others

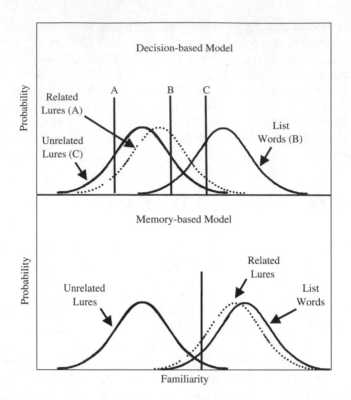

FIGURE 3.2 Two signal-detection models of false memories. Top panel: A decision-based theory. Related and unrelated lures are thought to have roughly similar levels of familiarity (represented here as normal distributions), whereas studied targets are more familiar. Subjects set their response criterion more liberally for related words, so that related lures (C) > list words (B) > unrelated lures (A). Bottom panel: A memory-based theory. Studying the list makes related lures more familiar than unrelated lures, and subjects use a single criterion.

(so that all three item types would be lures). This modification of the typical DRM task allowed for the calculation of SDT estimates of sensitivity (d[a], which is analogous to d', and is thought to reflect a "memory signal") and response bias (c2, which is analogous to C, and is thought to reflect decision processes) for each type of item. The main focus of Miller and Wolford's analysis was on the final recognition test (albeit confounded with prior recall tests).

The first finding was that sensitivity estimates were roughly the same for each item type (e.g., 1.63 for list items, 1.37 for related lures, and 1.34 for unrelated lures in Experiment 1), indicating that the memory strength of each item was greater when it was studied than when it was not studied. For related lures, this difference indicates that true recognition (i.e., when these items were studied) was stronger or more compelling than false recognition (i.e., when they were not studied). The second finding was that the estimates of response bias were more liberal for the critical related items than for the other items (−.35, −1.19, and +.42, respectively, with negative estimates indicating more liberal bias). Based mainly on this latter finding, Miller and Wolford (1999) argued that the high level of false recognition of related lures was due to liberal criterion shifts. They also proposed that this model could be extended to explain false recall of the related lure if a generate + recognize process was assumed (e.g., Bahrick, 1970; Kintsch, 1970). According to this type of hypothesis, the related lure is generated on the recall test because it is associated to other words, and then recognized via the aforementioned decision processes.

Miller and Wolford's (1999) article elicited strong reactions from other researchers in the area, and generated a deep theoretical discourse about the nature of false memories. Roediger and McDermott (1999) argued against the criterion-shift interpretation of DRM effects for several reasons. The first issue was one of semantics. They pointed out that, contrary to the implications of Miller and Wolford, a memory error does not need to be as strong or as compelling as a true memory in order to qualify as a false memory. Thus, the finding that the memory signal for the critical related item was greater when it was studied than when it was nonstudied (i.e., a significant d[a] value) does not contradict the idea that false alarms to this item (when it was not studied) should be considered false memories. In fact, it already had been demonstrated that presenting the critical related item at study would lead to a stronger memory for this word than would not presenting it at study (McDermott, 1997; McDermott & Roediger, 1998). Roediger and McDermott's position was that there always will be variability in the strength of both true and false memories, and any reasonable theory would predict that items that were studied will have more memory "signal," on average, than the same items when they were not studied.

The real issue at stake is why related lures are more likely to be falsely recalled and recognized than unrelated lures—what processes cause these systematic errors? To explain this relatedness effect, Miller and Wolford (1999) argued that subjects make liberal criterion shifts to related lures, as indicated by estimates of response bias. However, as pointed out by Wixted and Stretch (2000), such SDT estimates do not necessarily indicate criterion shifts. These estimates are based on the distance between the response criterion and the intersection of the memory distributions, so that either a criterion shift or a shift in the memory distributions could elicit more liberal bias. To illustrate, a simplified version of the latter SDT model of the DRM effect is presented in the bottom panel of Figure 3.2. Here the response criterion (or decision rule) is fixed, but because the related lure is more familiar than unrelated lures (i.e., the former distribution is farther right than the latter) the distance between the response criterion and the relevant distributions is different and would yield different estimates of bias. For more elaborate discussions of how this memory-based model would predict more liberal estimates of bias for related lures, in the absence of criterion shifts, the interested reader should refer to Wixted and Stretch (2000) and Wickens and Hirshman (2000). The main point to be made here is that SDT estimates of bias are ambiguous in this case (and indeed in many memory experiments), so that other evidence is needed to determine whether the criterion-shift model is viable.

☐ SUBJECTIVITY, PRIMING, AND WARNINGS

There are several lines of evidence against decision-based accounts of DRM false memory effects, and in favor of the idea that there is a memory signal for related lures. The major sets of findings discussed here are subjectivity, priming, warning studies, and some additional results motivated by SDT. Subjectivity already has been introduced. As demonstrated by Roediger and McDermott (1995) and others, falsely recognized related lures are more likely to elicit "remember" judgments than "know" judgments. If subjects were using knowledge of the list structure to accept related lures, instead of retrieved memories, then one would expect these lures to be given more "know" than "remember" judgments. These and other subjective judgments are discussed more thoroughly in Chapter 4, where evidence that subjects actually experience recollection for the nonstudied lures is reviewed.

The second line of evidence against a criterion-shift account is that the presentation of DRM study lists leads to priming of the related lure on a variety of implicit measures. On these tests subjects are not instructed to rely on their memory for the study lists, but, instead, memory for studied words and related lures is indirectly tested via facilitated processing of these words (relative to nonstudied and unrelated words) on an ostensibly unrelated task (e.g., completing word fragments, such as "sl__p" with the first word that comes to mind). Because these tests do not explicitly test memory for what was studied, response criteria and demand characteristics based on explicit decision processes are irrelevant. Nevertheless, as reviewed below, prior processing of the study list facilitates processing of the nonpresented related lure on implicit measures, indicating that there is a memory signal for the related lure.

Table 3.1 provides data from seven studies that have investigated priming of related lures after studying DRM lists (under the most typical conditions of these studies). McDermott (1997) found significant priming of related lures on a word association test (in which subjects had to generate the first word that came to mind in response to a nonstudied word) and a word-fragment completion test (see Diliberto-Macaluso, 2005, for similar effects in children). McKone and Murphy (2000), Smith, Gerkens, Pierce, and Choi (2002), and Tajika, Neumann, Hamajima, and Iwahara (2005) found significant priming for related lures on a word-stem completion task, Whittlesea (2002) and Hancock, Hicks, Marsh, and Ritschel (2003) found priming for related lures on a lexical decision task (where subjects had to quickly decide if a letter string was a word or not. Note that McKone (2004) and Zeelenberg and Pecher (2002) obtained null results with this task, but Tse and Neely (2005) replicated and extended related lure priming effects with this task, using a series of more rigorous controls), and Lövdén and Johansson (2003) found priming for related lures on an anagram solution task (using both reaction times and difficulty ratings). In some cases there was more priming for the related lures than for studied words, whereas in others the opposite pattern was found, but in most cases significant priming was obtained for related lures. These effects have been interpreted as reflecting long-lasting conceptual or lexical activation of the related lures, caused by studying the relevant list of associates (see Hicks & Starns, 2005, and Tse & Neely, 2005, for relevant findings and discussion).

A third line of evidence against a criterion-shift account comes from warning studies. Researchers have informed subjects about the false memory effect before the study phase, and warned them to avoid falsely recognizing related lures. Under these conditions subjects should avoid a strategic guessing strategy (on an explicit memory test), because they know that words related to the theme were not studied. Despite these strict instructions against making errors, such warnings do not eliminate the relatedness effect on false recognition (e.g., Gallo, Roberts, & Seamon, 1997; McDermott & Roediger, 1998). The warning results of McDermott and Roediger (1998, Experiment 2) are particularly striking (see also Multhaup & Conner, 2002). During the study phase, fully informed subjects were told to figure out the critical linking word for each list. Immediately after each list was studied, they were given the related lure and asked if it had been presented (in fact, this word was actually studied in half of the lists). Despite these strong warnings and the immediate single-item test, subjects still falsely recognized the related lure when it was not studied on 38% of the lists, and about half of these false alarms were made with high confidence.

TABLE 3.1 Priming Effects for Studied Words and Related Lures on
Implicit Memory Tests

Study	Task	Priming Effects		
		List Words	Related Lures	List vs. Related
McDermott (1997)				
Exp. 2	Word association	.08**	.08**	0[ns]
Exp. 3	Stem completion	.10**	.05*	.05*
Exp. 4	Fragment completion	.14**	.10**	.04[ns]
McKone and Murphy (2000)				
Exp. 1	Stem completion	.17**	.18**	.04[ns]
Exp. 2	Stem completion	.06[ns]	.06[ns]	−.02[ns]
Exp. 3	Stem completion	.25**	.15**	.12[ns]
Smith et al. (2002)				
Exp. 2	Stem completion	na	.19**	na
Exp. 3	Stem completion	.13*	.17*	−.04[ns]
Whittlesea (2002)				
Exp. 1a	Speeded naming	46 ms**	−5 ms[ns]	46 ms[nr]
Exp. 2a	Speeded naming	43 ms**	10 ms[ns]	33 ms[nr]
Exp. 1b	Lexical decision	69 ms*	57 ms**	−65 ms[nr]
Exp. 2b	Lexical decision	38 ms*	27 ms**	−45 ms[nr]
Exp. 2c	Lexical decision	na	24 ms**	na
Hancock et al. (2003)				
Exp. 1	Lexical decision	56 ms**	60 ms**	−19 ms**
Exp. 2	Lexical decision	63 ms[nr]	55 ms**	−19 ms**
Lövdén and Johansson (2003)				
Exp. 1	Anagram solution	1074 ms*	702 ms*	−372 ms[ns]
	Anagram solution	.16*	.08*	.08[ns]
Tajika et al. (2005)				
Single Exp.	Stem completion	.13*	.12*	.01[ns]

Notes: Priming for list words and related lures was measured as performance benefits relative to unrelated lures. The final column compares performance benefits for list words relative to related lures (here priming reflects positive numbers for proportions and negative numbers for latencies). In McKone & Murphy's (2000) Experiment 2, modality differed across study and test, and in Experiment 3 lists were studied five times. In Lövdén and Johansson (2003), McDermott (1997), and Smith et al. (2002), the estimates for studied words were based on responses to related lures when they had actually been studied. In the other studies, the estimates for studied words were based on typical DRM list words. (**$p < .05$, *$p < .10$, ns = nonsignificant, nr = no statistical results provided, na = not applicable).

This collection of arguments against the criterion-shift account is compelling, but the staunch believer could dismiss each piece of evidence. First, it has been argued that "remember" judgments sometimes reflect high-confidence responding, as opposed to recollection, and could themselves be modeled as criterion shifts (e.g., Donaldson, 1996; for discussion of this debate see Hirshman, Lanning, Master, & Henzler, 2002). By extension, related lures could yield "remember" judgments by eliciting extreme criterion shifts, even if they were not truly "remembered." (Setting aside, for now, additional evidence that illusory recollection is real.) Second, implicit priming of the related lures does not necessarily mean that these words would be more familiar on a recognition memory test (or otherwise have an episodic memory signal), especially if one assumes that familiarity and priming are different retrieval processes (see Wagner, Gabrieli, & Verfaellie, 1997, for discussion). Finally, although warnings did not eliminate false recognition, the false recognition effect was reduced significantly by warnings in the aforementioned studies, which is consistent with a criterion-shift account for at least part of the effect (i.e., warning subjects caused them to avoid a strategic guessing strategy, thereby reducing false recognition).

Gallo et al. (2001b) conducted a new warning experiment to further test the criterion-shift theory. In prior work, strong warnings always had been given prior to study, and thus could have influenced either encoding factors (e.g., figuring out the related lure for each list) or retrieval factors (e.g., criterion shifts). Gallo et al. used three primary conditions to tease these factors apart. In every condition, subjects studied several DRM lists for a final recognition test. The critical related item was studied in half of the lists (and hence was a target on the test), and was nonstudied for the other half of the lists (and hence was a lure). The difference between the conditions was in the instructions. In the standard condition, subjects were not informed about the false memory effect. In the remaining conditions, subjects were given explicit warnings to avoid false recognition, and were given a sample DRM list and its related lure as an example of the type of word that they were to avoid (cf. Gallo et al., 1997). In the warning-before-study group, this warning was given before study and so could have affected both encoding and retrieval strategies. In the warning-before-test group, the warning was given after study but before test, so that it could only influence retrieval strategies. In both warning conditions, subjects were told that the critical related word was studied in half the lists and was not studied in the other half. Thus, they had to carefully monitor their memories to determine whether this item had been presented, and could not avoid false recognition by simply responding more conservatively to any item that appeared to be related to the list (at least, not without lowering their hit rate to the critical related item when it had been studied).

When the critical related item was studied in the list, there were no differences in hit rates to this item across the three primary conditions. This finding suggested that subjects in the different conditions were not responding differently to critical related items, based solely on their perceived relatedness to the list (as might be expected from a criterion-shift account). In contrast, there were differences across conditions for those lists that did not contain the critical related item at study. These data are presented in Figure 3.3, after correcting for differences in false alarms to unrelated lures via subtraction. (The uncorrected data followed a similar pattern.) Whereas the hit rates to list items did not differ across these three conditions, false recognition of the related lure was significantly lower when given the warning before study (replicating Gallo et al., 1997 and McDermott & Roediger, 1998). It was argued that these subjects were able to strategically identify the related lure at study, and thereby avoid false recognition of this word (a topic discussed more fully in Chapter 5). More important for present concerns, the strong warning after study was ineffective at reducing false recognition. This last pattern was interpreted as strong evidence against the criterion-shift account. Because these subjects were given an analogous warning to those subjects that were warned before study, they also were motivated to reduce false recognition, and therefore should have avoided a strategic guessing strategy or liberal criterion shift at test. Nevertheless, these subjects were not able to reduce false recognition, suggesting that such decision processes are not the

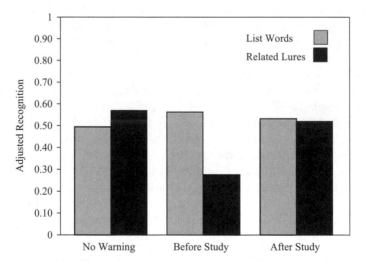

FIGURE 3.3   The effect of warnings on true and false recognition (adjusted for base rate false alarms) in Gallo et al. (2001b).

primary cause of the false memory effect. The warning after the study phase was too late—apparently the information that could lead to the false memory had already been encoded.

Other researchers also have found that giving a warning after study (but before test) does not lead to significant reductions in false recognition or false recall relative to a no-warning condition (Anastasi, Rhodes, & Burns, 2000, Experiment 3; Lee & Chang, 2004, Experiment 1; McCabe & Smith, 2002, Experiment 1; Neuschatz, Payne, Lampinen, & Toglia, 2001, Experiments 2 and 3; see also Whittlesea, 2002, Experiment 3a), although small effects of these warnings are sometimes observed (e.g., reduced confidence ratings). Two studies have found a significant effect of warnings after study (McCabe & Smith, 2002, Experiment 2; Whittlesea, 2002, Experiment 3b), but in both cases the related lure was never presented at study. Thus, unlike Gallo et al. (2001b) or McDermott and Roediger (1998), warned subjects could have avoided false recognition simply by responding conservatively to any item that they thought might be the related lure, even if there was a memory signal for this word (see Gallo et al., 2001b and Whittlesea, 2002, for comparisons of these two warning methodologies). Most important, robust relatedness effects on false recognition have been found in every warning study, and in almost every case the relatedness effect on false recognition or recall was not affected much by a warning after study. If one is willing to accept the assumption that motivated subjects who are strongly warned against guessing "old" to related lures (in the absence of a memory signal) actually *do* avoid such a guessing strategy, then the high levels of false recognition under these conditions cannot be attributed to such guessing strategies.

A final piece of evidence against the criterion-shift or guessing account comes from an additional SDT analysis. As Westerberg and Marsolek (2003b) argued, if the memory signal for related lures was equal to unrelated lures (i.e., if associative relationships do not influence the memory strength of nonstudied items), then studying related lures should yield the same increase in memory strength (or sensitivity) as does studying unrelated lures (or even a larger increase, if associations boost memory encoding). In three experiments, they included conditions (like Miller & Wolford, 1999) that allowed for the calculation of sensitivity estimates when each type of item was studied versus when it was not studied. Contrary to what they had predicted based on a criterion-shift or decision-based process, Westerberg and Marsolek found that it was harder for subjects to discriminate between studied and nonstudied (critical) related words than it was for them to discriminate between studied and nonstudied unrelated words. This result can be explained by theories that propose that there is a false memory signal for nonstudied related lures. Because these words already had a strong memory signal when they were not studied (bottom panel of Figure 3.2), there apparently was less room for memory to improve when they were studied, relative to unrelated words, and thus discrimination was more difficult. Further, these discrimination differences were found on a two-alternative forced-choice test (Experiment 2), on which criterion shifts based on perceived relatedness could not apply. An account that proposes a memory signal for nonstudied related lures is needed to explain these discrimination differences.

In sum, the evidence indicates that DRM false memory effects are not caused by decision processes or guessing strategies. Evidence that there is some form of memory for the related lure comes from subjective judgments, priming studies, warning studies, and SDT analyses. This is not to say, though, that criterion shifts play no role in this phenomenon, or that their consideration does not contribute to theoretical developments. In the Gallo et al. (2001b) warning study, it was discussed how a conservative criterion shift could reduce the frequency of responding to related lures, especially if subjects are told that related lures were never studied in the list. In this sense, the setting of a familiarity threshold (or response criterion) can be considered one type of diagnostic monitoring process that can reduce false memory effects (discussed in Chapter 5). The important point here is that strategically engaging in *liberal* criterion shifts does not seem to be the *cause* of these false memories, at least under standard conditions. Instead, some other factor (or set of factors) appears to create a false memory signal for the related lure, a topic that is addressed next.

☐ THE "THREE BIG" THEORIES

The three most common explanations of false memory effects in converging associates tasks are associative activation, thematic consistency, and feature overlap. Returning to Figure 3.1, these three theories differentially emphasize associations, themes, or semantic similarity, respectively. Each of these ideas can trace its origins to previous research literatures, well before the rise in the popularity of converging associates tasks as a way to study false memories. The following sections briefly sketch the origins of each theory, its central components, and how it is similar and different from the others. Evidence supporting one or the other theory will be presented in the final section, but these theories are not mutually exclusive. Also, in the spirit of fairness, each of these theories is afforded a considerable amount of explanatory flexibility. In previous works, advocates of one or the other viewpoint sometimes have furnished an oversimplified version of a rival explanation, in an effort to disprove that theory in favor of their own. For instance, advocates of gist-based explanations might oversimplify associative activation theories, or vice versa. The goal here is not so much to marshal evidence in favor of one or the other explanation, but instead to present the virtues and limitations of each theory, and to explore how far these theories can be pushed in an effort to incorporate the most illuminating findings.

Associative Activation

Although associative theories can apply to a variety of false memory effects, and the term "association" has several connotations (as discussed in Chapter 1), here the term "associative activation" is used very specifically. It refers to the activation of concepts stored in semantic memory due to the processing of other concepts found at the same conceptual level (e.g., one word activates another). Recent associative theories of false memories are related to Underwood's (1965) implicit associative response theory, although they have been elaborated with more modern cognitive explanations (e.g., Roediger, Balota, & Watson, 2001a). As a starting point, these theories assume that people develop an intricate lexicon, or mental dictionary, of frequently used words and concepts (represented as "nodes," or entries in the lexicon). This lexicon is often thought to be semantically organized, so that nodes with similar meanings or that are otherwise associated have stronger bonds than nodes that are relatively less associated (see Figure 3.4). This semantic assumption allows meaning-based similarity to be incorporated into the model, but other factors also contribute to the strength of an associative link (e.g., frequent co-occurrence in the language). A critical feature of this type of model is that the processing of one word (e.g., *bed*) activates its corresponding node in the lexicon, and this activation spreads to surrounding nodes (e.g., *sleep*), an idea popularized by Collins and Loftus (1975). Such spreading activation is thought to occur rapidly, relatively automatically, and to fade quickly. Evidence for such spreading activation comes primarily from semantic priming experiments, where the brief presentation of a prime word (e.g., lion) can facilitate subsequent processing of a related word (e.g., tiger), relative to an unrelated word (e.g., horse), on tasks such as lexical decision and speeded naming (e.g., Balota & Lorch, 1986; see Hutchison, 2003, and Neely, 1991, for reviews).

Such a model can explain how a nonpresented word (e.g., sleep) becomes mentally activated when a list of associates is presented (e.g., bed, rest, awake, etc.), but it needs additional assumptions to account for false recall and recognition in episodic memory tasks such as DRM. Semantic priming effects typically only last for a few hundred milliseconds of uninterrupted processing, which is much shorter than would be necessary to

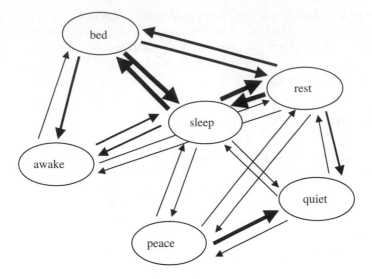

FIGURE 3.4 A schematic portion of the mental lexicon. Connections are pictured as bidirectional because one word might be more likely to activate another than vice versa. The hypothetical strength of each association is depicted by line thickness.

explain the false memory effects observed for related words (which have been found to occur minutes, days, or even months after the studied associates are presented; Seamon et al., 2002c; Toglia, Neuschatz, & Goodwin, 1999). There are at least two ways to explain long-lasting false recall and recognition memory effects via the associative activation theory.

The first explanation assumes that the related lure is activated during the study phase, and this activation causes the formation of a lasting memory representation. One idea is that, because several converging associates are studied, activation of the related lure summates (e.g., Seamon et al., 1998). If such activation becomes sufficiently strong, then the subject might consciously think of the related lure, and thereby encode this thought as a unique episodic memory. This representation could be long lasting, especially if the subject mistakenly rehearses the related item as having occurred (as observed by Goodwin, Meissner, & Ericsson, 2001, and Seamon, Lee, Toner, Wheeler, Goodkind, & Birch, 2002b). In this case, false remembering of the related lure would occur when the subject retrieves this episodic representation and mistakenly decides that the item had been presented in the list (a reality or source monitoring error; Johnson & Raye, 1981).

The second explanation assumes that the spreading activation that is responsible for false remembering occurs during the test phase, as opposed (or in addition) to the study phase (see Tse & Neely, 2005, and Whittlesea, Masson, & Hughes, 2005, for related discussions). According to this idea, the related lure could be activated on a recall or recognition test by the presentation (or recall) of its fellow associates that were studied (such activation would be predicted by associative models of retrieval, such as those developed by Anderson, 1983; Anderson & Bower, 1973; and by Nelson, McEvoy, and colleagues [e.g., PIER2], see McEvoy et al., 1999; Nelson et al., 2003). If the act of recalling list words sufficiently activates the related lure during the recall test, or if test-based activation facilitates processing of the related lure on a recognition test, then the resulting increase in processing fluency or familiarity of the related lure might be attributed to prior presentation in the study phase (cf. Jacoby, Kelley, & Dywan, 1989; Whittlesea, 2002). Note that studied associates might not need to be presented at test in order to activate the related lure on a recognition test. As long as the related lure can cue the episodic representations of its studied associates, these representations could, in turn, activate the related lure (Gallo & Seamon, 2004).

Thematic Consistency

The second major explanation focuses on the idea that each list is organized around a central theme. The subject extracts this theme as the list is presented and encodes it into memory. This aspect of the theory is similar to the aforementioned decision-based accounts (e.g., the criterion-shift theory), but the two accounts differ in how this thematic representation influences performance. The decision-based theory stipulates that thematic consistency causes the subject to guess (or strategically infer) that the related lure was presented (with no actual "memory" for the related lure). In contrast, the thematic consistency account stipulates that the consistency between the related lure and the theme of the list causes a memory signal for the related lure (this signal would be represented by a distribution shift in SDT, as opposed to a criterion shift). That is, the thematic knowledge activates the concept of the related lure (on a recall test), and/or makes the related lure feel familiar (on a recognition test), and the subject actually believes that they are remembering (as opposed to guessing or inferring). This difference is subtle but important. Under both accounts the subject might be consciously aware that the lure is related to a studied theme, but only under the thematic consistency account does the subject get the subjective sense that the related lure was previously encountered.

The thematic consistency explanation is similar to the prototype theories of categorization and false recognition discussed in Chapter 2, in the sense that the subject extracts a common representation across stimuli (in this case, a theme), and this representation affects performance to new (but related) stimuli. It also is similar to Bartlett's (1932) description of "schemas" in memory (see Chapter 1), although that concept has its own historical connotations and so the two probably should be kept separate (see Neuschatz, Lampinen, Preston, Hawkins, & Toglia, 2002).

In converging associates tasks, it is important to notice that the thematic consistency account has been primarily directed at explaining false recognition, and not false recall. That is, the experimenter presents the subject with a related lure; this lure feels more familiar due to thematic consistency, and thus is falsely recognized. In order to account for false recall effects, additional assumptions need to be made. For instance, some form of a two-stage generate + recognize process could be considered (as was discussed in terms of the criterion-shift theory). First, the related lure is mentally generated (i.e., it consciously "pops into mind"), and second, it is falsely recognized based on thematic consistency. Note, though, that this approach simply pushes the important question back a stage. How is the nonpresented lure mentally generated in the first place?

At this level the distinction between the associative activation theory and the thematic consistency theory gets blurred. To account for false recall, some appeal to activation processes in a pre-existing lexicon (or storehouse of general knowledge) is necessary. How else would a nonpresented word be mentally generated on a recall test, if not through some sort of mental activation? Any theory would need to make such an appeal. The associative activation theory proposes that activation spreads across associative links between nodes (or word representations) stored in memory. A theme-based theory could certainly incorporate this assumption in order to explain mental generation, and then appeal to thematic consistency to explain why this generated item is accepted as a retrieved memory. Alternatively, a theme-based theory could assume that the lure is activated by the thematic representation itself (which, by definition, contains features that generalize across many of the studied associates). The difference between these alternatives is that activation either spreads from one word representation to the other, or it spreads from a thematic representation to a word representation.

A popular theory that makes use of the notion of thematic consistency is fuzzy trace theory, originating with Brainerd, Reyna, and colleagues (e.g., Brainerd & Reyna, 1998, 2002; Reyna & Brainerd, 1995). This theory has contributed to research in memory, reasoning, and cognitive development (see Reyna & Brainerd, 1995), and has been popular in the false memory literature. According to this account, incoming stimuli are encoded into two qualitatively different types of traces: *verbatim* and *gist*. This distinction harks back to the psycholinguistic distinction between the surface-form of language (verbatim) and the meaning and substance of language (gist). In the DRM task, a verbatim trace represents the item-specific details of each presented item (e.g., perceptual attributes that uniquely identify each studied item, specific position in the list, etc.), and is associated with the subjective experience of recollection. A gist trace represents the overall similarity (e.g., overlapping conceptual or perceptual attributes) and relations between the studied words (e.g., the conceptual theme of the list), and is associated with the subjective experience of familiarity, or in some cases "phantom recollection" (discussed in Chapter 4).

The related lure is consistent with the gist of the list, and when it cues or activates this gist information at test the result is a memory signal for the lure. At this level of analysis, the idea of "gist" in fuzzy trace theory is similar to the idea of a "theme" in the thematic consistency account. However, in addition to the gist of a list (or global gist), some have proposed that each word has its own unique meaning or local gist that can cause false remembering (e.g., Lampinen, Odegard, Blackshear, & Toglia, in press; also see Neuschatz et al., 2002; Reyna & Lloyd, 1997). For instance, fuzzy trace theory has been used to explain false recognition effects even when only one associate is presented (e.g., remembering "hot" when "cold" was presented; see Brainerd, Reyna, & Mojardin, 1999), and thus there is no overall theme or gist of the list. In this sense, "gist" is being used more in terms of semantic feature overlap between the two words. As discussed in the next section, feature overlap is similar to thematic consistency, but there are important differences. To avoid confusion, the term "gist" is used here to refer to the extraction of a separate thematic representation of the list, and so the term should not be strictly interpreted as the gist parameter of fuzzy trace theory. Fuzzy trace theory maintains a rich set of operational definitions and mathematical formalizations that are beyond the present scope, and so these formulations will not be discussed in great detail. (Neither will the formulations of associatively based models, like PIER2, or feature-based models, like MINERVA2.) It also should be noted that, because of the verbatim–gist distinction, fuzzy trace theory is among the ranks of the numerous dual-process theories of memory. The dual-process nature of the theory provides one way of conceptualizing recollection-based monitoring processes that can reduce false memories, and these sorts of processes are discussed more in Chapter 5.

Feature Overlap

Like the thematic consistency theory, the feature overlap theory also was developed primarily to account for false recognition, but it does not necessarily appeal to either associative activation (within a lexicon) or to the extraction and encoding of a theme of each list (or a global gist representation). In fact, Anisfeld and Knapp (1968) proposed one version of this theory as an alternative to Underwood's (1965) associative account of false recognition, and a mathematical version of this type of theory (MINERVA2) was proposed as an alternative to the prototype explanation of the Posner and Keele (1970) categorization effects (Hintzman, 1986). Arndt and Hirshman (1998) extended the logic of this latter model to explain false recognition in the DRM task.

According to the feature overlap theory, events are encoded into memory as bundles of features (e.g., perceptual, conceptual, emotional attributes, etc.). At retrieval, the degree of overlap between the features of a test item (e.g., a lure on a recognition test) and the features stored in memory that correspond to each studied item determines the level of familiarity toward the test item. Similar processes are embraced by the encoding specificity principle, which proposes that the overlap between an encoded trace and a retrieval cue is critical for recall, and has been used to explain false recognition (see Tulving, 1983). In the DRM task the related lure shares semantic features with the studied words. The retrieval of these common features makes the related lure seem familiar, and thus causes the subject to falsely claim that the related lure was presented in the list. The critical difference between this theory and the thematic consistency theory is that a separate theme or gist trace (or prototype) does not need to be extracted and encoded from the studied items. Instead, only the studied items (or exemplars) are encoded into memory, and the overlap between their features and features of the related lure is the key contributor toward the memory signal for the related lure.

Much like the thematic consistency theory, the feature overlap theory needs to be elaborated to account for the mental generation of a nonpresented word on a recall test. An appeal to the activation of a pre-existing word representation is necessary, although spreading activation from one whole lexical entry to another (as in the associatively based theory) or from a thematic representation to a lexical entry (as in the theme-based theory) is not necessary. Instead, the semantic features of the related lure that overlap with studied words (and hence were encoded) might first be retrieved. If activation then spreads to the remaining (nonstudied) features of the related lure (i.e., its entire lexical entry), then the entire word could be generated on a recall test. As with the activation processes discussed under the thematic consistency theory, the distinction between the feature overlap theory and the associative activation theory gets blurred at this level of analysis. This point will be discussed more at the end of this chapter, after evidence that is directly relevant to these theories is reviewed.

☐ EVIDENCE FOR THE THREE BIG THEORIES

The difference between the three big theories is in their assumptions as to how words and concepts are represented and activated, and in how this activation gets translated into a false memory. Do lexical entries directly activate each other (associative theory), is there a separate thematic representation that can activate them (thematic theory), or does activation spread among the features that are bound to each lexical entry (feature theory)? Some version of activation needs to be proposed to explain the mental generation of the nonpresented lure on a recall test, or the priming of this lure on an implicit memory test, but the source of this activation differs across the three theories (see Buchanan, Brown, Cabeza, & Maitson, 1999, for related views). These theories also differ in their explanation of why the related lure is accepted as a memory (on a recall or recognition test). As discussed, a memory signal for the related lure could arise from associative activation, thematic consistency, or feature overlap, and this similarity makes the different theories difficult to disentangle. For instance, increasing the number of studied associates that correspond to the related lure increases false recall and recognition (as discussed in Chapter 2), but this increase could be explained by any of these three theories. In what follows the strongest evidence in support of one theory over the other in the DRM task is presented. The application of these theories to other converging associates tasks also is discussed, where relevant.

Associative Strength

As discussed in Chapter 2, Deese (1959b) showed that the associative strength between list words and the related lure (dubbed "backward associative strength," or BAS) was strongly correlated with false recall across lists ($r = +.87$), accounting for 76% of the variance. Deese concluded that "in the process of recollection, words and concepts associated with remembered items will be added" (p. 21) and that "the hypotheses arising out of the empirical relationship found in this study suggest ways of interpreting a wide variety of problems of patterning and organization in memory in terms of elementary associative frequencies" (p. 22). Needless to say, Deese favored an associative approach. Roediger et al. (2001c) replicated the relationship between BAS (as measured by the norms of Nelson, McEvoy, & Schreiber, 1998a) and false recall ($r = +.73$), and found that associative strength was the strongest predictor of false recall in a multiple regression analysis ($\beta = +.70$, sr = .60) relative to six other variables (mean inter-item associative strength [connections between list words, or connectivity], mean forward associative strength [connections from the related lure to the list words], and length, printed word frequency, and concreteness of the related lure). True recall was the second strongest predictor, correlating negatively with false recall ($r = -.43$, $\beta =-.40$, sr $= -.34$). The length of the related lure also was negatively correlated with false recall ($r = -.28$), but none of the other variables were significant predictors. BAS is the strongest predictor of false recall that has been found, and many researchers have reported a relationship between BAS and either false recall or false recognition (e.g., Arndt & Hirshman, 1998; Gallo & Roediger, 2002; and McEvoy et al., 1999). By comparison, forward associative strength is not a strong predictor of false recall or recognition across typical DRM lists. Brainerd and Wright (2005) have provided some evidence that forward associations can play a larger role than is usually attributed to them, but, as they discussed, they used short word lists and so their findings might not generalize to the typical DRM task (cf. Gallo, 2004). (The potential effects of connectivity are revisited at the end of this section, and the effect of lure length and true recall is discussed more thoroughly in Chapters 5 and 6, respectively.)

Roediger et al. (2001c) argued that the BAS correlation supports an associative activation theory of DRM false remembering. After all, BAS reflects the probability that subjects will mentally generate the related lure when presented with the list words on a free association task, and, as discussed, a similar process could occur during the study or test phase of the DRM recall task. They further suggested that the wide variability in these lists to elicit false recall is difficult to reconcile with a thematic consistency account (or gist). As a concrete example, they compared the lists corresponding to the related lure "bitter" (sweet, sour, taste, chocolate, rice, cold, lemon, angry, hard, mad, acid, almonds, herbs, grape, fruit) and "sweet" (sour, candy, sugar, bitter, good, taste, tooth, nice, honey, soda, chocolate, heard, cake, tart, pie). In both cases, they argued, the list contains words that converge on the general meaning or gist of the related lure, but nevertheless false recall norms (Gallo & Roediger, 2002; Stadler et al., 1999) indicate that "bitter" is almost never falsely recalled (1%), whereas "sweet" is falsely recalled more than half the time (54%). Other examples can be found, such as the "window" list (door, glass, pane, shade, ledge, sill, house, open, curtain, frame, view, breeze, sash, screen, shutter) and the "whiskey" list (drink, drunk, beer, liquor, gin, bottles, alcohol, rye, glass, wine, rum, bourbon, evil, bar, scotch). The first elicits one of the highest levels of false recall (65%), whereas the second elicits one of the lowest (3%). The critical difference, according to Roediger et al., is in associative activation as reflected by BAS: "sweet" and "window" are more likely to be generated as associates to list words on a free association task (mean BAS = 17% and 18%, respectively) than are "bitter" and "whiskey" (1% and 2%).

One limitation of these arguments is that they are based only on intu-itions about "goodness of theme" or gist. The correlation between BAS and false remembering, like all correlations, might not reflect a direct causal relationship. The correlation actually might be mediated by thematic consistency or feature overlap, as opposed to associative acti-vation. As was discussed in the context of these other theories, even if associative activation leads to the mental generation of the related lure while taking a recall test, other processes might lead to the false memory signal for this word (or the actual belief that it had been in the study list). Strong associates tend to be more similar in meaning than weak associ-ates, and so strong associates might share more overlapping semantic features or might create a more coherent theme. It might be this seman-tic similarity that makes related lures seem familiar and thus drives false remembering. These alternatives cannot be ruled out solely on the basis of the BAS correlation, but a comparison with other materials, discussed next, adds further weight to the idea that the strong relationship between BAS and false remembering is mediated by associative activation (from one word to another).

Categorized Lists

Evidence against a semantic similarity explanation of BAS effects, and thus against a feature overlap or thematic consistency account, comes from a comparison with false memories elicited by categorized lists (e.g., studying *sparrow, cardinal, blue jay*, etc., to elicit false recall of *robin*). All of the words in categorized lists share similar semantic features to the related lure, and by definition they all converge on a common theme or semantic gist that relates all of the words (i.e., the category). Despite these strong thematic relationships, relatedness effects on false recogni-tion from categorized lists (i.e., false alarms to related lures minus unre-lated lures) typically range from 20% to 30% (e.g., Brainerd et al., 2001; Dewhurst, 2001; Seamon et al., 2000), which are much lower than those that are typically observed with associative or DRM lists (40–60%). False recall also tends to be much lower from categorized lists than from DRM lists (e.g., Lövdén, 2003).

Buchanan et al. (1999) directly compared associative (DRM-type) and categorized lists and found that false recognition of related lures was greater in the former (.37) than in the latter (.19). They argued that the larg-er effects of associative lists on false recognition implicated an associative mechanism, as opposed to feature-based or category-based mechanisms.

In a similar vein, Smith et al. (2002) argued that false recall from DRM lists is dominated by associative activation of the related lures, whereas false recall from categorized lists (which was lower in their study) is dominated by semantically guided retrieval (akin to thematic consistency). Consistent with this argument, they found that DRM lists have higher associative strength than categorized lists, and that only DRM lists elicited priming on the implicit test of word-stem completion (which was thought to reflect associative activation of the nonstudied word).

Pierce, Gallo, Weiss, and Schacter (2005a) used a meaning test (e.g., Brainerd & Reyna, 1998) to directly measure the likelihood of related lures to cue the themes or gist of their corresponding study lists. After studying several associative and categorized lists (with greater BAS for associative lists), subjects were presented with studied words, related lures, and unrelated lures. Subjects in Experiment 1 decided whether each word was studied (typical recognition instructions), whereas subjects in Experiment 2 were instructed to indicate whether the test word was "similar to a central concept or theme that was studied," regardless of whether they thought the test word was studied. On the standard test, false recognition from categorized lists (38%) was lower than that from associative lists (60%), even though true recognition and false alarms to unrelated lures did not differ considerably across lists. A smaller difference was obtained on the meaning test (86% vs. 92%), and, even when a subset of associative and categorized lists were equated on their likelihood to be accepted on the meaning test (80%), large differences in false recognition persisted (28% vs. 59%). The finding that lists differed in terms of false recognition (and associative strength), but that judgments of thematic consistency did not differ, is more consistent with an associative activation view than with a thematic consistency view.

In another study, Park et al. (2005) argued that associative activation was responsible for the false memory effects from categorized lists. However, it was argued that the structure of the underlying associations was critical, in addition to associative strength. False memory was greatest when associations were at a coordinate level (e.g., from one exemplar to the next), but was minimal when associations were at a subordinate level (e.g., false recognition of a category name such as "fruit" was unlikely when studying a list of exemplars, such as "orange," "apple," etc.), even though associative strength was equated across the two levels of associations. It is difficult to explain these results with thematic consistency because, if anything, the category name should be most likely to activate the gist of a category. Unfortunately, a meaning test was not used in this study, so it is unclear whether cross-level associates were perceived at test as more or less consistent with the gist of the list than same-level associates.

Homophone Lures

Other evidence in favor of an associative activation theory, as opposed to similarity or gist-based theories, comes from a study by Hutchison and Balota (2005). In this study homophones were used as related lures (e.g., *fall*), so that half of the studied words converged on one meaning (*stumble, slip, rise, trip, faint, clumsy*) and the other half converged on another meaning (*autumn, season, spring, leaves, brisk, harvest*). False recall or recognition of these homophone lures was compared to that of DRM lures, in which all of the studied words converged on the same meaning. It was argued that the homograph lists had weaker gist or themes than the DRM lists, because they converged on two different meanings of a word instead of focusing on one. As a manipulation check, this difference in thematic coherence or gist was confirmed by comparing the related lures on a meaning test (similar to that used in Pierce et al., 2005a).

Consistent with any of the theories, false recall of related lures was equivalent across the two types of lists when only six studied words were used (i.e., six words converging on the same meaning of either the homophone or the DRM lure). However, when the list length was increased to 12, so that the 6 additional study words converged on a different meaning of the homophone lure but the same meaning of the DRM lure, the theories made different predictions. According to the gist-based theory, increasing list length should have enhanced false recall more for the DRM lists, because these lists had stronger gist than the homophone lists. According to an associative theory, though, false recall should have increased equally across the two types of lists, because the lists were equated on associative strength. Across five experiments, using various presentation times, blocked or mixed presentation, and recall or recognition tests, the results were more consistent with an associative activation theory. Adding additional studied words increased false memory rates equally across the two types of lists.

Nonassociative Convergence

Putting the arguments for associative activation in the DRM task aside, we do know that nonassociative mechanisms play an important role in false recognition. This claim is based on false recognition effects for materials that have no pre-existing mental representations, and thus cannot be associatively activated from semantic memory, such as lists of nonwords, random-dot patterns, nonfamiliar faces, or other abstract figures that are perceptually similar to a nonstudied lure (see Chapter 2). False recognition effects for these materials must be due to some other process, such as perceptual feature overlap or thematic consistency. Evidence for feature overlap alone comes from conditions where only one item from the abstract category was presented, and thus there is no theme that could contribute to false recognition, although such effects tend to be small or nonexistent (e.g., Budson et al., 2001; Koutstaal et al., 1999b). As in the DRM task (see Chapter 2), increasing the number of studied items can greatly increase false recognition with these materials, either because memory for the overlapping features is strengthened or because a coherent theme (or prototype) can be extracted more easily and further contribute to the false recognition effect. Given that thematic consistency or feature overlap plays a role in these other tasks, it often is assumed that one or the other also contributes to DRM false memory effects (although DRM lists involve conceptual as opposed to perceptual relationships).

Test-Item Context

Gunter, Ivanko, and Bodner (2005) found that testing only related words on a recognition test (i.e., DRM list words and related lures) resulted in lower false recognition of related lures, along with corresponding "remember" judgments, relative to a more typical condition where unrelated lures were included on the test. They argued that the typical procedure tended to encourage gist-based responding, because studied words and unrelated lures could be distinguished from each other solely on the basis of gist-based similarity (Tun et al., 1998, made a similar argument). Gunter et al. (2005) also found that true recognition was lower when only related words were tested. This finding suggests that subjects were more cautious overall in accepting any word related to the gist of one of the lists (analogous to some of the warning-after-study effects that were previously discussed). These effects are difficult to explain via associative activation processes, which if anything should have been greater when only related words were presented at test, and are more consistent with a gist-based theory.

Retention Interval

The effects of retention interval on false recall and recognition in the DRM task also have been used as a way to test between the theories. According to fuzzy trace theory, thematic or gist representations that support false remembering are more resilient to forgetting than the item-specific or verbatim representations that differentially support true memory (e.g., Brainerd,

Reyna, & Brandse, 1995a; Payne et al., 1996; Reyna & Brainerd, 1995), an assumption that originated in psycholinguistic research (e.g., Reyna, 1995; Reyna & Kiernan, 1994). This prediction also falls naturally from constructive theories of remembering, consistent with Bartlett's (1932) claim that memory for the details of a story fade over time but the overall gist or general meaning of the experience is retained. Feature overlap theories also predict that false memories can be more resilient to retention interval than true memories. The reasoning is that those features that are shared between several studied items (and support false memory of the related lure) will be forgotten less often than those features that are specific to each studied item (and thus support true memory), because there are more of the former than the latter (e.g., Hintzman, 1986). For similar reasons, test-based associative activation theories also could predict that false remembering will be more robust than true remembering over time, because activation of the related lure is summed across several studied words.

In contrast to these predictions, theories that are based solely on activation of the related lure at study (and subsequent source memory errors) predict greater decreases in false memories than in true memories across a retention interval. This prediction is based on the idea that, all other factors being equal, the recall of a word that was only mentally activated at study should not be as great as that of a word that was actually presented, because the latter would benefit from both associative activation and the perceptual features of presentation. It could be argued that study-based associative activation of the related lure is stronger than that of list words, and thereby surpasses the beneficial effects of actual presentation on memory (see Hancock et al., 2003, for relevant findings). Although this position can explain why false recall is sometimes as great as (or greater than) true recall on immediate tests (at least for words from the middle of the list), it cannot explain how false recall or recognition would be affected less by retention interval than true recall or recognition. As discussed, in order to explain false remembering at longer retention intervals a study-based activation account would need to posit a more lasting representation, ostensibly through conscious activation. However, when subjects are instructed to overtly rehearse the words during study, related lures are not rehearsed more often than list items (e.g., Seamon et al., 2002b). This finding suggests that the related lure is not consciously activated more often than list words during study. The most logical prediction from study-based activation theories therefore would be greater forgetting of related lures across a delay, relative to list words.

Table 3.2 summarizes the results from nine studies using the DRM task, divided into conditions using recall tests and recognition tests (all recognition data were corrected by subtracting the appropriate unrelated false alarms). All of these comparisons used relatively long delays

TABLE 3.2 Effects of Retention Interval (i.e., the Delay between Study and Test) on Recall and Recognition of List Words (LW) and Related Lures (RL) in 12 Studies

Study	Delay	Absolute Dec.		Prop. Dec.	
		LW	RL	LW	RL
Recall tests					
McDermott (1996, Exp. 1)[a]	2 days	.46	.34	.92	.74
Thapar and McDermott (2001, Exp. 1)	2 days				
Deep Study Task		.24	.08	.67	.33
Shallow Study Task (collapsed)		.06	.02	.67	.33
Brainerd, Payne, Wright, & Reyna (2003a, Exp. 2)	1 week				
List studied 1×/test 1		.10	.12	.50	.28
Lists studied 3×/test 1		.15	−.02	.47	−.11
Thapar and McDermott (2001, Exp. 1)	1 week				
Deep Study Task		.27	.10	.75	.42
Shallow Study Task (collapsed)		.06	.03	.67	.50
Toglia et al. (1999, Exp. 2)	1 week				
Study lists blocked by theme		.21	.03	.53	.06
Study lists mixed by theme		.16	.03	.52	.09
Seamon et al. (2002c, Exp. 1)	2 weeks	.10	.01	.59	.04
Toglia et al. (1999, Exp. 2)	3 weeks				
Study blocked by theme		.25	.05	.63	.09
Study mixed by theme		.21	−.07	.68	−.20
Seamon et al. (2002c, Exp. 1)	2 months	.13	.16	.76	.57
Mean		.18	.07**	.64	.24**
Recognition tests					
Payne et al. (1996, Exp. 1)	1 day	.18	.11	.35	.19
Lampinen and Schwartz (2000)[b]	2 days				
Exp. 1		.17	.11	.26	.16
Exp. 2		.24	.21	.38	.29
Neuschatz et al. (2001)	2 days				
Exp. 1 (collapsed)		.21	.22	.37	.46
Exp. 3 (no-warning condition)		.14	.08	.30	.22
Seamon et al. (2002c, Exp. 2)	2 days	.13	.17	.26	.29

(Continued)

TABLE 3.2   *(Continued)*

Study	Delay	Absolute Dec.		Prop. Dec.	
		LW	RL	LW	RL
Thapar and McDermott (2001, Exp. 2)	2 days				
Deep Study Task		.35	.15	.41	.24
Shallow Study Task (collapsed)		.11	.02	.32	.07
Brainerd et al. (2001, Exp. 2)	1 week				
Forward study order/no prior recall		.27	.27	.55	.42
Backward study order/no prior recall		.06	.27	.18	.47
Thapar and McDermott (2001, Exp. 2)	1 week				
Deep Study Task		.42	.17	.49	.27
Shallow Study Task (collapsed)		.11	.03	.32	.10
Seamon et al. (2002c, Exp. 2)	2 weeks	.22	.17	.44	.29
Seamon et al. (2002c, Exp. 2)	2 months	.41	.48	.82	.83
Mean		.22	.18[ns]	.39	.31[*]

Notes: Recognition scores were corrected by subtracting unrelated false alarms. "Absolute dec." reports the raw decrease between immediate and delay scores (negative numbers represent an increase). "Prop. dec." expresses the absolute decrease as a proportion of the initial score. For the mean differences between list words and related lures, **$p < .01$, *$p < .10$, ns = not significant.
[a]Immediate tests followed each study list (after a 30 s delay to eliminate the recency effect), whereas the 2-day delayed test covered all 24 of the studied lists.
[b]These data were estimated from figures, and were corrected (by the original authors) using the equation HITS - (FA/1 - FA).

(on the order of days) as opposed to brief delays (e.g., 30 s). Brief delays have been found to reduce true recall more than false recall (e.g., McDermott, 1996; McEvoy et al., 1999), but this simply may be due to a reduction of the recency effect in immediate recall (see Chapter 2). In Table 3.2, reductions in true or false memory over a delay are expressed both as absolute decreases and as proportions of the initial levels of true and false memory. This proportional score is one way to circumvent differences in initial levels of true and false memory that could have influenced relative differences in forgetting rates.

As can be seen from the table, regardless of the type of score one uses, the most frequent finding is that false memory was affected less by retention interval than true memory. For recall tests, this pattern was observed (at least numerically) in 11 out of 13 conditions for raw scores, and in all 13 conditions using proportional scores. Averaging across all of the experimental comparisons in the table (weighing each equally), the mean absolute decrease for list words (.18) was significantly greater than that for related lures (.07), t (12) = 4.63, $p < .01$, and this pattern also was found in proportional decreases (.64 vs. .24, t (12) = 7.09, $p < .001$). This pattern was not as consistent in recognition tests (and not always significant), although it was obtained in 9 out of 14 conditions for raw scores and in 10 out of 14 conditions for proportional scores. On absolute scores, the mean decrease for list words (.22) was not different than that for related words (.18) ($p = .20$), but the effect was larger on proportional scores (.39 vs. .31, t (13) = 2.11, $p = .06$). Thus, true recognition sometimes decreased more than false recognition over a delay, but not always. Collectively, these findings suggest that false recall is more persistent over time than true recall, and that false recognition is equally or more persistent than true recognition. These findings suggest that processes other than study-based associative activation are involved (e.g., test-based associative activation, gist or thematic consistency, or feature overlap).

Conscious Activation

Several other pieces of evidence suggest that DRM false recall or false recognition does not require conscious generation of the related lure at study, although such generation sometimes does occur and can influence false memory effects. Seamon et al. (2002b) had subjects rehearse the words aloud while they were studying the lists. They found high levels of false recall (.27) and false recognition (.74) even for those related lures that were never overtly generated at study, indicating that conscious thoughts of these words at study were not necessary for subsequent false remembering. The frequency of prior rehearsals did correlate positively with subsequent false recall (see also Goodwin et al., 2001), which is consistent with the idea that conscious generation of the related lure at study enhances false recall. Marsh and Bower (2004) obtained analogous results in false recognition, using a free-rehearsal procedure (as in these other studies) and also using a forced-generation procedure (in which subjects were instructed to generate associates for each word during study). Lampinen, Meier, Arnal, and Leding (2005) also presented evidence that subjects explicitly generate related lures during the presentation of the study words, and that these generations have consequences for subsequent recognition decisions.

Gallo and Seamon (2004) took a different approach. Subjects were presented with several DRM lists using rapid visual presentation (i.e., an entire list of 15 words was presented in less than 1 s, and masked by visual noise). After each list subjects were told to write down any words that they perceived, guessing if necessary. After several of these study/perception trials, subjects were given a two-alternative forced-choice recognition test, in which they were presented with the related lure and a control word for each list and had to guess which one had been presented (in fact, neither word had been presented). Gallo and Seamon found that, even for those lists where the subject did not generate the related lure on the immediate perception/recall test, selection of the related lure on the final test (57%) was significantly above chance (50%). Several other studies also have found memory effects for related lures following extremely rapid presentation of list words, in which conscious generation at study would have been minimal (see Chapter 5). In a related finding, Dodd and MacLeod (2004) reported robust false recognition of related lures following a well-disguised incidental procedure for the presentation of study lists, so that conscious generation of the related lures during study was unlikely. Collectively, these findings are consistent with the idea that conscious activation of the related lure at study is not necessary to cause false recall and recognition effects, but it seems to contribute under standard conditions.

An additional finding by Gallo and Seamon (2004) was that, contrary to prior work (Seamon et al., 1998), some form of conscious processing of the list words was necessary for significant recognition of the related lure (see also Zeelenberg, Plomp, & Raaijmakers, 2003). As shown in Figure 3.5,

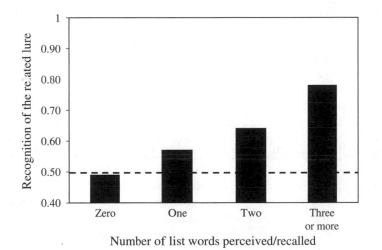

FIGURE 3.5   Recognition of the related lure as a function of the number of list words that were perceived/recalled during study in Gallo and Seamon (2004). Chance performance on the forced-choice test was 50% (dashed line). (Reproduced from Gallo, D. A., & Seamon, J. G. (2004). Are nonconscious processes sufficient to produce false memories? *Consciousness & Cognition, 13,* 158–168.)

recognition of the related lure was at chance (50%) when none of the list words were perceived/recalled at study, but increased steadily as more list words were perceived/recalled. These findings suggest that the short-lived semantic priming that may result from briefly presented list words, akin to that found in the semantic priming literature (e.g., Roediger, Balota, & Watson, 2001a), was not sufficient to cause longer-lasting recognition of the related lure in this study. Instead, conscious processing of the list words was necessary, perhaps because it provided even more associative activation of the related lure at study, or perhaps because it allowed for better encoding of overlapping semantic features or a thematic/gist representation (for additional discussion see Raaijmakers & Zeelenberg, 2004, which was a reply to Gallo & Seamon, 2004).

Another possible explanation for these findings is that conscious processing of list words at study allowed for the recollection of list words, at test. These recollections, in turn, could have activated the related lure (thereby increasing false memory). Although such test-based associative activation could contribute to typical DRM effects, other data indicate that it is not necessary for a memory signal for the related lures. As reviewed earlier, the related lure can be primed on implicit memory tests, in which it would be unlikely that subjects would try to recollect list words. Further, Cleary and Greene (2004) found that subjects were more likely to judge related lures as potentially studied than unrelated lures, even under conditions where subjects were unable to perceive the briefly flashed test words (i.e., a recognition-without-identification phenomenon). Because the test words were not identified in this task, corresponding recollections from the study phase were unlikely. This intriguing finding suggests that neither conscious recollection of list words (at test) nor conscious identification of the related lure (at test) is necessary for a memory signal for related lures. Much like the implicit memory studies, this task may have been sensitive to nonconscious priming of the related lure, due to the processing of its associates at study. Cotel, Gallo, and Seamon (2006) recently replicated Cleary and Greene (2004), and further showed that the recognition-without-identification effect for related lures (at test) did not require conscious generation of these items at study. They concluded that a false memory signal for the related lure could be created solely through nonconscious processes, although these effects were only found on immediate tests, suggesting that such nonconscious activation fades rapidly.

The evidence reviewed above indicates that conscious generation of the related lure at study is not necessary for false recall or false recognition. There are several pieces of evidence, though, that such generation does sometimes occur. (1) The overt rehearsal studies, discussed above, indicate that the related lure can be spontaneously incorporated into a subject's rehearsal. (2) Subjective reports obtained during the test also indicate that subjects think of the related lure at study (e.g., Brédart, 2000; Multhaup & Conner, 2002, see Chapter 5). (3) Lövdén and Johansson (2003) found priming for related lures on an anagram solution task under typical DRM presentation conditions, but in a second experiment these effects were eliminated when subjects engaged in articulatory suppression during study (even though priming for presented items was unaffected). The authors interpreted this pattern as indicating that priming for related lures depended on conscious generation of the word during study, which was minimized with articulatory suppression (see also Tajika et al., 2005). (4) Anaki, Faran, Ben-Shalom, and Henik (2005) found that, like studied words, low frequency related lures were more likely to be recognized than high frequency related lures, whereas false alarms to unrelated lures followed the opposite pattern (low frequency < high frequency). They argued that these effects implicated associative activation of related lures at study. (5) Part-set cuing and retrieval-induced forgetting effects on related lures also suggest that a memory representation for the related lure often is formed at encoding (see Chapter 6). All of these results point toward conscious generation of the related lure at study under typical DRM conditions.

□ SUMMARY AND CONCLUSION

The evidence indicates that associative activation plays a major role in the DRM false memory effect under typical conditions, and that thematic consistency and/or feature overlap processes also are involved. Although important questions remain to be answered, it should be stressed that these types of theoretical questions are not constrained to the DRM task. As discussed in Chapter 1, the debate between Underwood's IAR theory and Anisfeld and Knapp's feature-based theory of false recognition of synonyms was never resolved. The semantic priming literature provides another example. In a comprehensive review of that literature, Hutchison (2003) concluded that there is decent evidence for both feature overlap and associative activation. And yet again, the debate between feature-based and prototype-based (or thematic consistency) explanations of categorization still is active in the category learning literature (e.g., Zaki, Nosofsky, Stanton, & Cohen, 2003). Questions of this magnitude can be extended to other false memory tasks, too. Is false recognition for novel but perceptually related materials (e.g., Posner & Keele, 1970) due to feature overlap or to the generation of an abstract prototype? Is false recognition for similar or categorized pictures (e.g., Koutstaal & Schacter, 1997) caused by the activation of the common concept, or by overlapping perceptual features of the stimuli? Is false recognition of categorized words caused by access to a superordinate category representation, or by associations between the different words? And is false recognition for rhymes caused by pre-existing phonological associations, or by perceptual overlap between the words?

In all of these tasks, a major theoretical hurdle is that there is no universal agreement as to the type of information that is conveyed in an "association," a "theme," or a "semantic feature," and other relevant terms often are used in an ill-defined fashion (e.g., "meaning," "gist," "relational," "prototype," and the like). Many contemporary students of memory have expressed their discontent with this state of affairs, and these complaints are not without historical precedent. Tulving and Bower (1974) nicely captured this conceptual difficulty, in the context of a discussion of feature-based theories of memory errors:

> The problem of information overlap between features becomes considerably more complicated when the features cannot be described with reference to identifiable properties of the physical stimulus. For instance, how are we to classify semantic information? How many different "kinds" of semantic information are there? ... What is needed is a satisfactory taxonomy of "semantic" information which can then be validated through memory experiments. (p. 281)

In the same year, J. J. Jenkins (1974) published an insightful chapter, titled "Can we have a theory of meaningful memory?", in which he argued a similar point, based in part on research he had conducted that anticipated the levels-of-processing theory. He argued, "Meaningfulness must be regarded as a variable to be explained, not as an explanation" (p. 3). Despite these research prescriptions, we still lack a generally accepted taxonomy that could resolve these issues, and in the hands of different theorists these ideas tend to morph into each other. For instance, Arndt and Hirshman (1998) found that associative strength mattered, and considered associations to be an index of feature overlap in their model. Brainerd and Reyna (1998) found that related lures were more likely than other words to cue the gist of their corresponding list on a meaning test, and argued that this was because of the associative connections between the words.

The problem here is that there are multiple ways to conceptualize how words and concepts can be meaningfully related. Is a "theme" a collection of "semantic features" that were encoded from studied materials? If so, is this collection of features connected via "associations," in addition to the associative connections between words, and does "spreading activation" make all of this information available at retrieval? These fundamental questions have been difficult to answer, and for present purposes they might not be the right types of questions to ask. All of these theoretical constructs were created to explain and predict psychological phenomena, and they are critical for that level of analysis, but it is important to keep in mind that they are only metaphorical. At a physical level of analysis, we still have much to learn about how words and concepts, and their relationship to each other, are implemented in the biological substrate of the brain. It may be the case that there is no one-to-one mapping between these psychological constructs and their physiological correlates. In her review of this essay, Valerie Reyna (personal communication, September 15, 2005) adeptly made a related point, when considering the relationship between associative networks, features, and gist representations:

> ... constructs such as gist are not fundamentally opposed to assumptions about semantic features or networks because features or networks are possible ways in which semantic gist might be represented (especially if the nodes in a network represent conceptual relations rather than merely or only contiguity in experience). Fuzzy trace theorists have used phrases such as "cuing" or "activating" gist representations. These networks are, after all, metaphors rather than literally identical to specific neurons in the brain. Thus, evidence for networks or features or other ways of representing meaning are not evidence against gist per se, and vice versa.

Each of these mental constructs is a different way of realizing how the brain processes meaningfulness, and each is valid within its respective explanatory domain. However, when specific information processing assumptions are combined with these metaphors, or when precise operational definitions are made within an experimental context, the resulting theory can be tested (and can be wrong). In the case of converging associates tasks, the major information processing theories that have been based on these different conceptualizations of meaning are decision processes, associative activation, thematic consistency, and feature overlap. The findings discussed in this chapter provide some of the strongest evidence for or against these different theories.

The following conclusions can be drawn from the findings reviewed in this chapter. (1) Decision-based processes (e.g., criterion-shift or demand characteristics) cannot account for DRM false memory effects, and do not seem to play a major role in causing these effects, as indicated by subjective judgments, priming effects, and warning studies. (2) Activation of pre-existing representations plays a major role in the DRM task, as indicated by the generation of the related lure on a recall test and by priming on implicit tests. (3) Pre-existing associations at the word level seem to play a special role in this activation process, beyond any role of semantic themes, gist, or features, as indicated by the strong correlation between associative strength and false remembering, and comparisons with false memory effects for other types of semantically related materials (e.g., categorized lists and homophones). (4) Conscious activation or generation of the related lure during study does occur under typical task conditions (as suggested by studies of overt rehearsal, priming, subjective reports, word frequency effects, retrieval-induced forgetting, and part-set cuing), and influences false recall or recognition. (5) Conscious activation is not the only cause of these false memory effects (as suggested by studies of retention interval, overt rehearsal, incidental study phases, and rapid presentation rates). (6) Research with perceptually related stimuli (as opposed to semantically related stimuli) provides evidence that feature overlap and/or thematic consistency do influence false recognition, and by extension probably play a role in the DRM task. (7) The effects of test-item context in the DRM task are more consistent with gist-based theories of false recognition than with associative activation theories. (8) Research on the effects of retention interval in the DRM task suggests that some process other than associative activation during the study phase plays an important role, such as feature overlap, thematic consistency, or associative activation at test.

Another possibility to consider is that these different mechanisms might make different contributions depending on the type of test (recall or recognition) and other factors (e.g., encoding conditions, or the time of testing). McEvoy et al. (1999) have shown that lists with greater associative connections between studied items (inter-item associative strength) led to lower levels of false recall of the related lure, even when associative strength between studied items and related lures was held constant (note that Roediger et al., 2001c, failed to find this effect, but Deese, 1959a, 1961, also found negative correlations like those in McEvoy et al.). McEvoy et al. argued that, during the recall test, the shared associative connections between studied words caused them to activate each other, at the expense of activation of the related lure, whose recall was blocked by the greater recall of the studied items (i.e., an output interference mechanism, see Roediger, 1974). Surprisingly, these connections between studied items had the opposite effect on a recognition test, on which greater connections between studied items led to greater false recognition of the related lure. One explanation of this reversal is that lists with stronger inter-item associates form a more coherent thematic representation, and this process influences false recognition more than false recall. Other explanations also are possible, but the important point is that processes such as associative activation and gist-based similarity might differentially contribute to performance based on the task design. Gallo and Roediger (2002) made a similar point based on the observation that BAS was a strong predictor of false recall in their study, but had weaker effects (albeit still significant) on false recognition. They argued that the influence of overlapping semantic features and/or gist might be greater on delayed tests of false recognition than on immediate tests of false recall.

A final point to make is that, with the exception of the studies reviewed in this chapter, the three big theories all make very similar predictions for most of the false memory effects reported in the literature. All other factors being equal, as more associations, gist, or features that are relevant to the related lure are processed, more false memory of that related lure will result. Because of this similarity, the term "activation" will be used liberally in the remainder of this review, with the understanding that any of these three theories could cause a memory signal for the related lure in most situations (although the term "associative activation" will be used for that process alone, in those instances where these different processes should be distinguished). For many applications, the functional similarity of these three theories makes the distinction between them irrelevant. The mind uses pre-existing knowledge (e.g., associative relationships between concepts, similarity information) to understand the world, and the false memory effects discussed here clearly demonstrate that these relationships (however they are best characterized) can lead to memory errors. Thus, we can speak of the false recognition effect, and how some people are more or less susceptible to it, without a resolution to the mostly philosophical question regarding differences between features, associations, and gist. Other issues, such as the monitoring of false memories that is discussed in Chapter 5, also can be researched with indifference toward this issue. For many researchers, these functional issues are the more interesting research questions.

Illusory Recollection

One of memory's nastiest tricks is illusory recollection, or the detailed subjective experience that one had previously encountered an event that never occurred. Illusory recollection can cause errors on a memory test (false recall and recognition), but the two are not synonymous, as memory errors can occur without the experience of illusory recollection. For instance, in the DRM task one can falsely recall or recognize the related lure without recollecting specific phenomenological details of its presentation in the list. The lure only needs to "come to mind" to be given as a response on a recall test, and a vague feeling of familiarity is sufficient for false recognition. As discussed in Chapter 2, numerous studies have demonstrated that false recognition of the related lure is made with high confidence—not necessarily as high as that for list items, but always higher than that for unrelated lures (see also Brown et al., 2000, for similar findings using judgments of presentation frequency). These findings indicate that memory for related lures can be compelling, but such judgments could be based solely on a strong feeling of familiarity of the test stimulus (as opposed to recollection). Illusory recollection occurs when the related lure conjures subjective details (or "qualia") of its actual presentation in the study list, such as perceptual qualities of the seen or heard word, cognitive or emotional reactions to its presentation, and associations that were made to other items.

Illusory recollection has been demonstrated in a variety of false memory tasks (see Lampinen, Neuschatz, & Payne, 1998, for an excellent review), and it has been studied extensively in the DRM task. Unlike most other false memory tasks, related lures are not presented to subjects before the test phase of a DRM experiment, making the occurrence of illusory recollections for these events all the more intriguing. In some studies, subjects claim to remember details about the occurrence of related lures as often as they claim to remember details about the occurrence of studied words (e.g., Gallo et al., 2001a; Roediger & McDermott, 1995), although in other studies the subjects recollect more details for studied words than related lures (e.g., Mather et al., 1997; Norman & Schacter, 1997). Whether or not such differences are found is due to task parameters that can differentially influence true and illusory recollection (e.g., study modality or list length, as discussed below), and also due to the sensitivity of the measurements used to detect differences between true and false memories. The more important finding is that illusory recollection for related lures almost always is greater than illusory recollection for unrelated lures.

Researchers have used a variety of subjective judgments and source judgments to measure illusory recollection. The evidence for these illusory experiences is reviewed next, mostly in the context of the DRM task, along with the potential strengths and limitations of the various methods of measurement. Following those sections, theories of illusory recollection and factors that have been shown to influence illusory recollection will be discussed. It will be shown that the three big theories of false memories that were discussed in Chapter 3 go part of the way in explaining illusory recollection, but need to be embellished with additional processes in order to fully account for the phenomenon.

☐ "REMEMBER"/"KNOW" JUDGMENTS

The first demonstrations of illusory recollection in converging associates task were made by Roediger and McDermott (1995) and Read (1996), who had subjects make "remember" or "know" judgments on recognition and recall tests, respectively. As discussed in Chapter 2, the "remember"/ "know" technique was developed by Tulving (1985) as a means of distinguishing between two subjective states of awareness (note that Tulving's original proposal was made in the context of the episodic/semantic memory distinction, but these two judgments usually are used to reflect two subjective states within episodic memory tasks). "Remember" judgments are made when the subject can recall specific details about an event's prior occurrence, and are thought to reflect recollection (true or illusory). "Know" judgments are made when the subject cannot recall specific details about the event's prior occurrence, but nevertheless believes that it had occurred (e.g., it is familiar, but no details of its presentation can be recalled). These subjective judgments have been used extensively in memory research, and experimental dissociations have been taken as evidence that they truly reflect two different states of subjective experience (e.g., Gardiner & Richardson-Klavehn, 2000; Rajaram, 1993), as has their convergence with other methods to estimate recollection and familiarity (e.g., Yonelinas, 2001).

Roediger and McDermott (1995, Experiment 2) found that "remember" judgments were made for 53% of the falsely recognized related lures (considering only those that were not previously tested). This rate was much higher than that reported for falsely recognized unrelated lures (18%). Since then, at least 40 studies have measured "remember" judgments in the DRM false recognition task. Table 4.1 summarizes the results from 20 studies, with 32 separate experiments, using the most typical presentation

TABLE 4.1   The Probability of Giving a "Remember" (pR) and "Know" Judgment (pK), as well as IRK Estimates of Familiarity, in 32 Experiments using the DRM Task

		List words			Related lures			LW controls			RL controls		
		pR	pK	IRK	pR	pK	IRK	pR	pK	IRK	pR	pK	IRK
Auditory study/Visual test													
Gallo et al. (1997)		52	24	50	55	27	60	3	12	12	6	10	11
Gallo et al. (2001a)	Exp. 1	34	22	33	40	29	48	2	6	6	2	6	6
	Exp. 2	37	17	27	37	24	38	5	9	9	6	8	9
	Exp. 3	35	20	31	33	25	37	7	10	11	6	17	18
Gallo and Roediger (2002)	Exp. 3	44	27	48	53	30	64	12	17	19	19	27	33
Gallo et al. (2001b)		48	22	42	69	19	61	7	14	15	10	21	23
Intons-Peterson, Rocchi, West, McLellan, and Hackney (1999)	Exp. 1	37	30	48	32	39	57	2	8	8	3	12	12
	Exp. 2	43	26	46	39	39	64	4	9	9	3	7	7
Johansson and Stenberg (2002)	Exp. 1	32	34	50	34	39	59	1	6	6	1	7	7
Mather et al. (1997)	Exp. 1	38	37	60	34	45	67	9	11	12	9	11	12
Neuschatz et al. (2001)	Exp. 1	54	15	33	45	25	45	28	−4	−6	21	12	15
Norman and Schacter (1997)	Exp. 1	53	26	55	39	26	43	1	7	7	0	13	13
Payne et al. (1996)	Exp. 1	45	17	31	47	23	43	3	8	8	3	8	8

(Continued)

TABLE 4.1   (*Continued*)

		List words			Related lures			LW controls			RL controls		
		pR	pK	IRK	pR	pK	IRK	pR	pK	IRK	pR	pK	IRK
Roediger and McDermott (1995)	Exp. 2	41	24	41	38	34	55	2	9	9	3	13	13
Seamon et al. (2002c)	Exp. 1	39	28	46	45	32	58	4	14	15	5	14	15
Winograd, Peluso, and Glover (1998)		40	27	45	40	36	60	**3**	**7**	**7**	**3**	**7**	**7**
Visual study/Visual test													
Arndt and Reder (2003)	Exp. 1	71	18	62	52	25	52	4	6	6	6	11	12
	Exp. 2	66	27	79	41	38	64	4	12	13	7	14	15
	Exp. 3	68	19	59	44	28	50	5	10	11	9	14	15
	Exp. 3	73	15	56	47	21	40	3	9	9	4	15	16
Gallo et al. (2001a)	Exp. 1	31	27	39	36	28	44	**2**	**6**	**6**	**2**	**6**	**6**
	Exp. 2	45	15	27	35	16	25	5	9	9	6	8	9
	Exp. 3	39	17	28	23	24	31	4	8	8	7	13	14
Mintzer and Griffiths (2000)		67	18	55	54	24	52	4	5	5	5	5	5
Mintzer and Griffiths (2001a)		62	23	61	32	29	43	2	5	5	1	2	2
Mintzer and Griffiths (2001b)		67	21	64	41	19	32	4	6	6	2	8	8
Seamon et al. (1998)	Exp. 1	37	44	70	33	43	64	8	11	12	14	14	16
	Exp. 2	53	30	64	41	36	61	6	17	18	13	25	29
Seamon et al. (2002b)		56	19	43	49	24	47	5	11	12	9	23	25
Seamon, Luo, Schwartz, Jones, Lee, and Jones (2002d)	Exp. 1	20	39	49	15	40	47	1	4	4	3	12	12
	Exp. 2	33	23	34	23	28	36	4	10	10	2	13	13
Watson et al. (2003)	Exp. 3	39	23	38	27	26	36	3	11	11	2	14	14
Average (all)		27	24	47	40	29	50	5	9	9	6	12	13
Auditory study		42	25	43	42	31	54	6	9	9	6	12	13
Visual study		52	24	52	37	28	45	4	9	9	6	12	13

Note: Only conditions that approximated typical methods were included. Typically, younger adults intentionally studied several DRM lists (approximately 1–2 s per word, auditorily or visually) and were tested with a final visual recognition test. All lists contained at least 10 associates, blocked by theme. Some conditions were collapsed where appropriate, and conditions with warnings, source manipulations, or prior recall were not included. Bold numbers indicate that only a single base rate was reported for control items. Independent-remember-know (IRK) estimates of familiarity assume that recollection and familiarity are independent (IRK = pK/[1 − pR], see Yonelinas, 2002).

parameters (see table note for inclusion criteria). As can be seen from the table, the proportion of "remember" judgments given to related lures (mean = .40) was greater than that given to unrelated lures (.06) in every experiment, t (31) = 18.89, p < .001, and this inequality also was upheld when "remember" judgments were expressed as a proportion of the total probability of false recognition (means = .56 and .29, t (31) = 9.83, p <.001). These findings demonstrate the relatedness effect on illusory recollection for nonstudied lures. The related lure also was judged as more familiar than unrelated lures, using raw "know" judgments (means = .29 vs. .12, t (31) = 10.31, p < .001) or those that have been adjusted using the IRK procedure (means = .50 vs. .13, t (31) = 17.49, p < .001, see table note).

Three other sets of findings from the table are worth mentioning. First, although overall levels of true and false recognition did not differ (means = .73 and .71, t < 1, averaging across the means presented in the original papers), true recollection was greater than false recollection, measured as both "remember" judgments (means = .47 and .40, respectively, t (31) = 3.44, p < .01) and as proportional "remember" judgments (means = .64 and .56, respectively, t (31) = 6.67, p < .001). These patterns were maintained even when all of the subjective measures were corrected for those given to control items (via subtraction). Thus, even though illusory recollection can be quite compelling, true recollection was greater than illusory recollection on average. In contrast, the familiarity of true and falsely recognized words did not differ or was greater for related lures, depending on the measure (mean "know" judgments = .24 and .29, respectively, t (31) = 7.65, p < .001; IRK = .47 and .50, t (31) = 1.05, p = .30). Second, the base rate effect (false alarms to related lure controls > false alarms to list word controls) also was significant in overall false recognition (means = .20 and .15, respectively, t (31) = 5.12, p < .001), and was driven predominantly by familiarity differences ("know" means = .12 and .09, and IRK means = .13 and .09, respectively, both p < .001). Thus, although there are differences between list words and related lures when the corresponding lists are not studied, these differences tend to drive familiarity as opposed to recollection. Third, and finally, there were differences between the auditory and visual study modalities, so that "remember" judgments for related lures were made as frequently as those for list words following auditory study (both means = .42), whereas "remember" judgments for list words were greater than related lures following visual presentation (.52 vs. .37, p < .01). These modality effects are discussed more thoroughly in Chapter 5. They are mentioned here only to highlight the point that whether differences will be found between true and illusory recollection will depend on a variety of rather arbitrary task-specific conditions.

In contrast to the numerous studies using recognition tests, "remember"/"know" judgments are rarely obtained on recall tests. This discrepancy probably stems from the fact that Roediger and McDermott (1995) only measured subjective judgments after recognition, and also that recall is thought to depend heavily on recollection (and thus the distinction between "remember" and "know" is somewhat awkward). Nevertheless, Read (1996) and Pérez-Mata, Read, and Diges (2002) demonstrated illusory recollection on a recall test. For example, in Read (Experiment 1), falsely recalled related lures were rated as "remembered" 46% of the time, which was similar to judgments for list words in some of the comparisons. However, in Pérez-Mata et al., the proportion of falsely recalled related lures that were given "remember" judgments (40% in full attention conditions of Experiment 1) tended to be lower than that for list words (82%), and were roughly similar to "remember" responses to other recall intrusions (35%). It is difficult to explain the discrepancy in these findings, given that relatively few studies have used these subjective judgments on recall tests.

Warnings

Explicitly warning subjects to avoid false recognition after study (but before test) has been found to reduce "remember" judgments given to related lures, but even after such warnings a relatedness effect on "remember" judgments is still obtained (Anastasi et al., 2000; Gallo et al., 1997; Gallo et al., 2001b). For instance, in the primary warning-after-study condition of Gallo et al. (2001b) subjects gave "remember" judgments to 62% of the related lures that they had falsely recognized, compared to only 15% of the unrelated lures. The finding of significant levels of "remember" judgments for related lures even after such warnings is of critical interest. Researchers are notoriously skeptical about subjective judgments because it is difficult to independently assess the veracity of what the subjects report. The finding that fully warned subjects claim to "remember" details about the related lure's presentation helps to allay these concerns. These subjects knew that they might make false memories, and objective measures confirmed that they were strategically trying to avoid being "tricked" into falsely recognizing related lures. Thus, it is more difficult to dismiss these subjects' claims that they could recollect information about the related lure's occurrence. Looked at in this way, the important question is not "*Are* they remembering?" but rather "*What* are they remembering?"

Conscious Activation

Roediger and McDermott (1995) offered one explanation of these "remember" judgments on the basis of associative activation (see Arndt &

Reder, 2003, for related discussion). According to one version of this theory, subjects might consciously think of the related lure at study, and potentially rehearse this word along with the list words. If the subject later recalls rehearsing the related lure at study, then they might give this lure a "remember" judgment. In this case, the "remember" judgment would be based on the true recollection of their previous processing of the word, and thus would not necessarily be an instance of "illusory" recollection. Studies that have had subjects overtly rehearse the words during study are only partially consistent with this account (e.g., Goodwin et al., 2001; Lampinen et al., 2005; Seamon et al. , 2002b). These studies have demonstrated that subjects often rehearse the related lure during the study phase, and in Lampinen et al. (2005) these rehearsals were often reported (at test) as a justification for giving a "remember" judgment to related lures. However, Seamon et al. failed to find a relationship between the frequency of prior rehearsal of the related lures and subsequent "remember" judgments, and even when the related lure was not overtly rehearsed at study "remember" judgments were often made (e.g., 62% in a 2 s study rate condition). These findings indicate that "remember" judgments for related lures cannot be explained completely by conscious generation of the word at study.

Thoughts of the related lure during study might not be necessary to elicit "remember" judgments, but the true recollection of other aspects of the study phase might play a role. Typical instructions for "remember"/ "know" judgments are open-ended, asking subjects to make a "remember" judgment if they can retrieve any detail relevant to the word's prior presentation. Norman and Schacter (1997) provided relevant findings. In this study, subjects were asked to provide detailed explanations of what they recollected when making a "remember" judgment. Most explanations were dominated by vague claims of remembering associative information from study, and this was the case for "remember" judgments to both list words and related lures (see also Dewhurst & Farrand, 2004; Huron, Servais, & Danion, 2001; and Read, 1996). Lampinen et al. (2005) took a different approach, having subjects think aloud during the study and test phase. Analysis of these protocols indicated that, when claiming to "remember" a related lure, subjects often would provide details that originally were mentioned in the context of list words at study (and these errors persisted after a 48 hr retention interval). For instance, when presented with the word "sugar" at study, one subject thought, "It is fattening, but it is good." At test, this subject falsely recognized "sweet," and gave it a "remember" judgment "cause I remember liking sweets but thinking they are gonna make me fat" (p. 957). In cases like this, the reported recollection contained specific information, but this information was initially linked to associates that were presented at study.

Very specific details of presentation are sometimes reported for false memories in these sorts of tasks. For example, after studying categorized lists, one subject in Dewhurst and Farrand (2004) claimed to recollect an "image of trying to get a grand piano through the front door at home" (p. 408), even though they had never studied the word *piano*. Many other times, though, the reported recollections involved more general associations to other items in the list (e.g., for the nonstudied word *cousin*, another subject in this study gave a "remember" judgment "because I saw *brother* and *sister* as well," p. 408). These more general reports should not be too surprising, given that there are not as many details that could be remembered from word lists, relative to more complex events (such as autobiographical memories). In any event, these findings indicate that in many of the cases showing "remember" judgments for related lures, subjects might actually be remembering associations made to studied items (i.e., images, personal associations, list membership, etc.) that could reasonably apply to the related lure. As discussed later, true recollections might cause illusory recollection if the true recollections are erroneously attached or attributed to the false memory.

☐ SOURCE JUDGMENTS

Unlike "remember" judgments, which can be based on a variety of recollected details, source judgments are targeted at the recollection of very specific details of prior occurrence. Payne et al. (1996) were the first to document these types of illusory recollections in the DRM task. Subjects heard several DRM lists at study, with the words in some lists presented by a single voice (a blocked-source condition), and the words in other lists presented by two alternating voices (a mixed-source condition). For those words that were recalled on a final test, subjects indicated which voice presented the word or "don't know" if they were not sure. Despite the "don't know" option, subjects often attributed a voice to list words (94%) and related lures (87%). Most of the attributions for list words were accurate, and correct attributions were greater in the blocked-source condition (84%) than in the mixed-source condition (71%). This finding suggests that the knowledge that an entire list was presented by a single source helped to boost accurate source judgments for words from that list. Source judgments not only reflected the true recollection of the perceptual qualities of a word's presentation, but also were influenced by other clues afforded by the structure of the task. Source judgments for related lures did not benefit from this knowledge, as they were distributed more evenly across the two sources even in the blocked-source condition. However, this last finding is not characteristic of the rest of the literature (discussed below in the section "Congruency Effects"), in which related lures often were attributed to the source of their corresponding list (in blocked-source conditions). Most of these other studies have measured source judgments on recognition tests, as opposed to the repeated-recall procedure used by Payne et al.

Warnings

A study by Lampinen, Neuschatz, and Payne (1999) tested the idea that the source attributions to related lures were based on demand characteristics (i.e., "I'll attribute this word to a source because that is what the experimenter wants"), as opposed to actual beliefs or recollections that these lures were presented by a source. Subjects studied several DRM lists that were presented using male and female voices (mixed within each list). The critical aspect of the design for present purposes was that, on a final visual recognition test, subjects made "male"/"female"/"unsure" source judgments for each word that they recognized as "old." Then, after subjects had completed the test, the experimenter calculated the number of source attributions that were made (rightly or wrongly) and asked the subject to change 1/4 of these attributions, in an effort to correct their own errors. On the original (unchanged) source test, Lampinen et al. found that list words and related lures were more likely to be attributed to a studied source than were unrelated lures (i.e., a relatedness effect on source judgments). On the follow-up test they found that, even though subjects were more likely to change source judgments to related lures than to list words, a relatedness effect on source judgments to related lures persisted.

Neuschatz et al. (2001) used more direct warnings (between study and test) to encourage subjects to avoid false remembering. In their third experiment, subjects saw a videotape of two people reading DRM lists and then took a final recognition test with source judgments ("male"/ "female"/"unsure"). Subjects were instructed to try hard to recollect those characteristics (e.g., perceptual details) that should help to distinguish true from false memories. Despite these instructions, warnings had relatively little effect on the proportion of recognized words that were given source attributions. Source attributions for related lures (59%) were still considerably higher than those to unrelated lures (34%), although they were not as great as those to list words (76%). If the source test was instead given after a 48-hr delay, there were no differences in source attributions for related lures and list words (both 64%), even in the strong warning condition.

The findings reported by Lampinen et al. (1999) and Neuschatz et al. (2001) are analogous to the effects of warnings on "remember" judgments that were previously discussed. Subjects that were strategically trying to avoid false recognition were not able to eliminate a relatedness effect on subjective judgments. This unwillingness to greatly change source attributions to related lures provides strong evidence that these judgments reflect actual beliefs about the prior occurrence of the related lures. This is not to say that strategic or deliberate conscious inferences are not involved in source judgments for related lures. It does suggest, though, that (1) such deliberate inferences are fundamental to all source judgments (even for studied words), and so subjects are reluctant to abandon them, and/or (2) more automatic or unavoidable processes also are involved. Either way, the processes that cause illusory recollection of source seem to be central to the act of remembering source, in general.

Congruency Effects

Mather et al. (1997) presented several DRM lists using a blocked-voice or mixed-voice manipulation, and then gave a final visual recognition test (a "don't know" option was not given). Replicating Payne et al. (1996), they found that accurate judgments for list words were greater in the blocked-voice condition (.84) than in the mixed-voice condition (.65). Unlike Payne et al., in the blocked-source condition, they found that source judgments for related lures often matched the voice of the corresponding list (.83), and this rate was similar to that for list words (.84). Regardless of whether the word was studied, subjects were equally likely to attribute it to the voice that had presented the corresponding list (i.e., a "congruent" judgment). Gallo et al. (2001a) found analogous congruency effects in a situation where study lists were either heard or seen (a blocked-source condition), and subjects were given a final visual recognition test (a "don't know" option was included for source judgments). Results from the condition that did not involve prior recall testing can be found in Figure 4.1. Both list words and related lures were most likely to be attributed to the modality that had presented their corresponding list, and there were no differences in source attributions for list words and related lures. In contrast, unrelated lures that were falsely recognized were most likely to be given a "don't know" judgment (.86), and these false alarms were quite rare (.07).

Under blocked-source conditions, the studies by Mather et al. (1997) and Gallo et al. (2001a) indicate that source attributions to related lures are more similar (if not identical) to those for list words, relative to unrelated lures (see also Gallo & Roediger, 2003, and Roediger, McDermott, Pisoni, & Gallo, 2004). The situation is obviously different under mixed-source conditions. Here each list is associated with more than one source, so that there is no single source to which the related lure can be attributed.

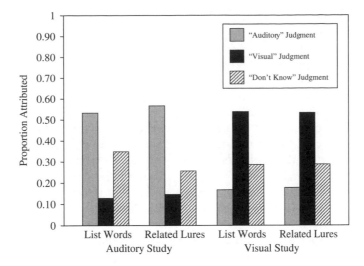

FIGURE 4.1 Modality attributions for each recognized test item as a function of the study modality of the relevant list in Gallo et al. (2001a, Experiment 1). Judgments for unrelated lures were .20 ("auditory"), .20 ("visual"), and .60 ("don't know").

Payne et al. (1996) and Mather et al. (1997) did not report source attributions for related lures in these conditions, but Hicks and Marsh (2001) did (see also Anastasi et al., 2000). Consistent with expectations, Hicks and Marsh found that the related lures were equally likely to be attributed to one or the other source when the two sources were comparable (i.e., one voice vs. another).

Roediger et al. (2004) reported source attributions in both blocked-source and mixed-source conditions (using auditory presentation at study and a visual test). Consistent with prior studies, they found that related lures often were attributed to the source of their corresponding list in the single-source condition, but were more evenly distributed across sources in a mixed-source condition. More important, the overall likelihood of making a voice attribution (as opposed to "don't know" responses) was similar across these two conditions (means = .38 and .40, respectively). This pattern is important because it indicates that subjects do not attribute related lures to a source simply because these words can be readily matched with that source (i.e., a blocked-source condition). Even when related lures were not obviously related to one source (i.e., their corresponding list was presented with two sources), subjects were more likely to attribute related lures to a source than they were to attribute unrelated lures.

Study/Test Match

Another factor to consider is the match between the study and test source. In all of the recognition findings discussed so far, words were presented visually at test. Roediger et al. (2004) presented lists auditorily at study, but manipulated whether test words were presented visually or auditorily (between-subjects), and also whether words on the auditory test were presented in the same or different voice as their corresponding study list (within-subjects). There did not appear to be any consistent effects of changing modalities between study and test on source attributions, although this variable was manipulated across experiments and thus is difficult to interpret. There were effects of whether the study and test voices were the same or different. In the blocked-source study condition, where entire lists were presented with one voice or the other, congruency effects were found for both list words and related lures (i.e., they often were attributed to the voice of the study list, regardless of the test voice). A different pattern was found in the mixed-source condition, where two voices were used to present each list at study. Here subjects were biased to attribute both list words and related lures to the voice that was used to present the word at test, regardless of the study voice. This finding makes sense for related lures, which could not be associated with a voice from the study phase in this condition, but is more difficult to understand for list words. Apparently, both true and false source attributions were a complex function of study and test variables. More work is needed to fully understand these study/test interactions (see Marsh & Hicks, 1998, for related findings and discussion).

Source Distinctiveness

The relative discriminability or distinctiveness of the sources that are used is an important consideration. In all of the findings discussed so far, with the possible exception of the study-modality manipulation (i.e., auditory vs. visual), the different sources that were used have been relatively similar (i.e., two different voices). As discussed, Hicks and Marsh (2001) found that source judgments for related lures were evenly distributed across two sources when only voices were used. However, when the two sources were more discriminable from each other (i.e., hearing list words vs. generating them from anagrams), they found that related lures were more likely to be attributed to the less distinctive source (i.e., hearing words; see Hicks & Marsh (1999) for analogous findings on a recall test, and Johansson & Stenberg (2002) for analogous findings on immediate recognition tests).

Johnson, Raye, Foley, and Foley (1981) dubbed this type of attribution bias the "it-had-to-be-you" effect. When faced with two alternative sources of information (e.g., words that the experimenter presented vs. words that the subjects generated themselves), subjects are more likely to attribute a questionable event to the external source (the experimenter). The idea is that generating words leaves a rich record of cognitive operations in memory, relative to simply hearing the words (i.e., "the generation effect"; Slamecka & Graf, 1978). As a result, subjects expect to have more detailed recollections for those words that they personally generated, so that the absence of these recollections leads them to infer that the word must have been presented by the experimenter (e.g., "You must have presented the word, because I can't remember generating it myself."). In Hicks and Marsh (2001), because related lures were not studied, they did not elicit detailed recollections of anagram solution at study, and thus subjects were more likely to attribute them to the less distinctive source. Such decision processes and memory monitoring are discussed more in Chapter 5.

□ MEMORY CHARACTERISTICS QUESTIONNAIRE

Another way to measure illusory recollection is to have subjects rate each test word on the basis of specific aspects or subjective details that can be remembered from the study phase. The most extensively used measure is the Memory Characteristics Questionnaire (or MCQ; Johnson, Foley, Suengas, & Raye, 1988). Each word that the subject recalls or recognizes is given a numerical rating (e.g., 1 through 5) indicating the vividness of their memories along various dimensions. For instance, Mather et al. (1997) had subjects rate their memories along four dimensions: "perceptual details," "emotional reactions," "associations," and "trying to remember (or rehearse)." It was stressed to subjects that MCQ judgments were not the same as confidence. Instead, they were to make their ratings on the basis of the vividness of their memory along each dimension. Norman and Schacter (1997), Neuschatz et al. (2001), and Gallo and Roediger (2003) also have used the MCQ to measure item-specific recollection in the DRM task, although the specific dimensions that were used to rate memories varied somewhat across studies.

Table 4.2 presents MCQ ratings from the conditions in these four studies that most closely resembled the typical DRM conditions: study lists were blocked by theme, each was presented by a single source (one of two voices in Mather et al., a single voice in Norman & Schacter, one of two

TABLE 4.2 Memory Characteristics Questionnaire Results from Four Experiments Using the DRM Task

Rating Scale:	Gallo & Roediger (2003) 1–5	Mather et al. (1997) 1–5	Neuschatz et al. (2001) 1–7	Norman & Schacter (1997) 1–7
Perceptual details				
LW	2.76	2.81	4.84	4.25
RL	2.68	2.57	4.30	3.35
URL	1.94	2.08	2.66	NA
Reactions/Feelings				
LW	2.71	2.64	3.69	5.18
RL	2.65	2.72	3.11	4.61
URL	2.01	2.13	1.93	NA
List Position				
LW	NA	NA	3.60	5.02
RL	NA	NA	3.05	4.14
URL	NA	NA	1.80	NA
Neighboring words				
LW	NA	NA	3.10	4.45
RL	NA	NA	2.74	4.11
URL	NA	NA	1.63	NA
Trying to remember				
LW	2.59	2.13	NA	NA
RL	2.43	2.11	NA	NA
URL	1.84	1.83	NA	NA
Associations				
LW	3.35	3.16	4.29	6.47
RL	3.36	3.57	3.72	6.22
URL	1.05	2.51	2.32	NA

Note: In many conditions, but not all, list words (LW) were rated higher than related lures (RL). In all conditions, related lures were rated higher than unrelated lures (URL). NA = not applicable.

videotaped experimenters in Neuschatz et al., and auditory or visual words in Gallo & Roediger), and MCQ ratings were measured on a final visual recognition test. Data from Mather et al. and Neuschatz et al. were based on 10-word lists, whereas data from 15-word lists are presented from Norman and Schacter and from Gallo and Roediger.

The main point to note from the table is that, in almost every comparison, list words were given the highest ratings, related lures were given ratings that were somewhat lower, and unrelated lures were given the lowest ratings. This pattern was consistently found for those judgments that pertained to the recollection of details regarding the actual presentation of the word (feelings/reactions and perceptual details), indicating reliable effects of actual presentation (list words > related lures), and reliable relatedness effects on illusory recollection (related lures > unrelated lures). One notable exception was in the rating of "associations," which did not differ between related lures and list words in Gallo and Roediger, and was greatest for related lures in Mather et al. Because related lures are highly associated to the list words, judgments of "association" for related lures probably reflected true memories of presented associates. Overall, these patterns speak of the validity of the MCQ. If subjects were simply rating items on the basis of familiarity, then differences between item types should have been constant across all of the dimensions. Differences between list items and related lures on "perceptual details" but not on "associations" suggest that the MCQ is a valid measure of these underlying constructs.

☐ THE CONJOINT RECOGNITION TECHNIQUE

Brainerd, Reyna, and colleagues have pioneered a more objective way to measure a type of illusory recollection that they call "phantom recollection," which is one of the ideas embedded within fuzzy trace theory. In this theory, the retrieval of a gist trace can lead to the subjective experience of familiarity (e.g., because the event is consistent with the studied theme, it feels "old"), but the retrieval of very strong gist traces or the repeated activation of a gist trace can lead to a more detailed subjective experience of recollection. These ideas were developed in earlier studies of false memories for inferences (see Reyna, 1995, 1998), and then later extended to the DRM task. In these later studies, phantom recollection has been mathematically modeled using a multinomial analysis of the conjoint recognition task (e.g., Brainerd et al., 1999; Brainerd et al., 2001; see also Brainerd et al., 2003a). Note that phantom recollection is a type of illusory recollection, but the term "illusory recollection" is used in other sections of this chapter as a more general term, so as not to be confused with the specific assumptions of fuzzy trace theory.

In the conjoint recognition task, subjects study a set of materials (e.g., DRM lists) and then take a recognition test under different instructional conditions. The procedure is analogous to Jacoby's opposition paradigm (e.g., Jacoby, 1991), in the sense that subjects are expected to recruit different memory processes across the instructional conditions. As a result, differences between the conditions are thought to reflect differences in the underlying processes (or the different subjective experiences that result from these processes), which can then be mathematically estimated. There are three different conditions. The "verbatim" condition is analogous to a standard "yes/no" recognition memory test, in which subjects are told to respond "yes" only to studied targets. In this condition, "yes" responses for related lures are thought to reflect either phantom recollection, familiarity, and/or response bias. In the "meaning" condition, subjects are told to respond "yes" to any test word that is somehow related to a studied word, but was not studied itself (i.e., related lures only). Under this condition, "yes" responses to related lures are caused by familiarity and response bias, but now phantom recollection leads to a "no" response, because phantom recollection would lead subjects to believe that the lure was studied, and hence should be excluded. Given these assumptions, the difference in "yes" responses to lures across the two conditions is due to phantom recollection (although the mathematical implementation of this basic idea is more complex). Finally, in the "verbatim + meaning" condition, subjects are told to respond "yes" on the basis of either memory for presentation or relatedness, and so "yes" responses for related lures would again be based on phantom recollection, familiarity, and/or response bias. The difference between this condition and the "verbatim" condition is that, in the verbatim condition subjects are thought to use true recollection of targets to reject lures (via monitoring processes discussed in Chapter 5), whereas true recollection would lead one to accept related lures in the verbatim + meaning condition (or in the meaning-only condition).

A more specific explication of the conjoint recognition model is beyond the scope of the present review, and the interested reader should consult the aforementioned papers for additional information. The main point to be made here is that, in several experiments using the procedure, Brainerd et al. (2001) have found significant estimates of phantom recollection using DRM lists (and other types of materials) in false recognition, and significant phantom recollection effects have been found using an analogous procedure on recall tests (Brainerd et al., 2003a). Moreover, in the DRM task, phantom recollection was found to be the dominant contributor to false recall and recognition of related lures, and persisted even after long delays (e.g., 1 week).

These findings are informative for several reasons, two of which are highlighted here. First, the conjoint recognition (or recall) procedure does not rely on direct subjective judgments. Instead, it relies on objective recognition discriminations under different instructional sets, with the assumption that different subjective criteria are used in each test. It there-fore provides converging evidence for illusory recollection using a very different set of assumptions and procedures. (For yet another type of mathematical model that provides evidence of phantom recollection, see Lampinen et al., in press.) Second, in order to administer the conjoint recognition instructions, all subjects were explicitly told that the recognition test would contain words that were not presented but were related to list words (i.e., related lures), or that they might recall these words on the recall tests, and they were given specific examples. Thus, these modeling procedures complement the warning studies mentioned earlier. In both cases, significant effects of illusory recollection were obtained even when subjects were "on the lookout" for related lures that were not studied.

☐ THEORIES OF ILLUSORY RECOLLECTION

In Chapter 3, three dominant theories of false recall or false recognition were discussed (associative activation, thematic consistency, and feature overlap). None of these theories sufficiently explains illusory recollection. These theories, at least in their simplest form, only address how the related lure will be generated (on a recall test), familiar (on a recognition test), or primed (on implicit measures). To account for illusory recollection, something needs to be said about the origin of the subjectively detailed recollections for nonstudied events. For instance, as discussed earlier, "remember" judgments might be based on the recall of vague or general associative information from the study phase, and source judgments might be based on knowledge-based inferences (e.g., knowing the modality of the corresponding list). Such processes could go part of the way in explaining the origins of illusory recollection, but they cannot explain more specific recollections for related lures, such as "perceptual details" and "feelings." Similarly, fuzzy trace theory proposes that gist traces cause false memories, but by definition only verbatim traces contain recollected details. The fact that illusory recollection persists under strict warnings or conjoint recognition instructions indicates that subjects actually believe that they are remembering aspects of the lure's presentation at study. Where does this detailed (and yet false) information come from?

Here we discuss two logical sources of this detailed information, dubbed *content borrowing* and *imagination*. Content borrowing is a term originally used by Lampinen and colleagues (e.g., Lampinen et al., 2005), and others have proposed related ideas (e.g., Gallo & Roediger, 2003; Reyna & Titcomb, 1996; Schacter et al., 1998a). The idea is that the features that subjects recollect for related lures actually were encoded into memory as a result of processing the list words. When the related lure is encountered at test (or generated at study), details that originally corresponded to the presentation of list words are retrieved and erroneously attributed to the presentation of the related lure. For example, the subject might have thought "I'm tired" when the word "bed" was studied, but at test they may have recalled this reaction when they encountered the related lure "sleep," and then erroneously attributed this reaction to the presentation of "sleep" at study. Such content borrowing implies a breakdown of feature binding, analogous to the classic binding errors observed in perceptual tasks (e.g., Treisman & Schmidt, 1982). Features that are loosely bound to list words are retrieved and then erroneously bound to the memory for the related lure.

Fuzzy trace theory provides one way to conceptualize this illusory binding phenomenon. In this theory, verbatim traces can disintegrate over time, so that perceptually specific information that was once associated with studied items can become bound to gist traces (e.g., Reyna & Titcomb, 1996). When presented with a related lure, the retrieval of these detailed gist traces would result in an illusory recollective phenomenology (phantom recollection). In this conceptualization, content borrowing could occur at some point prior to the retrieval of the phantom recollection. For instance, repeatedly activating a gist representation could cause it to become associated with verbatim fragments, resulting in the storage of a detailed gist trace that could later be retrieved as a phantom recollection at test. Alternatively, the actual binding of verbatim details to a gist trace might occur during retrieval, resulting in the online creation of the phantom recollection when memory is tested. For example, Lampinen and colleagues have proposed a familiarity + corroboration mechanism (e.g., Lampinen et al., 1999; Lampinen et al., 2005; Odegard & Lampinen, 2004). The idea is that encountering a familiar lure at test leads one to search memory for supporting details. Once these details are retrieved from list words, they can be attributed (consciously or nonconsciously) to related lures. Note that fuzzy trace theory appeals to gist-based processes to explain illusory recollection, but other mathematical models that focus on associative activation (e.g., PIER2) or feature overlap (e.g., MINERVA2) also can accommodate this sort of illusory binding (see Hicks & Starns, 2006, for discussion).

Imagination is the other potential source of the subjective details of a false memory, and is known to cause false remembering in other tasks (e.g., Goff & Roediger, 1998). In contrast to content borrowing, where the details are recollected from the study phase, it is not necessary for imagined features to have a "true" memory component (e.g., Gallo & Roediger, 2003). Instead, when subjects are asked about their recollections of various characteristics of a test item's presentation (e.g., perceptual details), they imagine the test word's presentation in an effort to remember. Illusory recollection is created when this imagination is mistaken for a memory (e.g., a reality monitoring error). For example, subjects might imagine how "sleep" would have sounded had it been spoken by the experimenter at study, and then falsely recognize this image as an actual recollection. Memory for the list words could certainly inform such a process (e.g., one has to remember what the experimenter's voice sounds like), but this is not necessarily the case (e.g., the word "sleep" might conjure an image of sleeping in class, and this could be accepted as a memory even if no such image was formed at study). This account is very similar to Lampinen et al.'s (1999) familiarity + corroboration account, in the sense that both explanations focus on the creation of illusory recollections at retrieval. The main difference between the two explanations is the origin of the subjective details (imaginations vs. true recollections).

Although there are important differences between content borrowing and imagination, they both involve attribution processes. In a seminal chapter on memory attributions, Jacoby et al. (1989) argued that the subjective experience of remembering was not stored in a memory trace, but rather involved a sort of unconscious inference. Although their attributional framework was focused mainly on explaining the subjective experience of familiarity, it broadly applies to all acts of remembering, including illusory recollection (see Higham & Vokey, 2004). Take the following example offered by Jacoby et al.:

> For example, consider trying to answer a question such as "Did you eat dinner at La Casa a few weeks ago?" An image of sitting at a table in a restaurant might readily come to mind, but that image may not be sufficient to specify a particular visit to the restaurant. You then might elaborate on that train of thought until your elaborations narrowly specify an event. An additional detail might come to mind, such as "oh yes, we were discussing the election results" that would allow you to infer that you were truly "remembering" a specific event from several weeks ago. An image is fluently generated, and that image includes specific details that are diagnostic of a particular experience. The transfer is assumed to occur between the actual event several weeks before and later fluent imagining of the event. But even the fluent generation of details can be open to error, as in the case of confabulation and errors of reconstruction. (p. 398)

The point is that memory is not simply retrieved from stored traces, but instead the subjective experience of remembering is created "online" at the time of retrieval. As such, it is influenced by the cognitive context at both encoding and retrieval. Under these conceptualizations, the sharp distinction between "memory signals" and "decision processes" discussed in

Chapter 3 becomes blurred. The subjective experience of remembering can be influenced not only by the retrieval of information from memory, but also by attributions that occur automatically and/or through more explicit decision processes.

Misattributions are thought to drive a wide variety of memory errors, and attributions play a central role in many theories of human memory (e.g., Johnson & Raye, 1981; Whittlesea & Williams, 1998). Extended to the DRM task, the idea is that the related lure is processed more fluently than unrelated lures (because of associative activation, thematic consistency, and/or feature overlap), and fluency causes one to misattribute perceptual details (borrowed or imagined) to actual presentation. In a sense, attributions have to be involved at some level in the DRM task (see Whittlesea, 2002, for discussion). Because related lures were never presented, detailed recollections of their occurrence must come from another source and then be misattributed to the related lures. The more critical—and testable—idea is that these attributions are caused by enhanced processing fluency of the related lures.

☐ FACTORS AFFECTING ILLUSORY RECOLLECTION

According to the attribution theory, details will be attributed to a memory for a lure depending on how fluently the lure is processed. Due to associative activation, thematic consistency, and/or feature overlap, related lures are processed more fluently than unrelated lures, and thus more illusory recollection is experienced for related lures than for unrelated lures. This theory predicts that variables that influence the activation of the related lure, and hence processing fluency, also should influence illusory recollection. This prediction has been borne out in a few studies.

As discussed in Chapter 3, the strength of the associative connection from the list words to the related lure (BAS) has been identified as the largest predictor of false recall and recognition (e.g., Deese, 1959b; Roediger et al., 2001c). Gallo and Roediger (2002, Experiment 3) had subjects study lists that were either high or low on associative strength, and then had them make confidence judgments or "remember"/"know" judgments on a final recognition test. They found that "remember" judgments were greater for related lures from strong lists (.59) than from weak lists (.33), and a similar difference was observed in confidence ratings. Brainerd et al. (2003a) reported analogous effects on recall tests, where estimates of phantom recollection (via the conjoint-recall methodology) were greater for lists with greater associative strength.

Other variables that influence activation of the related lure also have been found to influence various measures of illusory recollection. Mather et al. (1997) showed that blocking the study lists led to more "remember" judgments and greater MCQ ratings for related lures, relative to mixing the words from different lists at study. Brainerd et al. (2001) found that increasing the number of studied categorized words that were related to a nonstudied exemplar increased estimates of illusory recollection via conjoint recognition. Similarly, Gallo and Roediger (2003) found that increasing the length of the study list (from 5 to 15 items) increased levels of false recognition in the DRM task, and also increased (1) the proportion of falsely recognized items that were attributed to a source and (2) the ratings that these items were given on various MCQ dimensions. Finally, using a repeated-recall technique similar to the conjoint-recall technique, Brainerd et al. (2003a) found that estimates of illusory recollection were influenced by a variety of factors (e.g., blocked vs. mixed study, repeated tests, and study repetition).

Although these various findings are consistent with a fluency-based attribution theory of illusory recollection, there are two limitations to this line of reasoning. First, the assumption that each of these variables influences the processing fluency of related lures could be wrong. The fact that related lures are primed on implicit memory tests (reviewed in Chapter 3) suggests that they are processed fluently, but whether some of the aforementioned manipulations (e.g., blocking) also influence fluency has not been directly measured. (Some of these variables were reviewed in Chapter 3, and others will be discussed more in Chapters 5 and 6). Second, all of the aforementioned variables influenced overall levels of false recall and recognition, in addition to illusory recollection. If illusory recollection causes false recall and recognition, then a positive correlation between illusory recollections and overall error rates must necessarily be obtained. This relationship is problematic when a variable is only assumed to have influenced fluency because of its ultimate effects on memory errors. In these cases, the logic is circular.

One way around this circularity is to manipulate illusory recollection under conditions where overall levels of false recognition are held constant. Hicks and Hancock (2002) presented subjects with DRM lists, with one voice reading half of the items from the list, and another reading the other half (a mixed-source condition). The critical manipulation was that one source presented the items that were strongly related to the related lure, and the other source presented the items that were weakly related. Although attributions for list words were equally accurate for the two sources, related lures were more likely to be attributed to the strong source (.48) than to the weak source (.34). Because source was manipulated within a list, this strength effect on source attributions cannot be explained by different levels of false recognition of the lure, or to different levels of activation. Instead, Hicks and Hancock proposed that the strong items would be more likely to generate thoughts of the related lure at study, and the lure would then be attributed to the source of those items. Other possibilities are that related lures were more likely to borrow perceptual features from strongly associated items, or that subjects were more likely to imagine the lure in the source that had presented the stronger associates. In all of these cases, a fluency-based process could have driven the attribution, but again this process was not directly measured. Regardless of the exact cause, Hicks and Starns (2006) recently have replicated the basic effects of Hicks and Hancock (2002), and provided evidence that source judgments for related lures are due to the illusory recollection of source-specific information, as opposed to a strategic guessing or conscious inference process.

To conclude this chapter, it should be noted that theoretical understanding of illusory recollection is still in its infancy relative to our understanding of false recall and recognition errors. This difference probably stems from the fact that false recall and recognition are objectively measured using tasks that are commonly accepted (recall and recognition), whereas illusory recollection is measured from subjective judgments ("remember"/"know" or MCQ) or other types of judgments (e.g., source judgments, conjoint recognition) that are not used as frequently and can be more difficult to interpret. This is an unfortunate state of affairs, because illusory recollection is one of the most intriguing aspects of false memories (indeed, it is thought to be the proximal cause of these recall or recognition errors in the first place). The fact that illusory recollection is reliably demonstrated using a variety of measurement techniques, even when subjects are strategically trying to avoid false remembering, suggests that it is a tractable psychological phenomenon. The door is therefore wide open for inventive research in this area, and for the development of new measurement techniques to broaden our understanding of illusory recollection.

CHAPTER

Processes that Reduce False Memory

In the previous chapter the idea of attribution processes was introduced as central to the creation of memory errors. A nonstudied event may conjure illusory recollection and/or a feeling of familiarity, and these subjective experiences can cause a false memory if they are attributed to the past. The flip side to this idea is that if one can avoid attributing familiarity or illusory recollection to the past, then false memories can be avoided. Researchers have uncovered a host of variables that help subjects avoid false memories, by enhancing retrieval monitoring or editing processes. These processes fall under the broad umbrella of "metamemory," "metacognition," or "cognitive control." As they are applied to false memory monitoring, these terms often (but not always) refer to conscious or deliberate decision processes that use various types of information to reject an event as false.

Two frameworks that have a heavy influence on research and theory in this domain are the dual-process framework and the source monitoring framework. The dual-process framework posits that memory retrieval (and the resulting subjective experience) can involve the recollection of specific details of prior occurrence or a decontextualized feeling of familiarity (Atkinson & Juola, 1974; Jacoby, 1991; see Yonelinas, 2002, for a comprehensive review). Although dual-process theories are typically applied to recognition memory, they also can apply to memory on a recall test if a generate + recognize model is adopted (e.g., Bahrick, 1970; Jacoby & Hollingshead, 1990; Kintsch, 1970). False memory is typically thought to arise from familiarity (illusory recollection rarely being addressed, see Higham & Vokey, 2004), whereas recollection is thought to support accurate memory that can, under certain circumstances, reduce familiarity-based errors. In most conceptualizations, this type of recollection-based monitoring is thought to be a consciously controlled or strategic process. As discussed in Chapter 3, fuzzy trace theory is a type of dual-process theory, and it includes a mechanism through which true recollections can suppress or edit false memories that otherwise would be caused by gist-based similarity (e.g., "recollection rejection," discussed more in a subsequent section). Unlike more classic dual-process theories, though, the monitoring process in fuzzy trace theory is not necessarily conscious.

The source monitoring framework focuses less on the distinction between recollection and familiarity. According to this framework, retrieval involves the recall or recollection of various features or attributes of a memory (e.g., perceptual details, emotional reactions, and cognitive operations involved at encoding). These features are recalled to varying degrees, depending on the situation and the type to-be-remembered information, and they are attributed to different sources (e.g., the evening news, a conversation, or a daydream) depending on monitoring processes that operate on this information. These monitoring processes can be systematic (relatively conscious and deliberate) or heuristic (relatively fast and automatic), and depend on the available information (Johnson & Raye, 1981; Johnson et al., 1993). Memory errors occur when monitoring processes go awry, and false memories are avoided when monitoring processes "get it right." The activation-monitoring framework developed by Roediger, McDermott, and colleagues has emphasized these sorts of monitoring processes, in addition to associative activation processes, in an effort to explain many of the findings in the DRM task (e.g., McDermott & Watson, 2001; Roediger et al., 2001c).

Dual-process theories and source monitoring theories have developed in mostly separate lines of research, and there are many ways to conceptualize the relationship between the two. Most important for present purposes is that each framework has been responsible for generating a wealth of research that is relevant to two different types of false memory monitoring processes. Based on a distinction drawn by Gallo (2004) and Gallo, Bell, Beier, and Schacter (in press), these processes will be referred to as *disqualifying* and *diagnostic* monitoring. These two monitoring processes are thought to represent two fundamentally different decision processes through which true recollection can be used to avoid false memories. This hypothetical distinction is meant to be categorical, distinguishing different monitoring processes (or different effects that are thought to be due to monitoring processes) on the basis of the logic of the underlying decision process.

Disqualifying monitoring occurs when the true recollection of one event logically allows one to reject a more questionable event as having occurred. For example, a questionable event may seem familiar (e.g., "I bought plane tickets for vacation."), but could be rejected as false if inconsistent information is recalled ("No, I reserved them online, but I couldn't have bought them because I recall losing my credit card."). Dual-process research has capitalized on this type of decision process by the use of exclusion tasks. For instance, the list-based exclusion task allows one to reject a word as having occurred in one context (List 1) if they can recall that the word was presented in a different context (List 2), and if a word could have been presented only in one list or the other (Jacoby, 1991). The changed-pluralization task allows one to reject a lure (computers) if they can recall that a singular form of the word was studied (computer), and if a word could have been studied only in one form or the other (Hintzman & Curran, 1994). Finally, the associative recognition task allows one to reject test pairs (plant-guitar) if they can recall that these words were studied in different pairs (plant-road; candle-guitar), and if words were presented only in one pair at study (Rotello et al., 2000; Yonelinas, 1997). In all of these situations, the task is designed so that the recall of the item in one context is mutually exclusive with its occurrence in the other context, and therefore allows the rejection of the item as having occurred in that other context. This type of disqualifying monitoring process often is dubbed recall-to-reject, and is thought to be an explicit or strategic process that involves a conscious decision.

Diagnostic monitoring occurs when the failure to recollect expected information logically allows one to infer that the questionable event did not occur. Even though an event might be plausible (e.g., "I told you I lost my credit card."), the absence of expected recollection can lead one to decide that the event did not occur ("No, you didn't tell me, because I would remember if you did."). In this case, the decision process is based on the absence of the expected recollection. Brown, Lewis, and Monk (1977) presented a classic demonstration of diagnostic monitoring. In their experiment, subjects were unlikely to falsely recognize their own name as having been studied on a list of common names. Brown et al. argued that subjects expected to be able to recollect their own name, which would be very memorable, and could therefore reject it as having occurred based on the absence of such expected recollections. Related diagnostic monitoring processes were discussed in Chapter 4 in the context of the "it-had-to-be-you" effect in source memory literature (e.g., Hicks & Marsh, 2001; Johnson et al., 1981; see also Brown et al., 2000; Ghetti, 2003), and have been referred to as "memorability" heuristics (e.g., Hicks & Starns, 2006) or the "distinctiveness" heuristic (described more in a later section). Importantly, these effects occur even for events that were never studied, so that there can be no "true recollection" of the event that would allow subjects to disqualify it as having occurred in one source or the other. Instead, diagnostic decision processes are used to reason that the lure was not presented, or to decide (in the absence of expected recollections) that it probably was presented in one source and not another. Much like disqualifying monitoring, this process usually is thought to occur in an explicit or strategic way, although it sometimes is thought to occur at a more automatic level too.

These two decision processes focus on how true recall or recollection can be used to monitor memory accuracy, but it should be noted that other types of knowledge (e.g., beliefs, plausibility) also could be used to reject questionable events. For instance, someone might dismiss a false recollection of alien abduction by reasoning "I don't think aliens exist, so I could not have been abducted." In this case, they would have rejected the memory based on a belief, instead of the presence or absence of recollected information. Familiarity-based expectations also can be considered a form of diagnostic monitoring, in the sense that subjects will reject a test item if it is not deemed sufficiently familiar to have been studied (as illustrated by the setting of a response criterion in classic SDT). Despite these other possibilities, most of the basic research in false memory tasks has focused on how recall or recollection can be used to monitor memory accuracy, and these studies are reviewed below. Findings that can be explained via disqualifying monitoring are presented first, followed by those that can be explained via diagnostic monitoring. Of course, alternative conceptualizations of these effects also are possible, and some of these are discussed at the end of the chapter. Note that the terms "recall" and "recollection" are used somewhat interchangeably here, to refer to the retrieval of any specific information from the past that is not present in the retrieval cue, although "recall" often is used to refer to the retrieval of studied words, whereas "recollection" is used to refer to the retrieval of details associated with those studied words.

☐ DISQUALIFYING MONITORING

At least three different ways that recall can disqualify the related lure as having occurred have been demonstrated in converging associates tasks (using DRM or categorized list tasks). These are reviewed here under the labels *identify-and-reject*, *source-based exclusions*, and *exhaustive-recall-to-reject*. The first process is demonstrated by warning studies. As discussed in Chapter 3, several studies have found that informing subjects about the false memory effect, before they study the lists, can considerably reduce false recognition relative to a group of unwarned subjects. Gallo et al.

(1997) reasoned that informed subjects could have strategically encoded the study lists, trying to identify the related lures and mentally tag them as "not presented." At test, subjects could avoid false recognition of such a related lure by recalling their earlier discovery that this was a nonpresented item. In support of this idea, Gallo et al. found that informed subjects often claimed to have used such a strategy on an open-ended post-test questionnaire (7 out of the 16 subjects reported using this strategy). Interestingly, 5 out of 32 uninformed subjects also reported such a strategy, suggesting that a minority of unwarned subjects will spontaneously use this strategy in the typical DRM task.

Multhaup and Conner (2002) presented additional evidence for such an *identify-and-reject* process. They found that, when given the appropriate response option, subjects often identified test items as those that they had generated at study but that were not presented. Also relevant is Brédart (2000), who showed that subjects who did not falsely recall a related lure (nonpresented names, in this case) were later likely to produce these items when asked to recall words that were not presented but that had been identified as related to other words on the list (see also Libby & Neisser, 2001; Mukai, 2005). Neuschatz, Benoit, and Payne (2003) took a different approach. They reasoned that it should be easier for subjects to identify the related lures from some lists than others, and that false recognition from these lists should be affected more by warnings (given before study) if an identification strategy was used. Consistent with the prediction, they found that lists with highly identifiable related lures (as measured via a separate identification task) were affected more by before-study warnings (mean false recognition = .53 for an unwarned group and .22 for a warned group) than were lists with less identifiable related lures (means = .45 and .38, respectively). These findings, along with the previous findings, indicate that an identify-and-reject strategy is used when warnings are issued before study.

A second way that recall-to-reject has been demonstrated in converging associates tasks is by modifying the procedure so that it allows a *source-based exclusion rule*. In Smith, Tindell, Pierce, Gilliland, and Gerkens (2001, Experiment 1), subjects studied several lists of categorized words for a final category-cued recall test. Prior to the study phase, an ostensibly unrelated word-rating task occurred in which subjects rated various words for either pleasantness (a "deep" level of processing) or number of vowels (a "shallow" level of processing). Unbeknown to subjects at this time, the critical missing exemplars from some of the study categories were presented in this phase. On the final cued recall test, subjects were given one of three instructions. In the standard group, subjects were asked to recall all of the items studied from the categories during the study phase, and no mention was made of the relationship between the study phase and the incidental phase. In the inclusion and exclusion conditions, subjects were told at test that the incidental phase contained some words that were not in the study phase but were exemplars of the study categories. Subjects were told to include these incidentally studied exemplars into their recall (inclusion instructions) or to avoid recalling these items (exclusion instructions).

Results from these three conditions can be found in Figure 5.1. In the standard condition, false recall of related lures was greater when they had been "primed" by the incidental phase, after both shallow processing (means = .19 nonpresented and .30 presented) and deep processing (.24 vs. .38, respectively). These effects demonstrate source confusions, whereby presenting the related lure in an incidental task made these items more accessible and/or familiar on the recall test, and this enhanced memory signal was erroneously attributed to presentation in one of the categorized study lists. Even greater effects of incidental presentation were found in the inclusion condition, in which subjects were told to include these incidentally studied exemplars into their recalls. Most important, when subjects were told to exclude incidentally presented items from their recalls, they were able to reduce the incidental presentation effect for items that had been shallowly processed (.29 vs. .35, respectively), and to eliminate the effect of incidental presentation for items that

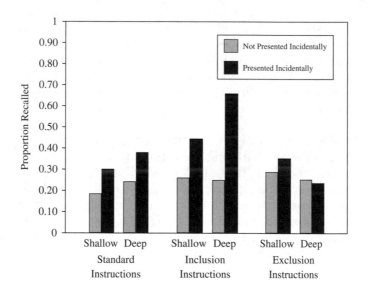

FIGURE 5.1   Recall of related lures as a function of whether they were studied in the incidental list and test instructions in Smith et al. (2001, Experiment 1).

had been deeply processed (means = .25 nonpresented and .23 presented). Thus, subjects were able to overcome source confusions when they were instructed to use a recall-to-reject strategy, and they were most effective for deeply presented items (which were easier to recall).

Dodhia and Metcalfe (1999) also presented evidence for a recall-to-reject exclusion rule. Subjects studied two DRM lists (presented in different colors) before each exclusion recognition test (i.e., respond "yes" to words from the target list [blue], and "no" to words studied from the exclusion list [red] or to nonstudied words). On some trials, the related lure was studied in the to-be-excluded list, whereas several of its associates were studied in the target list. Even though subjects were not specifically told that the lists were mutually exclusive, false recognition sometimes was reduced when the related lure was presented in the nontarget list compared to a condition where it was never studied. This finding is consistent with the idea that subjects had used a recall-to-reject rule, such that if they recalled the word from the nonstudied list they rejected it as having occurred in the target list. Gallo et al. (in press) reported analogous results in a similar DRM task, in which subjects were explicitly instructed to reject related lures that were presented in a to-be-excluded list.

The recall-to-reject processes discussed so far can be thought to rely on the application of an exclusion rule, whereby the recall of the related lure from one context allowed subjects to reject or disqualify it as having occurred in another context. With the aforementioned warning studies, the related lure was rejected by recalling that it had been personally generated and identified as "not presented," and with the source-based exclusion studies the related lure was rejected by recalling that it had been studied in the nontarget source. A third demonstration of recall-to-reject processes in converging associates tasks comes from those situations where the related lure is not necessarily recalled from any context. This situation arises when the subject can exhaustively recall all of the studied items that were presented in a list, and therefore knows that the related lure could not have been presented in the list (an *exhaustive-recall-to-reject* process).

Gallo (2004) reported evidence for such an exhaustive-recall-to-reject process in a converging associates task, where subjects studied several lists of categorized words for a final recognition test. In Experiment 1, each critical studied category contained three items and thus subjects could frequently recall all of the items that had been presented in a category (recall was measured using a separate cued recall test). Under these conditions, there was a negative relationship between false recognition and true recall, so that categories that elicited correct rejection of the non-studied exemplars were associated with greater levels of true recall than were categories that elicited false recognition (see Tulving, 1983, Chapter 15, for analogous results in a single-associate task, and Reyna & Kiernan,

1995, for analogous results when testing memory for metaphors). Further, false recognition was lower for those categories that were exhaustively recalled (mean = .12, collapsing across conditions) compared to those categories that were not exhaustively recalled (mean = .41). These patterns suggest that subjects were most likely to reject a related lure when they could recall all of the words that had been studied from the relevant category. In Experiment 2 of Gallo (2004), each critical category was longer (five words), so that subjects could rarely exhaustively recall all of the items from a category, and thus they could not use exhaustive recall to disqualify the lure. Consistent with this idea, there was no association between true recall and false recognition in this second experiment. When subjects could not apply the logic of mutual exclusivity (i.e., "I remember all the words that were studied from this category, so this test item could not have been studied."), they were unable to use recall to reduce false recognition (see Libby & Neisser, 2001, for related findings).

The general conclusion from all of these studies is that subjects can reduce false recognition by recalling information that is inconsistent with the occurrence of the lure's occurrence in the target list. Given that subjects can use recall-to-reject in other tasks (e.g., list-based exclusion, changed-pluralization, and associative recognition), it is perhaps not too surprising that they also can use such a strategy in a converging associates task. However, these findings are important to keep in mind for at least two reasons. First, subjects often experience illusory recollection in converging associates tasks (as discussed in Chapter 4), whereas familiarity is thought to cause false recognition in these other tasks. The finding of recall-to-reject under conditions that are prone to illusory recollection indicates that subjects can differentiate true recall from illusory recollection. Second, there was evidence that subjects had used recall-to-reject to reduce false recognition even without special instructions (e.g., Dodhia & Metcalfe, 1999; Gallo, 2004; Gallo et al., 1997; see also Rotello et al., 2000). These findings suggest that (1) subjects often spontaneously use recall during recognition memory tasks, in contrast to models of recognition memory that are based solely on familiarity, and (2) recall-to-reject must be considered a potential factor in any study using the DRM task, at least in the sense that subjects might generate the related lure and identify it as "nonstudied."

☐ DIAGNOSTIC MONITORING

In contrast to a disqualifying recall-to-reject process, diagnostic monitoring refers to those situations where the *absence* of the recall (or recollection) of information is used to reduce memory errors. As discussed, these processes play a central role in the source monitoring framework, where memory attributions are believed to be a product of decision processes that compare recollected information to that which is expected to be recollected from the different sources (e.g., Mitchell & Johnson, 2000). Several studies indicate that such processes are involved in converging associates tasks, but whether diagnostic monitoring can reduce false memory depends, in part, on the type or quality of the recollections that the study materials afford (and hence that the subjects expect to retrieve). For this reason, reductions based on source monitoring manipulations are sometimes but not always observed, as reviewed in the next section.

Following the discussion of source tests, other variables that are thought to reduce false memory via diagnostic monitoring will be reviewed. The strongest case that diagnostic monitoring processes are involved can be made from investigations that have manipulated presentation format at study (e.g., pictures, fonts, vocalization, writing, and modality) or related lure characteristics (e.g., emotionality, word length, or concreteness). Research that has manipulated study presentation rate, number of repetitions of the study lists, number of study/test repetitions, and response time at test also is reviewed. As will be discussed, these latter manipulations are somewhat ambiguous because they could influence either diagnostic monitoring processes or disqualifying processes (or both).

Source Tests

One way to demonstrate diagnostic monitoring has been to show that memory confusions are lower on a source memory test, in which subjects must decide between the potential sources of a memory, than on a standard memory test, in which subjects either recall or recognize all studied words regardless of the source (Dodson & Johnson, 1993; Lindsay & Johnson, 1989). The general idea is that source tests force the subject to more carefully monitor their memories for the recollection of details that are characteristic of one source or the other, thereby reducing errors through diagnostic decisions.

Surprisingly, research in converging associates tasks indicates that encouraging source monitoring does not necessarily yield reductions in false recognition. As discussed, Gallo (2004) failed to find evidence that recalling some (but not all) of the items from studied categories could reduce false recognition. It was thought that recalling some of the studied items would focus subjects on those details that would be diagnostic of presentation, thereby helping them to realize that they did not recollect such details for related lures. No evidence for such a process was found. Using a separate tactic, Hicks and Marsh (2001) had subjects study several DRM lists using one of two presentation sources, and then take either a standard "yes"/"no" recognition test or a source test. The results from their Experiment 2B (using male and female sources) are presented in Table 5.1. In contrast to the source monitoring prediction, they found elevated false recognition on the source test, relative to the standard test. Neuschatz et al.'s (2001) findings, discussed in the previous chapter, also are relevant. In that study, warning subjects to avoid false recognition before test, and instructing them to focus on the recollection of those features that could potentially help discriminate true from false memories, had little effect on false recognition of related lures. Collectively, these studies provide little evidence that focusing subjects on source monitoring processes at test can reduce these sorts of false memory effects.

Multhaup and Conner (2002, Experiment 2B) did find reductions in DRM false recognition, compared to a standard "yes"/"no" recognition condition, by giving subjects four response options on a source test ("I did not hear this word"; "I did not hear this word but I generated it on my own"; "I heard this word and generated it on my own"; "I heard this word"). However, this source test was given after each of several study lists, so that after the first study/test list these subjects might have been more likely to try to identify such lures on subsequent study trials. Thus, it is unclear whether the obtained reductions were due to the adoption of an "identify and reject" strategy (at study), or to source monitoring processes (at test), or both.

There are two potential reasons why source monitoring manipulations only sometimes have reduced false memories in these studies (and usually have been ineffective). The first is that subjects might spontaneously use diagnostic monitoring processes in standard conditions, in the absence of special instructions or response options. As discussed by Gallo

TABLE 5.1 Increases in True and False Memory on Source Memory Tests in Hicks and Marsh (2001, Experiment 2B)

| | List Words | | Related Lures | Unrelated |
	Male	Female		Lures
Recognition test	.69	.65	.76	.05
Source memory test	.78	.80	.90	.17
Difference	.09	.15	.14	.12

Note: Study presentation voice (male or female) was varied within each list, and type of test ("yes"/"no" recognition or "male"/"female"/"new" source judgments) was manipulated between-subjects.

(2004), if subjects naturally use recollective expectations when making memory decisions, then having them recall some of the studied words prior to a test decision, or focusing them on to-be-remembered details of studied words, might not add any useful information. Lampinen et al. (2005) presented compelling evidence that subjects do use these sorts of monitoring processes on their own. Typical DRM procedures were used, with the exception that subjects were asked to think aloud during the experiment. Evidence for recollection-based monitoring processes was found for many of the trials where subjects correctly rejected lures. For instance, when rejecting the lure "view," one subject indicated "because I used to have a good view in my California apartment, and I do not remember saying that" (p. 958). This justification is a clear example of the formation of a recollective expectation, and then using the absence of this expected recollection to reject the lure (i.e., diagnostic monitoring). As discussed later in this chapter, the specific decision process used to justify the rejections of related lures was not always obvious in this study. Nevertheless, these results indicate that subjects spontaneously engaged in recollection-based monitoring processes, without the prompting of the experimenter.

The other potential reason that source monitoring manipulations have only sometimes reduced false memories is that, under typical DRM conditions, there might not be enough recollective detail for these monitoring processes to work effectively. One common feature to many of these investigations, especially the conditions discussed above, was that the studied materials were presented using relatively homogenous sources. That is, all of the studied items were words presented either visually (on the computer screen) or auditorily (by one voice or two). Diagnostic monitoring processes might not be that effective in these situations because true recollection does not vary enough across studied items. If studied materials are made more heterogeneous, so that there are more features or attributes to potentially recollect from each studied item, then research indicates that diagnostic monitoring processes can have larger effects on false memories.

In line with this reasoning, Hicks and Marsh (1999) showed that presenting DRM lists with alternating sources could reduce false recall, but only if the sources were different enough. Experiment 3 in their series was particularly telling. Words from each list were presented visually or were solved from anagrams. For one group of subjects, the two sources alternated across lists (a blocked-source condition), whereas the source alternated within each list for the other group (a mixed-source condition). Each list was tested with immediate free recall. As discussed at the beginning of this chapter, studies have shown that subjects are more likely to attribute nonstudied events to an external source (hearing) than to anagram solution. This "it-had-to-be-you" effect indicates that different sources elicit different recollection-based expectations, and that these expectations contribute to source attributions (see Chapter 4). Hicks and Marsh reasoned that these source monitoring processes might lead to overall reductions in false recall, even when subjects are not explicitly required to make source attributions at test. Consistent with this hypothesis, they found that false recall was reduced considerably in the mixed-source condition (.22) compared to the blocked-source condition (.42, collapsing across the sources). In contrast, when the two sources were less discriminable (e.g., male vs. female voices in Experiment 2a), they failed to find a significant reduction (means = .45 and .46, respectively).

Hicks and Marsh's (1999) findings highlight the importance of stimulus characteristics for diagnostic monitoring processes. Whereas explicit instructions to engage source monitoring processes at test have been relatively ineffective on their own (e.g., Hicks & Marsh, 2001; Neuschatz et al., 2001), presentation manipulations that influence the type of information that is encoded from studied materials can greatly affect false memories, ostensibly by fostering more accurate diagnostic monitoring. Several manipulations of the method of study presentation influence false memories in converging associates tasks (i.e., presentation format, presentation rate, study repetitions, and study/test repetitions). Importantly, in many of these cases, the manipulations are not thought to influence associative activation, thematic consistency, or feature overlap, or are thought to influence these processes in a way that cannot explain the observed patterns of false recall or false recognition. Additional monitoring processes must be involved, by default, as reviewed next.

☐ STUDY FORMAT MANIPULATIONS

With some format changes, it is thought that the presentation manipulation makes the studied materials elicit more distinctive, feature-rich, or detailed recollections. This enhancement sometimes leads to greater levels of true memory for list words, but not always. Either way, it is believed that the format change allows subjects to expect richer or more distinctive recollections before attributing a test item to the study phase, relative to a less distinctive condition, and thereby reduce false recall or recognition of nonstudied items that are unlikely to elicit such recollections. The absence of expected recollections is used as information when making a memory decision, and the more information one expects to recollect, the more diagnostic the absence of such recollection is of nonoccurrence. Another way to look at these diagnostic monitoring effects is via illusory recollection. The more distinctive the studied materials, the less likely there will be compelling illusory recollection of the related lure occurring in that distinctive format.

These types of format effects were discussed in Chapter 4, to explain why falsely remembered related lures were more likely to be attributed to a more distinctive source (e.g., anagrams) than a less distinctive source (reading) in Hicks and Marsh (1999, 2001) and Johansson and Stenberg (2002). Similar processes are thought to occur in the following cases, with the exception that the distinctiveness of the studied materials was manipulated between-subjects (in most cases), and instead of a source test (i.e., choosing between one source and another) the decision was usually "yes" or "no" recognition. In these situations, the tendency to avoid attributing the related lure to distinctive sources translates into fewer "old" judgments, and hence lower levels of false recognition. Note that these diagnostic monitoring processes also might occur during the study phase of the DRM task, if the subject generates the related lure but immediately rejects it as having occurred when studied materials are more distinctive (although the available evidence suggests mostly a test-based locus). Also note that the difference in false recognition between a relatively nondistinctive and a distinctive study condition is taken as evidence for enhanced diagnostic monitoring, but this is not to say that such monitoring does not occur in the nondistinctive condition. By one view, subjects are always engaged in this type of retrieval monitoring, and the difference in conditions simply reflects a greater degree of success (due to enhanced distinctiveness). The rest of this section reviews research on format changes, starting with picture manipulations that have been investigated most extensively. In those instances where a study involved several variables, only the results from those conditions that most purely reflect the construct of interest are presented (e.g., recognition tests that are unconfounded with prior recall tests). As with most of the other experiments discussed in Chapters 1–6, results from healthy college-aged adults are discussed below (or control subjects in neuropsychological studies).

Pictures

Schacter and colleagues used the term "distinctiveness heuristic" to explain why false recognition was reduced following the use of a perceptually distinctive study format (Schacter, Israel, & Racine, 1999, see also Israel & Schacter, 1997). In Schacter et al. (Experiment 1), each DRM list was auditorily presented to subjects. In the word-only condition, each auditorily presented word was simultaneously presented as a visual word

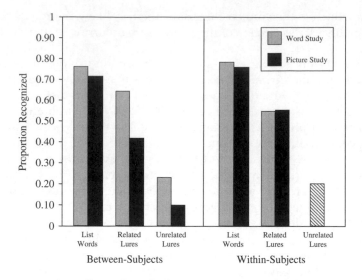

FIGURE 5.2 The effect of study format on true and false recognition in Schacter et al. (1999). False alarms to unrelated lures are collapsed across list word controls and related lure controls. There was only one false alarm rate to unrelated lures when study format was manipulated within-subjects.

on the computer screen. In the picture condition, each auditorily presented word was simultaneously presented as a picture. At test, words were either presented in the auditory format (i.e., subjects in the picture condition could rely on familiarity and/or search their memory for picture recollections), or in the auditory and visual format (i.e., pictures were presented at test in the picture condition). The left panel of Figure 5.2 presents recognition data as a function of study format in the auditory test condition. True recognition of list words did not vary as a function of study presentation, but false recognition of related lures dropped considerably from .64 in the word-only study condition to .41 in the picture condition. False recognition to unrelated lures also was lower in the picture condition (.26) than in the word condition (.08). Similar (or even greater) results were obtained with visual presentation at test, ostensibly because presenting novel pictures for lures would make the absence of recollections of those pictures even more salient (although subjects in this condition could have relied on familiarity of the presented test pictures, as opposed to recollection-based responding, and so it is unclear whether these effects should be attributed to recollective distinctiveness). Schacter et al. argued that subjects in the picture condition were able to demand more distinctive recollections than subjects in the word-only condition, and thus were better able to reduce false recognition. That is, the absence of picture recollections helped subjects to decide that the related lure was not presented.

To test the distinctiveness heuristic hypothesis, Schacter et al. (1999) ran an additional experiment with study format manipulated within-subjects (i.e., some lists were presented in the word-only format, and others were presented in the picture format). It was thought that, when study format was manipulated within-subjects, subjects would be less likely to invoke a distinctiveness heuristic because they could not expect to recollect distinctive pictures from all studied items. The data from this condition (again with an auditory test) can be found in the right panel of Figure 5.2. Again, true recognition did not differ following the two presentation conditions, but, more important, false recognition did not differ across the word and picture lists either. Schacter et al. argued that this was consistent with a global application of the distinctiveness heuristic at test. Subjects in the within-subjects design may have tried to apply a heuristic, leading to suppressed levels of false recognition relative to the standard word-only condition (in the between-subjects design), but this reduction was observed for both word and picture lists. The pattern of results in Figure 5.2 has been replicated by Schacter, Cendan, Dodson, and Clifford (2001), and Gallo et al. (in press) have demonstrated the separate influences of a distinctiveness heuristic and a recall-to-reject strategy in a single experiment (discussed more in Chapter 8).

It is worth mentioning that the picture-superiority effect on true memory (pictures > words, Mintzer & Snodgrass, 1999; Paivio, 1971) was not always found in the verbal testing conditions of Schacter et al. (1999, 2001) or Israel and Schacter (1997). This null result may have been due to the fact that test items were presented verbally, and thus items studied in the word-only condition had the benefit of study-to-test format matching (e.g., the encoding specificity principle; Tulving & Thomson, 1973). When test items were presented visually, so that pictures were now represented at test, the typical picture-superiority pattern was obtained in each of these three studies.

Arndt and Reder (2003) questioned decision-based accounts, such as the distinctiveness heuristic or other diagnostic monitoring processes, as explanations for distinctive format effects on false recognition. As an alternative, they proposed that presenting study words in more distinctive formats might lead to more item-specific processing, which would serve to reduce relational-processing (e.g., Einstein & Hunt, 1980; Hunt & McDaniel, 1993). In the present terms, reducing relational processing of a DRM list would reduce activation of the related lure, and thus reduce the memory signal for the related lure (e.g., it would not be as familiar). As a result, false recall and recognition would be lower following the distinctive study format. In Arndt and Reder's experiments, presenting studied words in distinctive fonts (e.g., each list item was presented in a different font) reduced false recognition relative to less distinctive conditions (e.g., each list was presented in the same font). Because these effects were obtained when distinctiveness was manipulated both between-subjects and within-subjects, they argued that these effects could not be explained through the use of a global distinctiveness heuristic operating on all of the test words, and instead they proposed a "memory-based" account (i.e., reducing relational processes at study reduced a memory signal for the related lures). This reduced relational processing account is different than arguing that subjects relied more on item-specific memory following a distinctive study format, without a cost to relational processing. Relying more on item-specific memory to reduce false recognition would be akin to demanding more distinctive recollections, and thus is equivalent to a diagnostic monitoring process such as the distinctiveness heuristic.

Although the relational processing account might apply to the distinctive font manipulation used by Arndt and Reder (2003), as well as other manipulations (see the "Encoding Context" section in Chapter 6), several pieces of evidence suggest that it cannot entirely explain the distinctive picture manipulation. First, as discussed, studying some lists in the picture format and other lists in the word-only format did not selectively reduce false recognition (i.e., the within-subjects conditions of Schacter et al., 1999 and 2001). If studying pictures reduced relational processing, then the picture lists should have reduced false recognition regardless of the format of other lists in the study phase. Second, Schacter et al. (2001) directly tested this reduced gist account by switching to a meaning-based test, as opposed to a standard recognition test. On the meaning test, subjects were instructed to say "yes" to any test word that appeared to be related to the list words (i.e., any word that was consistent with the theme or gist of the lists), regardless of whether or not they thought the test word itself was actually studied. This meaning test removed the need to monitor whether a word was studied (and thus should have eliminated the distinctiveness heuristic), but it still was sensitive to differences in relational processing across conditions. Schacter et al. (2001) did find some reductions in the picture condition relative to the word-only condition on this meaning test (means = .75 and .87, respectively), suggesting that there may have been some relational processing impairment, but this effect was much smaller than that on the standard recognition test (means = .28 and .66, respectively). Because of this interaction, which persisted on scores that were corrected for base rates, they argued that the distinctiveness heuristic still was needed to explain the reduced false recognition following picture study on the standard recognition memory test.

A final piece of evidence that is consistent with the diagnostic monitoring account is that studying pictures reduces false recognition (relative to studying words-only) in other tasks that do not rely on converging associations. Dodson and Schacter (2002a, 2002b) used the repetition-lag task to elicit familiarity-based false recognition. In this task, subjects study a list of unrelated items and are then given a recognition memory test. On this test, some of the lures are repeatedly tested (i.e., they appear more than once in the test list). Repeating these lures makes them more familiar and/or increases source confusions, and thus makes subjects more likely to falsely recognize them as having occurred in the study phase. Consistent with the distinctiveness heuristic, Dodson and Schacter (2002a, 2002b) found that subjects were less likely to falsely recognize repeated lures if the studied items were presented as pictures, compared to a word-only study condition. Because this task does not use converging associates to elicit false memories, a relational processing account cannot explain these effects of studying pictures. Similarly, Gallo, Weiss, and Schacter (2004b) provided evidence for the distinctiveness heuristic in a source-confusion task that they dubbed the "criterial recollection task." In those experiments, it was shown that subjects were less likely to falsely recognize lures when subjects expected to recollect pictures (i.e., a picture recognition test), as opposed to words (i.e., a word recognition test). Importantly, these effects were obtained even when words were made more familiar than pictures. This last finding indicates that the distinctiveness effect on false recognition was based on recollection-based expectations, as opposed to familiarity or strength-based expectations (i.e., a familiarity-based criterion shift). Gallo et al. also found that, on source tests, subjects were more likely to attribute falsely recognized lures to the less distinctive source (words) than the more distinctive source (pictures), analogous to the "it-had-to-be-you" effect in the source monitoring literature.

Considered as a whole, the evidence indicates that expecting distinctive picture recollections can reduce false recognition compared to expecting less distinctive recollections (e.g., words). Given this wealth of evidence in false recognition, it is surprising that analogous effects have not been consistently reported in false recall. Ghetti, Qin, and Goodman (2002) found that false recall for subjects that had heard lists read by the experimenters (15%) was no different than false recall for subjects that heard the lists and were presented with pictures (15%). However, this study used seven-item lists in order to test children, so that performance was close to ceiling for younger adults (true recall was around 90%). Hege and Dodson (2004) did find an effect on recall tests, but they also found a large effect on a meaning-based recall test (i.e., recall all of the items that are similar in meaning to those that you studied). This latter finding suggests that a relational processing account might offer a viable alternative in the recall test situation. Thus, although there is converging evidence that the distinctiveness heuristic is involved in the picture/word effect on false recognition, across several different tasks, more work is needed to investigate these effects on recall tests.

Modality

Smith and Hunt (1998) were the first to report that presenting list words visually at study reduced false recall (on written tests) and false recognition (on visual tests) relative to presenting the list words auditorily. Since then, there have been at least four published studies (Cleary & Greene, 2002; Gallo et al., 2001a; Kellogg, 2001; Smith, Lozito, & Bayen, 2005), with a combined total of ten experimental conditions, that have demonstrated this effect in free recall on written tests. Further, these effects have been demonstrated on visual recognition memory tests in at least four published studies, with effects in six different experimental conditions (Cleary & Greene, 2002; Gallo et al., 2001a; Gallo & Roediger, 2003). In the majority of cases, visual study suppressed false recall and recognition by about 10% relative to auditory study. There is one published reversal of these modality effects in recognition (Maylor & Mo, 1999), and Clearly and Greene found a reversed modality effect for weakly related lures (visual study > auditory study), but these patterns are unexplained exceptions to the rule.

The study modality effect on visual recognition tests is so robust that it is found even in cross-experiment comparisons. In Table 4.1 the recognition results from 32 DRM studies were reported, broken down in terms of auditory or visual study. If one calculates the mean proportion of related lures that were falsely recognized in the two sets of studies, then a reliable modality effect is obtained (mean auditory presentation = .75, visual presentation = .67, t [30] = 2.90, $p < .01$), and this effect also is apparent on data that were corrected for base rate false alarms. Interestingly, visual study also led to greater true recognition (.77) than did auditory study (.68), t [30] = 2.44, $p < .05$, but such modality effects on true recognition are not always obtained (see Gallo et al., 2001a, for discussion). Because the test used visual presentation in these studies, the effect of study modality on true memory might simply reflect the match between study and test presentation modality (e.g., the encoding specificity principle; Tulving & Thomson, 1973).

To explain the effect of study modality on false recognition, Smith and Hunt (1998) proposed that visual presentation led to more distinctive or item-specific processing of the list words, and hence suppressed false remembering. For instance, if subjects mentally generated the related lure while studying the list, then it might be easier to discriminate this thought from actual presentation when words were presented visually than audi-torily. Gallo et al. (2001a) echoed these sentiments, and suggested that modality effects also might result from monitoring processes at retrieval, similar to the distinctiveness heuristic. This conclusion was based, in part, on their finding that modality effects were obtained with visual recognition tests, but not when test items were presented auditorily (see also Israel & Schacter, 1997). It was suggested that visual test presentation made the processing of distinctive visual information more salient, and thereby facilitated the monitoring processes that could suppress false recognition (much like pictorial presentation at test can enhance the picture/word effect on false recognition, as discussed).

Kellogg (2001) provided analogous study/test interactions on recall tests. In those experiments, the modality effect on false recall was replicated with written recall tests, but it was not obtained with spoken recall tests. Kellogg argued that written recall made distinctive orthographic features of words more salient than did spoken recall, and thus facilitated those monitoring processes that could suppress false recall. Further support for the "distinctive visual information" explanation came from Kellogg's second experiment. Having subjects visualize (or imagine) the letters of the list words at study eliminated the modality effect on written recall, even though the modality effect was replicated in a control condition that also employed a secondary study task (repeated counting from 1 to 5). Kellogg argued that the visualization task allowed subjects to encode distinctive orthographic information for list words in both the auditory and visual conditions, and thus eliminated the advantage of visual presentation.

As was the case with the picture/word effect, an alternative explanation of the study modality effect on false memory is reduced relational processing. Presenting the list words in the visual modality may have reduced relational processing at study, and therefore reduced relatedness effects on false memory. The existing evidence does not support this possibility. If visual processing reduced relational processing, then lists that were studied visually should have reduced false memories regardless of the test modality. However, the interaction between study and test modalities (Gallo et al., 2001a; Kellogg, 2001) indicates that retrieval processes (such as diagnostic monitoring) play a critical role. Other evidence against a reduced relational account comes from Pierce et al. (2005a). In this experiment a typical study modality effect was obtained on a standard recognition test, but the effect was eliminated when subjects instead were given a meaning test (which did not require the monitoring of study presentation at retrieval). As discussed above in the context of the picture/word effect, a relational processing account would have predicted a modality effect on the meaning test. Pierce et al. also found that the study modality effect (on a recognition test) generalized to false recognition for categorized lists, and argued that this finding is consistent with a retrieval monitoring explanation (as opposed to monitoring during the study phase, which was thought to occur less often for categorized lists; see Smith et al., 2002, see Chapter 3).

Even though the study modality effect on false recall and recognition (with visual tests) is well documented, one outstanding question remains. If the modality effect is caused by the global application of a diagnostic monitoring process such as the distinctiveness heuristic, then the effect should not be found when study modality is manipulated within-subjects (but between lists), as was the case with the picture/word effect (e.g., Schacter et al., 1999). In contrast to this prediction, Gallo et al. (2001a) found an equivalent modality effect on visual tests when study modality was manipulated within-subjects (Experiment 2) and between-subjects (Experiment 3). To explain this result they argued that subjects might have accessed list-specific information at test, and thus applied a distinctiveness heuristic at a more local level. However, it then becomes unclear why subjects did not use such list-specific information to apply the distinctiveness heuristic in the picture/word conditions of Schacter et al. (1999). Other evidence that the study modality effect operates differently than picture/word effect is discussed in the context of aging effects on monitoring processes in Chapter 9.

Vocalization

Dodson and Schacter (2001) presented study words visually to subjects and had them read each word aloud (to promote distinctive encoding) or silently (a control condition). Analogous to Schacter et al. (1999, 2001), they found that false recognition was selectively reduced (read-silently > say-aloud) when the distinctive format was manipulated between-subjects, but not when it was manipulated within-subjects. Also like Schacter et al. (1999, 2001), they found that false recognition was lower overall in the within-subjects conditions compared to the low-distinctiveness between-subjects condition (read-silently). Unlike these previous studies, though, they did not find a comparable effect on base rate false alarms to unrelated lures. Overall, Dodson and Schacter took these findings as additional evidence for a distinctiveness heuristic on false recognition.

Other evidence supports the idea that overtly verbalizing the studied materials leads to lower levels of false recognition, although these effects are not as clear-cut as the picture/word effect, and the effects on false recall also are tenuous. Cleary and Greene (2002) reported relevant conditions. Subjects studied several DRM lists for immediate recall tests, with presentation format manipulated within-subjects (but across different study/test blocks). They reported no difference in false recall of related lures for lists that subjects had silently read (.27) than for those that they had read aloud (.24) in their first experiment, and a null result also was obtained in their second experiment (means = .21 and .23, respectively). No effects were found on false recognition of related lures, either, but that test was confounded with prior recall. For weakly related lures (those which were unlikely to have been recalled earlier), the predicted effect (read-silently > say-aloud) was found in both experiments, providing some evidence for the distinctiveness effect of vocalization on false recognition. Seamon et al. (2002b) also is relevant. In their experiment, subjects either read words and rehearsed them silently, or read the words and rehearsed them aloud. They failed to find evidence for differences in false recall or false recognition of the related lures between these two conditions. However, because subjects sometimes generated related lures in the overt rehearsal condition, "say-aloud" information could later be recollected for related lures, and this would have undermined a distinctiveness heuristic (which is based on the absence of such recollections). Consistent with this interpretation, there was an effect of vocalization on false alarms to unrelated lures on the recognition test (silent rehearsal > overt rehearsal). Thus, for those lures that were not likely to be verbalized at study, false recognition was lower when the studied materials were verbalized than when they were not.

Writing

Seamon et al. (2003) compared a variety of format manipulations, one of which was analogous to saying aloud each word, except words were written down instead of said aloud. In Experiment 1, subjects studied several DRM lists for a final recall test. One group of subjects heard the lists, and another group heard the lists and simultaneously wrote the words down on a sheet of paper. (A third group wrote down the second letter of each word, which might be considered a more distinctive encoding condition. Results from that group were similar to those from the group that wrote the whole word.). On the first study/test trial, they found that true recall of list words did not differ between the hear-word (.37) and hear + write conditions (.33). More important, false recall was lower in the write-word conditions (.20) than in the hear-word condition (.38), although this effect was significant only after several study/test trials. This finding is consistent with the idea that writing each word down (much like saying each word aloud) provided more distinctive recollections than simply hearing the words at study. Similar results were obtained in Experiment 2, where a recognition test was given. On the first study/test trial, true recognition did not differ across the hear (.76) and hear + write (.77) conditions, whereas false recognition was lower with the latter (means = .75 and .55, respectively). Note that, because a similar result was obtained on false alarms to unrelated words (means = .17 and .09, respectively), the difference in corrected false recognition was not significant. However, correcting for base rates is problematic in these situations. A distinctiveness heuristic could affect false alarms to all lures (related and unrelated), as demonstrated by Schacter et al. (1999, 2001), so that correcting for base rates would essentially factor out the effect of interest.

☐ LURE CHARACTERISTICS

Emotionality

Various characteristics of the related lure are thought to influence false recall and recognition via diagnostic monitoring processes. For instance, Pesta, Murphy, and Sanders (2001) created lists of words that were orthographically similar to neutral or emotionally valenced lures (e.g., "bark," "dark," "hark," etc. were studied for the related lure "park," and "bell," "dell," "fell," etc. were studied for the related lure "hell"). Even though lures were equated on word frequency, length, and number and density of orthographic neighbors, Pesta et al. (Experiment 1) found that emotionally distinctive related lures were less likely to be falsely recognized (mean = .18) than were neutral lures (.64). These differences also were obtained in base rate false alarms to these same lures when the corresponding list of similar words was not studied (means = .05 vs. .33, respectively), and these effects were replicated in three other experiments. Pesta et al. argued that emotional words were more distinctive than neutral words, and as a result subjects could avoid false recognition of these words by realizing that they were not studied. In the terms used here, emotionally valenced words could facilitate diagnostic monitoring processes in the form of an item-based distinctiveness heuristic. Subjects could reason "I didn't study 'hell,' because that would be a very memorable word, and I'd remember it if it had been presented." Consistent with this distinctiveness account, Pesta et al. found that reducing the distinctiveness of emotionally valenced lures, by presenting other emotionally valenced lures in the study list, reduced the effect of emotionality on false alarms (for analogous results, see Lenton, Blair, & Hastie, 2001). Kensinger and Corkin (2004) replicated and extended these effects in false recognition, but found smaller effects in false recall. They also argued that distinctiveness underlies the effect, although they noted that either emotional distinctiveness or conceptual distinctiveness could have been involved.

Word Length

In the typical DRM task, Roediger et al. (2001c) found that length and orthographic distinctiveness of the related lure correlated negatively with false recall and recognition (mean bivariate correlations = −.37 and −.27, respectively), although only the recognition effect remained significant when other factors were taken into consideration in a multiple regression analysis (see Chapter 3). Madigan and Neuse (2004) reanalyzed the dataset used by Roediger et al., and found that the relative length of the related lure (compared to list words) was an even stronger predictor of false recognition than absolute length. They also replicated these length effects in separate recognition experiments. Roediger et al. argued that longer and more distinctive related lures such as "butterfly" were less likely to be falsely recalled than shorter and less distinctive lures such as "soft" because more distinctive words would facilitate source monitoring processes. In the terms used here, this process again could be considered an item-specific distinctiveness heuristic.

Concreteness

Pérez-Mata et al. (2002) had subjects study several DRM lists that were modified so that both the list words and related lure either would be concrete words (e.g., subjects studied "butter," "food," "sandwich," etc. for the related lure "bread") or abstract words (e.g., "rest," "awake," "tired" for the related lure "sleep"). On an immediate recall test, under full-attention study conditions, they found that concrete lists yielded greater true recall than abstract lists (means = .65 and .56 in Experiment 1), replicating the classic concreteness effect in word recall (ostensibly because concrete words benefit more from spontaneous mental imagery; see Paivio, 1971). Of greater interest was that false recall of concrete related lures was lower than that of abstract related lures (means = .31 and .43, respectively). These effects were replicated in a second experiment, and also were found when attention was divided at study (the effects of divided attention are discussed in Chapter 6). One explanation for this finding is that there was more diagnostic monitoring for concrete words, analogous to the picture/word distinctiveness heuristic reviewed above. That is, subjects were more likely to expect to recollect a mental image for concrete lures than for related lures, and the absence of such an image was diagnostic that the lure did not occur. It should be noted, though, that Roediger et al. (2001c) did not find a relationship between related lure concreteness and false recall or recognition in their multiple regression analysis.

☐ OTHER RELEVANT MANIPULATIONS

Study Rate

Slowing presentation rate allows more time to process list words, and thus should enhance true recall or recognition. According to the three big theories of false remembering in the DRM task, the additional processing of list items also might increase false remembering of related lures, by allowing more time to meaningfully process the list items and therefore increase activation of the related lure. However, increased processing of list items also might allow subjects to expect more distinctive or item-specific recollections of each studied item, and therefore facilitate diagnostic monitoring processes that would reduce false remembering. McDermott and Watson (2001) manipulated a wide range of presentation rates across subjects (from approximately 50 ms per item to 5 s) and found that, as expected, true recall steadily increased. However, false recall from DRM lists followed a nonmonotonic function (see Figure 5.3). Within the very rapid range, slowing presentation led to increased false recall. This finding is consistent with the idea that processing of the list items was minimal at the most rapid rate, resulting in minimal activation of the related lures, and

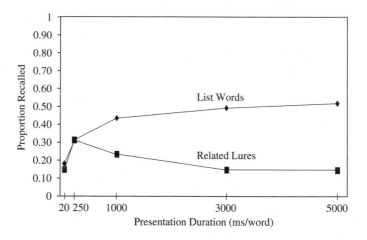

FIGURE 5.3 The effect of study presentation duration on true and false recall in McDermott and Watson (2001). The proportions of other recall intrusions were not reported. (Reprinted from *Journal of Memory & Language, 45,* McDermott, K. B., & Watson, J. M., The rise and fall of false recall: The impact of presentation duration, 160–176, 2001, with permission from Elsevier.)

slowing rate allowed more processing of the list items and hence more activation of the related lures. More important for present concerns, when rate was slowed even further, a separate cognitive process began to contribute and led to reductions in false recall. McDermott and Watson argued that this separate process was a monitoring component. Gallo and Roediger (2002) also showed that slowing presentation rate (from 500 ms per item to 3 s per item) decreased false recall, and Seamon et al. (2002b) reported similar results using rates of 2 and 5 s (but only when subjects had overtly rehearsed items at study).

Rate-related decreases in false recall implicate monitoring processes, but at least two questions remain. First, it is unclear whether these are diagnostic monitoring processes or disqualifying monitoring processes (or both). As discussed, slower rates might contribute to diagnostic monitoring, by increasing the processing of list words and hence increasing the amount of expected recollected detail. However, they also might contribute to an identify-and-reject strategy, by giving the subjects more time to "figure-out" the related lure and later reject it as having occurred. Second, the effect of rate on false recognition has been less consistent than that on false recall. Several studies have shown that decreasing presentation rate from very rapid rates (i.e., less than a second per item) to slower rates (e.g., 2–3 s per item) leads to increased false recognition (Arndt & Hirshman, 1998; Kawasaki-Miyaji & Yama, in press; Seamon et al., 1998, 2002d; Zeelenberg et al., 2003), consistent with the idea that activation of the related lure is enhanced by additional processing of the list words. However, significant effects of presentation rate are not always obtained in false recognition (e.g., Gallo & Roediger, 2002; McCabe & Smith, 2002; Seamon et al., 1998, 2002b, 2002d), and unlike false recall none of these studies found that false recognition eventually decreased with slower rates.

Study Repetitions

Another way to enhance memory for studied items is to repeat the study lists before the memory test is given. Much like presentation rate, one could hypothesize that repetitions would (1) increase processing of list items, and hence increase activation of related lures, but (2) increase monitoring processes that could reduce false remembering. Benjamin (2001, Experiment 2) nicely demonstrated these two opposing processes in the DRM task. On a standard recognition test with self-paced responding, repeating list words three times increased true recognition but decreased false recognition (see the left panel of Figure 5.4). This decrease in false recognition is consistent with the idea that repetition enhanced monitoring processes that suppressed false recognition. Repetition also reduced false recognition in studies by Mintzer and Griffiths (2001c) and Seamon et al. (2002d), and repetition reduced false recall in studies by Brainerd et al. (2003a) and McKone and Murphy (2000); see also Cleary and Greene (2002).

In a separate condition of Benjamin (2001), subjects were exposed to the same study conditions but now they were forced to make their recognition decisions very rapidly (around 750 ms). Under these conditions, presented in the right panel of Figure 5.4, both true and false recognition increased with repetition. Benjamin reasoned that speeded subjects were forced to rely on familiarity, as opposed to recollection (or recollection-based monitoring processes). Repetitions increased the activation of related lures, and hence their familiarity, leading to more false recognition when diagnostic monitoring processes could not keep this familiarity in check. Seamon et al. (2002d, Experiment 1) also demonstrated these two opposing effects of repetition. In the standard presentation rate conditions of that study, repeating lists five times increased false recognition relative to once presented lists (means = .65 and .54, respectively), ostensibly by increasing the activation of the related lure, whereas even more

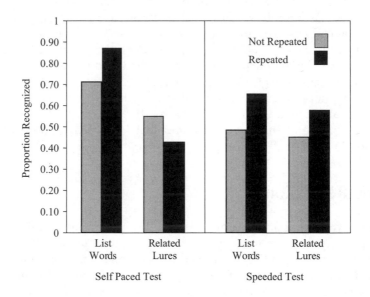

FIGURE 5.4 The effect of study repetitions on true and false recognition in Benjamin (2001, Experiment 2, approximated from Benjamin's Figure 2). False alarms to unrelated lures were approximately .10 in the self-paced condition and .20 in the speeded condition. (Benjamin, A. S., On the dual effects of repetition on false recognition. *Journal of Experimental Psychology: Learning, Memory, & Cognition, 27*, 941–947, 2001, APA, reprinted with permission.)

repetitions (ten) decreased false recognition (mean = .46), ostensibly due to monitoring processes. This nonmonotonic function was replicated in Seamon et al.'s (2002d) second experiment, and because repetition was manipulated within-subjects, there were no base rate false alarm differences across the repetition conditions (hence, the same pattern was obtained on base rate corrected data). These competing effects of repetition on false remembering are analogous to those that were reported by McDermott and Watson (2001) in the context of presentation rate, and they might explain why some earlier studies did not find repetition-related reductions on false recognition (Shiffrin et al., 1995; Tussing & Greene, 1997).

As was the case with presentation rate, it is unclear whether repetition increases a diagnostic monitoring process or a disqualifying monitoring process. Repetition would afford more processing of the list items, and hence increased recollective distinctiveness and diagnostic monitoring processes. However, repetition also might afford more opportunities to "figure-out" the related lure, and thus to use an identify-and-reject strategy. Again, no evidence exists to favor one account over the other.

Study/Test Repetitions

Rather than repeating the study lists before a single test, some investigators have repeated the entire study/test cycle. McDermott (1996, Experiment 2) had subjects study three blocked DRM lists and then take a recall test. After subjects had recalled words from the three lists, they then restudied the three lists and took another recall test, and this procedure was repeated for five study/test cycles. True recall of list words increased across the five study/test trials (mean recall, estimated from McDermott's Figure 5, was 39% for the first trial and 85% for the fifth trial), but false recall steadily decreased across trials (approximate means = 58% and 31%, respectively). These effects have been replicated in recall by Seamon et al. (2003) and Kensinger and Schacter (1999), and in recognition by Budson, Daffner, Desikan, and Schacter (2000); Budson, Sullivan, Mayer, Daffner, Black, and Schacter (2002c); Kensinger and Schacter (1999); Schacter, Verfaellie, Anes, and Racine (1998b); and Seamon et al. (2003).

As was the case with study repetition alone, these repeated study/test cycles suggest that monitoring processes suppressed false recall, but some combination of disqualifying and diagnostic monitoring processes may have been involved. The repetition of testing cycles adds an additional complication, in the sense that false recall and recognition on subsequent trials might have been due to source confusions from processing the related lure on an earlier test. Such source confusions do not compromise the effects discussed here, because if anything they would have led to increased false recall or recognition across repetitions, as opposed to the observed decreases. However, these source confusions will be important to keep in mind when research on other populations (e.g., older adults, Alzheimer's patients) is reviewed.

Speeded Responding

Heit, Brockdorff, and Lamberts (2004) used the response-signal procedure to determine how varying amounts of response time at test could influence true and false recognition. With this procedure, subjects studied several DRM lists and then took a recognition test under varying amounts of time pressure (i.e., after the presentation of each test word, subjects were signaled to respond at times ranging from 500 to 1400 ms). The motivating idea for this sort of procedure is that subjects are thought to rely on familiarity of the test stimulus at early response windows, but when given more retrieval time additional recollective information is thought to accrue and thereby influence the recognition response (cf. Benjamin, 2001; Hintzman & Curran, 1994). The results from two of the conditions in Experiment 2 are presented in Figure 5.5.

In the inclusion condition, subjects were told about the construction of the DRM lists and were instructed to respond "old" to list words and related

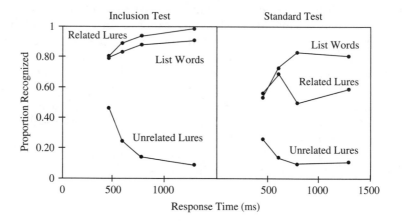

FIGURE 5.5 The effect of response time on true and false recognition in Heit et al. (2004). Subjects in the inclusion condition were told to respond "old" to list words and related lures, whereas subjects in the standard condition were given typical instructions ("old" to list words only).

lures and "new" to unrelated lures. From the figure (left panel) it can be seen that subjects followed this instruction at all response times. As is typically found with this response-time procedure, "old" responses to studied words (list words) increased as more response time was given, ostensibly because of the retrieval of additional information. By comparison, "old" responses to unrelated lures decreased, potentially owing to the use of more elaborate retrieval expectations with additional response time. That is, because subjects expected to recollect more information at slower times, they were better able to reject unrelated lures via diagnostic monitoring processes. Of critical interest was the pattern of responses to related lures. As instructed, subjects said "old" to these words, and, like list words, additional retrieval time increased the influence of information that supported this recognition decision (e.g., familiarity or illusory recollection).

Turn next to the results from the standard condition (right panel), in which subjects were instructed to respond "old" only to list words. As was the case in the inclusion condition, true recognition of list words increased across the response times, and false alarms to unrelated lures decreased. However, false recognition of related lures did not show an increase across response times, as one would have expected given the fact that the memory signal for these words would have had more time to accrue (as shown by the inclusion results). Instead, false recognition of related lures was relatively flat across the response times. This pattern suggests that additional gains in familiarity (or illusory recollection) with slower response times were offset by additional monitoring processes, such as the diagnostic monitoring process discussed above to explain the reduction in false alarms to unrelated lures (see Dodson & Hege, 2005, for analogous findings in a study of the distinctiveness heuristic). A disqualifying monitoring process also might have been more likely at slower response times in Heit et al. (2004), as in Benjamin (2001), but that cannot be determined from these data alone. A separate condition where subjects were warned (before study) to avoid false recognition was more relevant to this issue. The data suggest that the warning was somewhat more effective at the slowest window, but this effect was not significant. Along these lines, Endo (2005) allowed even longer response times (4 vs. 8 s), and reported that the effect of warnings on false recognition was greater in the slower condition.

☐ OTHER MONITORING ISSUES

The findings reviewed in this chapter have been organized around two different types of decision processes, diagnostic and disqualifying. Although this distinction applies to many of the recollection-based monitoring processes that have been reported in the literature, the decision process is not always obvious. A good example comes from the think-aloud protocols of Lampinen et al. (2005), discussed previously. When rejecting the lure "trash," one subject noted, "that is new, I do not remember *trash* because it was *garbage*" (p. 958). The decision process in this situation is ambiguous. Although the logic of a mutual-exclusivity rule was not applicable (i.e., both "garbage" and "trash" could have been presented in the study list), the thought process nonetheless was characteristic of a disqualifying decision (e.g., recalling one associate excluded the other from having been presented). One explanation is that disqualifying monitoring processes sometimes are applied even when they do not perfectly apply to the situation. Another explanation is that the decision was perfectly rational, but the subject did not fully verbalize the reason for the rejection. Maybe they recollected thinking of "trash" at study, in response to "garbage," and mentally tagged it as nonpresented (a disqualifying decision). Or maybe they simply did not think that their recollection of "trash" was as vivid as that for "garbage" at test (a diagnostic decision). The verbal report did not describe these processes, but that does not mean that they did not occur.

Recollection Rejection

An important body of evidence for recollection-based monitoring that has not been considered in depth in the aforementioned sections comes from fuzzy trace theory (e.g., Reyna & Kiernan, 1994, 1995). As discussed at the outset of this chapter, fuzzy trace theory is a dual-process framework. Under certain situations, the retrieval of a verbatim trace can override the influence of a gist trace, leading to the rejection of related lures (a process dubbed "recollection rejection," e.g., Brainerd & Reyna, 2002; Brainerd et al., 2001; for a review see Brainerd et al., 2003b). When subjects encounter a related lure, they might retrieve one (or many) of the related studied words. According to the theory, the retrieval of a studied word can result in a "nonidentity" judgment, or a feeling of contrast between what was actually studied and the test lure. Although explicit decision processes could inform these rejection decisions, they are not necessary under the theory. Instead, it is proposed that the feeling of contrast can lead to the rejection of the related lure even when an explicit or logical justification for this decision is not available to the subject.

This recollection rejection process has been modeled using the conjoint recognition task (discussed in Chapter 4), and Brainerd et al. (2003b) have shown that a variety of manipulations such as presentation duration of the studied words, presentation repetition, and study-to-test delay systematically affect estimates of the recollection rejection parameter in predictable ways. Brainerd et al. (2003b) also provided evidence for "false recollection rejection," or the erroneous rejection of studied words based on a misapplication of the rejection process. Using a different modeling technique, which involves the calculation of receiver operating curves (ROCs) in signal detection theory, Lampinen et al. (in press) have provided additional evidence for recollection rejection. This large (and growing) body of findings provides converging evidence for recollection based monitoring processes in converging associates tasks and others (e.g., Lampinen, Odegard, & Neuschatz, 2004).

The strength of these modeling approaches is that they allow for the calculation of precise estimates for the underlying processes. One limitation, though, is that the decision process that contributes to recollection rejection has been underspecified (see Lampinen et al., 2005, for discussion). Some combination of diagnostic and disqualifying monitoring processes could have contributed to many of the manipulations that have been used in these modeling exercises, as well as the more automatic feelings of contrast that have been hypothesized. This under-specification is not inherent to the models, but instead is due to the fact that they are relatively new. The treatment of monitoring processes in the activation-monitoring framework (e.g., McDermott & Watson, 2001) also has been underspecified, or at least overly general, for much the same reason. Future elaboration of these different theories will help to broaden our understanding of false memory editing, and in particular how the different types of decision processes discussed here (e.g., diagnostic, disqualifying, or other) can contribute to retrieval monitoring.

Monitoring versus Attribution

Up to this point monitoring processes have been couched in terms of metacognitive decision processes that influence memory attributions, but the exact relationship between decision processes and attribution processes is open for speculation. In some cases the subject might experience familiarity or illusory recollection towards the related lure as the result of a relatively automatic attribution process, but these subjective products of retrieval are then monitored and rejected via metacognitive decision processes. Consider the picture/word distinctiveness heuristic as an example. The related lure might feel very familiar in the context of the picture study condition, but, nevertheless, expecting distinctive recollections might allow one to avoid false recognition, by rejecting this familiarity as a sufficient memory signal for an "old" response. In other cases, metacognitive processes might override the attribution process and prevent the feeling of familiarity or illusory recollection in the first place, leaving nothing to be "edited" through more explicit decision processes. For example, when subjects are consciously trying to base their responses only on distinctive pictorial recollections, the related lure might not "feel as familiar" as when subjects are not demanding such distinctive recollections (this idea is similar to proposals made by Whittlesea et al., 2005).

Using the terminology of Jacoby, Kelley, and McElree (1999), the first example would be a "late correction" monitoring process, in the sense that monitoring processes are engaged only after the subjective products of retrieval (familiarity or illusory recollection) are experienced. Another term used to describe this sort of process is post-retrieval monitoring. In contrast, the use of recollection to circumvent or prevent the erroneous subjective state from occurring would be an "early-selection" model of memory monitoring, or a pre-retrieval orientation effect. Johnson and colleague's distinction between "systematic" and "heuristic" source monitoring that was discussed earlier in this chapter also is relevant, with post-retrieval effects potentially being more systematic, and pre-retrieval effects potentially being more heuristic. At the heart of the issue is the complex interaction between automatic attributions and conscious decision processes during memory retrieval, which seems to be separable in some instances but not in others.

An additional theoretical issue is that a relatively constrained view of "monitoring" has been used in this review (and often in the literature), in the sense of using recollection to oppose erroneous responses. Koriat and Goldsmith (1996) have advocated a more general use of the term, using it to describe a complex set of decision processes that ultimately determine whether or not the subject will respond on a memory test. The important idea for present purposes is that the subject might decide that they cannot make a good memory decision, and therefore withhold responding altogether. On recall tests, this decision might translate into fewer responses overall, whereas on a recognition test it might translate into more "new" responses, or more "don't know" responses if that option is given. From this view, simply looking at the quantity of memory errors is not enough. The overall quality of memory performance (i.e., the number of errors relative to the number of accurate responses) also is important. Consider the following thought experiment. Who is more "accurate": a subject who recalls 70% of the list words and 40% of the related lures, or a subject who recalls 30% of the list words and 20% the related lures? On an absolute level, the first subject has falsely recalled 20% more related lures than the second, but the proportion of false recall to true recall is 10% greater in the second subject than in the first. The answer to the question, of course, depends on one's definition of "accuracy," which in turn will depend on the point one is trying to make.

This interpretative issue has not been an issue in the monitoring effects discussed so far, at the group level, because those variables that have been shown to reduce absolute levels of false recall and recognition (e.g., study repetitions) have either increased true remembering or not affected it. Thus, the absolute decreases in false recall or recognition that were discussed also could have been expressed as proportional decreases, and so the effects of these variables on memory accuracy were the same with either measure. This interpretative issue is more important to understanding differences between individuals or groups that have different levels of true and false memory, as will be discussed in subsequent chapters.

Additional Study and Test Manipulations

The previous three chapters reviewed research findings that could easily be couched in terms of the causes of false remembering, illusory recollection, or monitoring processes. Some variables, such as associative strength and number of studied associates, were believed to have their effects predominantly on the encoding of information that will cause false remembering (via associative activation, thematic consistency, or feature overlap). Other variables, such as study format and study repetitions, were believed to have their effects predominantly on the encoding of information that will help to reduce false remembering (via diagnostic or disqualifying monitoring processes). Needless to say, these processes are all interrelated, and whether a variable was discussed in one or the other context depended on the net result (i.e., whether false remembering increased or decreased), which in turn depended on the specific conditions of the task.

This chapter serves as a "catch-all," reviewing the effects of several additional variables on false recall or false recognition (mostly in the DRM task). For simplicity, these variables have been divided into experimental manipulations that occur during the study phase, those that occur during the test phase, those that involve multiple tests, and those that are relevant to recall in social (or group) settings. In most of these cases the obtained effects can be explained by more than one process. Thus, unlike the findings reviewed in previous chapters, the theoretical implications of the findings reviewed in this chapter are not always evident. Nevertheless, many of these findings have been cited heavily in the literature, and many of the manipulations have been used by other studies (reviewed in subsequent chapters). A description of these basic findings and possible explanations therefore are necessary.

☐ STUDY FACTORS

List Blocking

One variable that influences false memory effects is whether the associates are blocked or grouped into themes at study or presented in a mixed fashion. Using a final free recall test, McDermott (1996, Experiment 2, Trial 1) found that blocking the lists led to greater levels of false recall than mixing the lists (means approximated from McDermott's Figure 5 = .58 and .30, respectively), and there was a similar, but smaller, effect on true recall (.39 and .30). The effect of blocking failed to reach statistical significance in this study, but Toglia, Neuschatz, and Goodwin (1999) and Brainerd et al. (2003a) both have reported similar effects of blocking on true and false recall, as well as the interaction, and analogous effects have been reported on final recognition tests. When only one speaker read the lists, Mather et al. (1997) found that blocked lists led to greater false recognition than mixed lists (means = .80 and .62, respectively), and a smaller effect was found in true recognition (.76 and .69). However, there were no blocking effects when two speakers alternated reading the items from each list. Tussing and Greene (1997) also found that blocking the lists led to greater false recognition than mixing the lists (means = .90 and .74, respectively), but the smaller effect on true recognition was not significant (.83 and .80, respectively).

As discussed by McDermott (1996), there are several explanations of these blocking effects. Blocking study associates might encourage associative activation, because relational processing of the list words would be encouraged and associative activation could potentially summate across the study items. Such activation would increase false remembering and, to a lesser extent, also could increase true remembering of the list words (i.e., by facilitating inter-item associations and organization). Blocking the associates at study also would encourage the encoding of a thematic or gist representation of the list, or the encoding of overlapping semantic features, and could therefore increase false remembering via these mechanisms. True remembering also would be facilitated, but to a lesser extent, especially if one assumes that thematic consistency has greater effects on false memory (e.g., Brainerd et al., 2003a). Explanations based on monitoring processes are possible, but more tenuous. One might argue that mixed presentation encouraged item-specific processing, and thus subjects reduced false remembering by expecting more distinctive item-specific recollections (a diagnostic monitoring process). The difficulty with this explanation is that true recall and recognition sometimes were greater following blocked presentation, so one could argue that recollection-based monitoring should have been greater in this condition.

Levels of Processing

Although the majority of DRM studies have used intentional encoding instructions, in which subjects were asked to remember the materials for a subsequent memory test but were not given any particular study strategies, several researchers have investigated the influence of different encoding tasks on false remembering. The most frequently investigated encoding tasks have been those that fall under the levels-of-processing framework (Craik & Lockhart, 1972; Lockhart & Craik, 1990), and have compared "shallow" processing (focusing on perceptual or orthographic/phonological details of words) to "deep" processing (focusing on the meaning or semantic details of words). It is well established that deep levels of processing can enhance true recall and recognition of words, and in single-associate false recognition tasks several early studies demonstrated that deep processing also led to greater false recognition (Coltheart, 1977; Elias & Perfetti, 1973; Parkin, 1983). This pattern has been observed in DRM false recognition. As illustrated in Figure 6.1, Thapar and McDermott (2001, Experiment 2) found that deep levels of processing (pleasantness ratings) led to greater levels of true and false recognition than did shallow levels of processing (vowel or color judgments). Because the level of processing was manipulated within-subjects in this study, differences in base rate false alarms across conditions were not an issue. Tussing and Greene (1997) did not find effects of pleasantness ratings and vowel judgments on false recognition, but they also failed to find a levels-of-processing effect on true recognition, suggesting that their study was not sensitive to levels-of-processing effects.

Patterns analogous to those in Figure 6.1 also have been reported on true and false recall. Toglia et al. (1999) had subjects study each list and make pleasantness ratings for each word (a deep task) or decide whether each word contained the letter "a" (a shallow task). On immediate free recall, they found that true recall was greater for the deep task (77%) than for the shallow task (66%). False recall also was greater following the deep task (58%) than the shallow task (44%). Rhodes and Anastasi (2000)

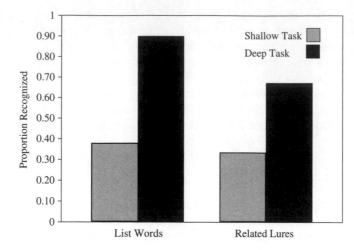

FIGURE 6.1 The effect of level of processing on true and false recognition in Thapar and McDermott (2001, Experiment 2, immediate test). Pleasantness judgments were used for the deep orienting task, and vowel or color judgments were used for the shallow task (because they yielded similar results, data are collapsed across the two shallow tasks in the figure). The false alarm rate to unrelated lures was .04.

obtained similar patterns, using vowel counting as the shallow task and either concrete/abstract ratings (Experiment 1) or categorization judgments (Experiment 2) as the deep task. Finally, Thapar and McDermott (2001, Experiment 1) replicated these patterns, using the same encoding tasks as in their recognition study. True recall was affected more than false recall in Thapar and McDermott, but Rhodes and Anastasi (Experiment 1) found larger effects on false recall than true recall, and Toglia et al. and Rhodes and Anastasi (Experiment 2) found the same absolute effect on true and false recall. Thus, deep levels of processing lead to greater true and false recall in all of these studies, but it is unclear if the effect is of the same magnitude for true and false recall.

As was the case with the blocking effect, there are several explanations of these levels-of-processing effects on false recall and recognition. Semantic processing could have facilitated associative activation and/or the encoding of semantic themes or features, as well as the reliance upon such information at retrieval, and any of these would have increased false memory effects. Alternatively, it might be the case that shallow processing led to more item-specific information that thereby reduced false recognition via diagnostic monitoring processes. This last explanation seems less likely, though, given that some believe that "deep" processing (i.e., pleasantness ratings) encourages item-specific encoding (see Smith & Hunt, 1998, as discussed below).

It should be stressed that all of these levels-of-processing effects on false recall and recognition have relied on semantically related lures. However, in the single-associate studies mentioned earlier, researchers also had included phonological or orthographically related lures on the recognition tests. For these types of lures, it generally was found that false recognition was greater following shallow processing than deep processing (Coltheart, 1977; Elias & Perfetti, 1973; Parkin, 1983). Chan, McDermott, Watson, and Gallo (2005) nicely demonstrated this crossover interaction in converging associates tasks, by crossing list type (semantic or phonological associates) with processing type (meaning vs. rhyme). Semantic processing increased false remembering of semantically related lures, whereas more perceptual processing increased false remembering of perceptually related lures. These are important observations, because they imply that there is nothing inherent in deep or semantic processing, per se, that necessarily leads to greater levels of false remembering. This general pattern is consistent with the transfer-appropriate processing framework's explanation of levels-of-processing effects (e.g., Morris, Bransford, & Franks, 1977), and is analogous to similar findings on implicit memory tests (for further discussion see Roediger & Gallo, 2001).

Encoding Context

As discussed in Chapter 5, Arndt and Reder (2003) found that presenting list words in different fonts reduced false recognition, relative to a single-font condition. They proposed that presenting each list word in a different font increased item-specific processing, and in turn decreased relational processing. This sort of manipulation could reduce false recognition in one of two ways. First, with more item-specific processing, subjects might expect to remember more distinctive information from study, thereby reducing false recognition via diagnostic monitoring processes at test (such as the distinctiveness heuristic). Second, by reducing relational processing at study, the memory signal itself might be reduced for the related lure (e.g., less associative activation or impoverished gist-based memory). Although there is evidence against this latter possibility as the sole explanation for findings such as the picture/word effect or the auditory/visual effect (see Chapter 5), the reduced relational processing account provides a plausible explanation for other effects, such as the font manipulation.

Goodwin et al. (2001) conducted a relevant experiment. They paired each list word with an associate that was inconsistent with the associative structure of the original list. For instance, for the list of associates to the related lure "soft," the list words "hard," "light," and "pillow" were paired with the words "hat," "bulb," and "case." In a comparison condition, these same list words and fillers were studied, but in a different order that did not bias the encoding of each original list word (i.e., the DRM words were studied first, followed by the filler words, as in Robinson & Roediger, 1997). Goodwin et al. found that disrupting the associative structure of the original list increased true recall, probably because studying each list word in the context of a unique associate (e.g., "hard-hat," "light-bulb," "pillow-case") facilitated elaborational processes. More important, this manipulation decreased false recall, perhaps because the filler items decreased the encoding of semantic information (e.g., associations, gist, or features) that is relevant to the related lure. Enhanced diagnostic monitoring processes also might have contributed to the effect (e.g., "I do not remember 'soft' being paired with another word at study, so it probably was not studied"), but pairing filler items with only some of the studied words also reduced false recall, with the size of the reductions being directly related to the number of studied words that were paired with fillers. In these cases subjects should not have expected to recall a study pair for all of the study words, so it is unclear whether they would have invoked such diagnostic monitoring processes.

Thomas and Sommers (2005) reported analogous effects of filler studied words on subsequent false recognition. When the filler words biased encoding away from the associative structure of the list (e.g., "river-bed," as opposed to "mattress-bed," for the list of associates to "sleep"), false recognition of related lures was reduced. This result provides additional evidence for a relational processing account of this sort of manipulation, as opposed to diagnostic monitoring (which should not have varied across these two encoding conditions, because in both cases word pairs were studied). Unlike Goodwin et al. (2001), true memory was not affected by the context words at study, perhaps because a paired associate was used in each condition of this study. Thomas and Sommers also found that presenting studied words in the context of sentences reduced false recall or false recognition of related lures, relative to using only words at study, again by potentially reducing the associative or relational processing of each list during study. False recall of unrelated lures was not affected, and true memory was reduced by the presentation of sentences.

Bruce, Phillips-Grant, Conrad, and Bona (2004) also found that pairing list words with additional verbal information at study reduced false recognition, as did the addition of other contexts at study, such as different fonts, background colors, or other visual stimuli. In the absence of other measures, though, it is difficult to know whether these context effects were due to impaired relational processing at study, enhanced distinctiveness (and hence diagnostic monitoring at test), or both.

Item-Specific versus Relational Processing

In the section on encoding context it was proposed that presenting list words with unique contexts (e.g., different fonts, context words, etc.) enhanced item-specific processing at a cost to relational processing. As a result of this reduced relational processing, false memory effects for related lures decreased. In these instances the effect of the contextual manipulation on relational processing was indirectly inferred from the pattern of results. McCabe, Presmanes, Robertson, and Smith (2004) took a more direct approach, by manipulating the instructions given during study. Subjects studied several DRM lists, under instructions to either relate all of the words in the list to each other or to encode each word in such a way that item-specific features would be central. Neither true recognition of list words nor false recognition of unrelated lures was affected by the encoding task, but false recognition of related lures was greater following relational encoding (.79) than following item-specific encoding (.61). McCabe et al. argued that reduced relational processing impaired those mechanisms that would otherwise support false recognition (such as associative activation or gist). Of course, diagnostic monitoring processes also might have been involved, with subjects expecting more distinctive recollections in the item-specific conditions. Similar effects were found if the encoding task was manipulated between-subjects or within-subjects (but on different lists), arguing against a global diagnostic monitoring process (such as the distinctiveness heuristic), but list-specific monitoring processes such as those discussed in the context of the modality effect were not ruled out.

Generation Effects

Hicks and Marsh (1999, 2001) and Johansson and Stenberg (2002) manipulated whether list words were heard or seen or were instead generated from anagrams. Presenting some of the words in each list as anagrams did reduce false recall or recognition in these studies, but entire lists that were studied with one encoding task or the other were not directly compared within a single experiment. Soraci, Carlin, Toglia, Chechile, and Neuschatz (2003, Experiment 1) directly compared a generation task (seeing words with one letter missing and typing the entire word) to a copy task (seeing and typing intact words), with the generation task manipulated across lists (but within-subjects). On a final recognition test, they found that true recognition was greater for the generate condition than the copy condition (means approximately .90 and .78, as estimated from their Figure 1), consistent with the established generation effect on true memory. However, there were no false recognition differences across conditions (both means approximately .70). This pattern was replicated in a second experiment, and was generalized to free recall in a third experiment.

The Soraci et al. (2003) findings are inconsistent with the idea that generation should be a more distinctive encoding task, and hence should reduce false remembering via diagnostic monitoring processes. However, as was discussed in Chapter 5, such distinctiveness patterns (at least for the picture/word effect) are typically larger when distinctiveness is manipulated between-subjects. Because Soraci et al. manipulated the two encoding tasks within-subjects, a between-subjects reduction was not tested. If this line of reasoning is correct, then between-subject manipulations of generation at study should yield reductions in the false memory effect.

Miscellaneous Encoding Tasks

Libby and Neisser (2001, Experiment 3b) had subjects study several DRM lists under an intentional encoding condition or under conditions where they were to selectively rehearse only words that began with a particular letter. Unbeknown to the subjects, the target letter was either the first letter of the related lure or another letter. They found that there was a small interference effect of the selective rehearsal instructions on recall of list words (control mean = .71, mean for both rehearsal groups = .65). More important, selective rehearsal decreased false recall of the related lure, but only when the target letter was the same as that of the related lure (control mean = .20, rehearsal of other letter = .18, rehearsal of same letter = .07). Libby and Neisser argued that focusing subjects on those words that began with the same letter as the related lure allowed them to reject the lure because they would have realized that they did not study (and rehearse) this word. One could view such an effect as a diagnostic monitoring process ("I did not study this word, because I do not have a vivid memory for rehearsing it.").

Read (1996) had subjects perform one of three encoding tasks at study: serial learning (learn the words in order), elaborative rehearsal (focus on the meaning of each word), and maintenance rehearsal (always keep the last word presented in mind). On an immediate free recall test, Read found that elaborative rehearsal led to the greater recall of list words (.70) than did maintenance rehearsal (.62), which in turn led to greater true recall than serial learning (.57). False recall was greater in the elaborative rehearsal group (.73) and maintenance rehearsal group (.76) than in the serial learning group (.50). The difference between the elaborative and serial learning groups (on true and false recall) might reflect a levels-of-processing effect, but it is unclear why maintenance rehearsal (which could be viewed as a "shallow" task) did not lead to lower levels of false recall compared to the elaborative group.

Other patterns across encoding tasks are even more difficult to understand. Newstead and Newstead (1998) had different groups of subjects perform a variety of encoding tasks (intentional encoding, elaborative encoding, making personal associations to each word, forming images of each word, and chaining each word into a story). Elaboration and chaining significantly enhanced recall of list words compared to the control condition (means = .74, .76, and .68, respectively), but there were no other differences between groups on true recall, and no differences in false recall, either. These results suggest that, when all of the encoding tasks were relatively "deep" or meaningful, false recall was relatively stable across tasks. In contrast, Hicks and Marsh (1999, Experiment 4) reported that false recall of related lures was significantly greater from lists that were encoded with pleasantness ratings (.19) compared to those encoded with frequency of usage ratings (.12), both of which might be considered "deep" tasks. To further complicate matters, Smith and Hunt (1998, Experiment 3) found that false recall of related lures was reduced by pleasantness ratings (mean = .15, collapsed across study modalities) relative to intentional encoding (mean = .31). They argued that pleasantness ratings afforded more item-specific processing of each word, which would have increased the discriminability between list words and related lures. One mechanism for such enhanced discrimination might be diagnostic monitoring (e.g., "I do not remember making a pleasantness rating for that word, so it probably was not studied."). However, it then becomes unclear why Hicks and Marsh found that pleasantness ratings led to greater false recall than frequency judgments. Are frequency judgments more "item-specific" than pleasantness judgments? Without a priori predictions about the effect of an encoding task on false remembering, it is easy to fall into circular logic when trying to interpret these types of results.

Dividing Attention

One might think that dividing attention during study would increase false memories, by reducing memory for what had happened and thereby impairing the use of recollection-based monitoring processes. This expectation has been borne out in false memory tasks that rely on source-confusion (e.g., mistakenly claiming that an item studied in List 1 had occurred in List 2). Studies have found that such errors increased when attention is divided at study, via some concurrent task or memory load (e.g., Jacoby, 1999).

Results from dividing attention in the DRM task deviate from this expectation. Seamon et al. (1998) provided some of the earliest evidence. Subjects studied several DRM lists for a final recognition test, under conditions of full attention (i.e., subjects were instructed to remember the words for a subsequent test) or a concurrent memory load (i.e., subjects rehearsed a seven-digit number while studying the words, and following study, they had to recall the number before taking the recognition tests). Concurrent load was manipulated between-subjects in Experiment 1 and within-subjects in Experiment 2, and presentation rate also was manipulated. In Experiment 1, collapsing across rate, the concurrent load impaired recognition of list words relative to the no-load condition (means = .58 vs. .67, respectively), and a similar result was obtained on related lures (.69 vs. .81). The same pattern also was obtained when these recognition rates were corrected for base rate false alarms (via subtraction), but these load effects were not found at all presentation rates, and they were not significant in Experiment 2. Other null effects of divided attention on false recognition have been reported. Dodd and MacLeod (2004) found that dividing attention at study (via a color-naming task) reduced true recognition but had no significant effects on false recognition of related lures in the DRM task, and Koutstaal, Schacter, and Brenner (2001a) found a similar pattern in a similar-pictures task.

Seamon et al. (2003) used a different approach, investigating the effects of several encoding conditions. Subjects studied several DRM lists and then took either a final recall test (Experiment 1) or a final recognition test (Experiment 2), and this procedure was then repeated several times. For present purposes, the most relevant conditions were the "hear" condition, where subjects simply listened to the list words for an upcoming memory test, and the "number" condition, where participants counted backwards by threes and kept a written tally of their count in pace with the presentation of the list words. On the first recall trial, the divided attention task reduced true recall (.37 vs. .14, respectively). A similar pattern was found on false recall (.38 vs. .28, respectively), but this effect was not significant. These patterns also were obtained on the first recognition trial, with true recognition impaired by the divided attention task (.76 vs. .39) and similarly for false recognition (.75 vs. .51), and both of these effects were significant when recognition rates were adjusted for base rate false alarms (via subtraction).

Pérez-Mata et al. (2002) provided evidence that dividing attention at study increased false recall of related lures. Subjects heard several DRM-type lists at study, under either full attention or divided attention (i.e., they monitored a video clip for changes in camera perspective), and were given a free recall test after each list. Lists were modified to consist of either concrete or abstract list words (see Chapter 5). For both types of lists, divided attention impaired true recall relative to full attention (means = .38 vs. .61, respectively), but divided attention increased false recall of related lures (.61 vs. .37), and a similar effect was observed on noncritical intrusions. This same pattern was replicated in a second experiment, using visual presentation of the lists and an auditory divided attention task (monitoring a sequence of digits and numbers).

Considering all of these results, the effects of dividing attention at study on false recall and recognition are mixed. The effects were not always significant, and when they were, dividing attention was found to reduce false recognition in some conditions, but to increase false recall in others. One difficulty in comparing these effects is that different secondary tasks were used across studies. The theoretical significance of these differences (if any) is unknown, and more comprehensive research is needed to understand how divided attention influences these sorts of false memories.

Stress

Another variable that has important implications for memory distortions in everyday living is psychological stress. Psychological stress can cause episodic memory impairments (see Nadel, Payne, & Jacobs, 2002), potentially because stress causes the release of glucocorticoid hormones that disrupt the functioning of memory systems in the brain (the neural mechanisms of memory are discussed more in subsequent chapters). In a study on stress and false recognition, Payne et al. (2002) had subjects study several DRM lists for immediate recognition memory tests (administered after each list was studied). Just prior to the task, stress was induced in half the subjects by having them deliver a speech in front of a one-way mirror under stressful conditions (i.e., with minimal preparation, without notes, and with the understanding that they were being watched and videotaped). Although true recognition did not differ across groups, false recognition of related lures was significantly greater in the stressed group (.77) than in the control group (.61). False recognition of unrelated lures was at floor levels and did not vary across conditions. These results suggest that stress made subjects more prone to false recognition, potentially by impairing monitoring processes at encoding or retrieval, but two caveats must be made. First, cognitive processes might have caused the influence of stress on performance (e.g., preoccupation with the stress-inducing procedure, leading to divided attention) instead of neurochemical effects on memory systems, per se. Second, Wenzel, Jostad, Brendle, Ferraro, and Lystad (2004) failed to find differences in false recall or recognition for a group of socially anxious individuals, relative to nonanxious individuals, under conditions where social anxiety was elicited (e.g., by telling subjects they would have to give a speech after the memory task). Additional work is needed to fully understand the potential role of stress on memory accuracy.

Mood

Storbeck and Clore (2005) investigated the effects of positively and negatively induced mood (prior to study) on false recall. Subjects listened to Mozart to induce the positive mood (8 min of *Eine Kleine Nacht Musik*), and a different group listened to Mahler to induce the negative mood (8 min of *Adagietto*). They then studied several DRM lists (using a relatively rapid 250 ms presentation rate) for immediate recall. An affective questionnaire administered after the memory task provided a manipulation check of the induced mood states. In Experiment 1, it was found that false recall was reduced in the negative mood group, relative to the positive mood group and a control group that received no music (false recall did not differ between these latter two groups, and true recall did not differ across any of the groups). The methods of Experiment 2 were similar, except subjects were asked to recall studied words and any word that came to mind during the study phase, even if it was nonstudied (in this way, retrieval-based monitoring processes would not have contributed to the results). Under these conditions, recall of critical lures still was lower in the negative mood group relative to the positive mood group.

The authors argued that these effects were consistent with a gist-based explanation. When studying the lists under a negative mood, subjects may have been more likely to process item-specific information, at the expense of relational information, thereby reducing the encoding of an overall theme or gist of each list. However, as with many other findings in this chapter, an associative activation or feature-based explanation is equally plausible, and the possible enhancement of item-specific processing could have boosted diagnostic monitoring, too. A study by Wright, Startup, and Mathews (2005b) also has found that mood can influence DRM false recall, but these effects were highly sensitive to test instructions (and in some conditions, subjects in a negative mood were more likely to falsely recall related lures). Importantly, unlike Storbeck and Clore (2005), Wright et al. (2005b) induced the mood after study lists had been studied, but before the lists were recalled (so the mood manipulation did not affect relational processing at study). This procedural difference might explain the discrepancy across studies, but it does not explain the specific findings in each. As with the effects of stress on false remembering, further work on the effects of mood on false memories seems warranted.

Directed Forgetting

In a directed forgetting task, subjects are explicitly instructed to try to forget newly learned information. Directed forgetting instructions typically decrease recall of the to-be-forgotten material, relative to a condition where subjects are not given forgetting instructions, either because retrieval of the to-be-forgotten material is inhibited or because it is rehearsed less often (e.g., Bjork, 1970, see MacLeod, 1998, for a review). Using the DRM task, researchers have investigated how instructions to forget affect false recall of lures that are related to the to-be-forgotten words.

Seamon et al. (2002e) had subjects study several lists and then gave a "forget" cue for those lists (i.e., they were told that the experimenter mistakenly presented the wrong lists, and they were to forget them). After the forget cue, these subjects studied several additional lists. After studying the second set of lists, they took a final free recall test for all of the lists (subjects were not told that they would be tested on all of the lists until this time). A second group of subjects was treated identically, except no "forget" cue was provided—they were simply told to keep remembering the list words in between the study sets. As expected, Seamon et al. found that instructing subjects to forget the first set of lists led to lower levels of true recall from that set (.19) relative to subjects who were instructed to remember all of the lists (.24). In contrast, there were no effects of directed forgetting on false recall of related lures from the to-be-forgotten list (both means = .26). A similar pattern of results was obtained using a within-subjects comparison.

Unlike Seamon et al. (2002e), Kimball and Bjork (2002) had subjects study a single DRM list which was followed by either a "remember" cue (they were told that memory for this list would be tested) or a "forget" cue (they were told that this list was only for practice), and then a second DRM list was studied. On a final recall test, subjects were instructed to recall items from either the first list or the second list. As expected, true recall of the first list was greater for "remember" subjects (.58) than for "forget" subjects (.46), whereas true recall of the second list was greater for "forget" subjects (.51 vs. .60, respectively), owing to less proactive interference from the first list. In contrast to the results of Seamon et al., false recall from the first list was considerably greater when subjects had been instructed to forget this list (.70) than when they had been instructed to remember it (.37). It is unclear why Kimball and Bjork obtained an effect on false recall, whereas Seamon et al. reported no effect.

As one explanation of the directed forgetting effect on false recall, Kimball and Bjork (2002) proposed that trying to forget the list words did not affect associative activation of the related lure, but did influence source monitoring. One interpretation would be that forgetting the list words would lead to less distinctive recollections, and thus impair diagnostic monitoring processes that otherwise could reduce false recall. An alternative explanation is that, owing to impaired recall of list words, subjects relied more heavily on semantic or thematic information following the forget cue, and this elevated levels of false recall. Still a third possibility is that, because true recall was suppressed in the directed forgetting condition, there was less output interference to suppress false recall (cf. McEvoy et al., 1999, as discussed in Chapter 3). All of these explanations are further complicated by the more recent publication of a study demonstrating that directed forgetting *reduced* the DRM memory illusion (Marche, Brainerd, Lane, & Loehr, 2005), albeit using a different type of directed forgetting instruction than Kimball and Bjork (i.e., the item-specific method), and with the publication of a study showing that directed forgetting reduced the DRM illusion in children (Howe, 2005). If these directed forgetting effects on false memories are to be understood fully, more research is clearly needed.

☐ TEST FACTORS

True Recall

As discussed in Chapter 3, Roediger et al. (2001c) found a negative relationship between true and false recall across DRM lists—lists that were better recalled (although rarely exhaustively recalled) led to lower false recall of related lures. As one explanation, they suggested that enhanced true recall might facilitate monitoring processes that could reduce false recall. In Chapter 5, several uses of recall to reduce false memory were discussed, such as when the subject can identify the lure at study and later recall this as the "nonpresented" word (a disqualifying strategy), or when the absence of distinctive recollections (e.g., pictures) allows one to infer that the lure was not presented (a diagnostic monitoring process). However, in the absence of a recall-to-reject situation or a distinctiveness manipulation, there is little evidence that simply recalling studied words or focusing on potentially recallable features of studied words can reduce false recognition in converging associates tasks (e.g., Gallo, 2004; Hicks & Marsh, 2001; Neuschatz et al., 2001, see Chapter 5). Thus, unless it is assumed that recollection-based monitoring processes exert a larger influence on immediate free recall tests than on final recognition tests, these other studies suggest that a recollection-based monitoring process was not responsible for the negative correlation between true and false recall in Roediger et al. Other possibilities should be considered. For instance, McEvoy et al. (1999) argued that enhancing true recall can reduce false recall via output interference mechanisms (see Chapter 3). A similar mechanism might have contributed to the negative correlation between true recall and false recall observed by Roediger et al. In any event, given the wealth of research on false memories in the DRM task, it is striking that the cause of the negative correlation between true and false recall (across lists) is not yet understood.

Part-List Cuing

Another test-based factor that has been investigated, one that is related to output interference, is part-list or part-set cuing (e.g., Slamecka, 1968; see Roediger & Neely, 1982, for review). The part-list cuing technique involves the re-presentation of some of the studied words on the recall test, in an effort to provide recall cues for the remaining words in the study list. Contrary to what might be expected, the presentation of some studied words at test actually impairs the recall of the remaining studied words, ostensibly by blocking or interfering with recall of the remaining items. Reysen and Nairne (2002) presented several DRM lists to study, each for an immediate recall test (delayed by 15 s of math problems). They found that, relative to a free recall situation, re-presenting half of the list words as part-list cues impaired both true recall (means = .50 vs. .44, respectively, in Experiment 1) and false recall (.41 vs. .21). These results were replicated in a second experiment. Kimball and Bjork (2002) and Bäuml and Kuhbandner (2003) reported similar results. Kimball and Bjork further found that increasing the number of part-list cues (from 4 to 8) led to larger reductions in false recall, and that cues with stronger associative connections to the related lure, those studied at the beginning of the list, interfered more with false recall. Part-list cuing effects are not always obtained on false recall (Marsh, McDermott, & Roediger, 2004), but the several significant demonstrations indicate that the effect is real.

As one explanation, Kimball and Bjork (2002) proposed that the part-list cues provided retrieval competition for both the uncued list words and the related lures. Much like the output interference effects discussed above in the context of the negative relationship between true recall and false recall, providing some list words during the test would interfere with retrieval mechanisms that would otherwise produce recall of list words and related lures. For instance, the presentation of part-list cues would make memories for those items more salient or accessible, and thereby block the retrieval of other words. Note that this explanation implies that the related lure is consciously generated at study, so that its subsequent recall can be blocked by part-list cues (just like list words). Otherwise, the presentation of additional list words at test would have been thought to increase activation of the related lures, and thereby increase false recall (as opposed to the observed decreases).

Retrieval-Induced Forgetting

When subjects receive practice recalling a subset of words from a list, recall of unpracticed words suffers (e.g., Anderson, Bjork, & Bjork, 1994). One explanation for this effect is that, like part-list cues, retrieval strengthens the memory representation for practiced words, thereby increasing the likelihood that they will block the retrieval of nonpracticed words. However, evidence also suggests that retrieval practice inhibits nonpracticed associations that would otherwise support the recall of nonpracticed words. Replicating the basic effect, Bäuml and Kuhbandner (2003, Experiment 2) found that practice retrieving some DRM list words (via word-stem cues) reduced subsequent recall of the remaining list words, relative to a condition without retrieval practice (.50 vs. .60). They also found that retrieval practice reduced false recall of related lures (.28 vs. .36). Bäuml and Kuhbandner argued that practice retrieving the list words inhibited the memory representation for related lures (ostensibly formed via conscious generation during study), resulting in lower false recall. Starns and Hicks (2004) reported analogous findings using false recognition and cued-recall techniques, and like Bäuml and Kuhbandner they argued that retrieval practice resulted in inhibition of a stored representation for the related lure. As with the part-list cuing effects, and other effects reviewed in Chapter 3, these results support the notion that related lures are sometimes generated at study, thereby forming a memory representation that can potentially be inhibited (or at least blocked from retrieval).

Test-Item Order

One variable that could be predicted to influence false recognition is the ordering of the test items (which is usually random). Presenting list words at test might activate a subsequently tested related item (or otherwise make it familiar), and hence serve to increase false recognition. These effects have not been consistently observed in the DRM task. Marsh and Hicks (2001) reported no difference in false recognition of related lures that were tested in the context of their corresponding list words and those that were not. Marsh et al. (2004) also failed to find significant testing effects on false recognition (Experiment 1) and false cued recall (Experiment 2) of related lures. However, they did find a significant testing effect for false recognition of unrelated lures. These items were more likely to be falsely recognized when they had been preceded by related test lures (.49) than when they had not (.31). This finding is consistent with the idea that test words can activate each other, but it is unclear why a similar effect was not found on lures that were related to the study lists. More recently, Coane and McBride (in press) have demonstrated significant increases to false recognition of related lures as a function of the number of prior list words that were tested, providing stronger evidence for the effect.

Another factor to be considered is that the testing of list words before the related lure might cause a false recognition suppression effect. Brainerd, Reyna, and Kneer (1995b) used a single-associate task, and showed that testing the studied item (e.g., cat) just prior to testing the related lure (e.g., dog) led to significant decreases in false recognition of the related lure, relative to a condition where the related lure was tested without having recently been tested for the studied word. They argued that the recent testing of the relevant studied word caused subjects to compare their memory for the related lure to that of the studied word, and thereby realize that the lure had not been presented. This finding was interpreted as evidence for a "nonidentity" judgment, consistent with the recollection rejection idea in fuzzy trace theory (see Chapter 5).

Although such monitoring is a possibility, several uncertainties remain. First, Wallace, Malone, Swiergosz, and Amberg (2000) failed to replicate these false recognition reversal effects in several conditions (see also Gunter et al., 2005). Second, as was discussed in Chapter 5, Gallo (2004) showed that recalling list words immediately prior to making a recognition decision for a related lure was effective at reducing false recognition only when all of the corresponding list words could be recalled (and hence, the subject could deduce that the lure was not studied). This disqualifying monitoring strategy could have operated in Brainerd et al. (1995b), because each lure was related to only one instantiating target.

Language Shifts

Cabeza and Lennartson (2005) presented DRM lists in either French or English to bilingual subjects. This variable was then crossed with the language that was used during the recognition test (French/English), with all language variables manipulated within-subjects. At test, subjects were instructed to indicate "old" only if the exact same word had been studied (i.e., in the same language). Consistent with the instructions to only accept words that were studied in the same language as was used at test, subjects were more likely to accept list words if they were studied and tested in the same language (.64) than if they were not (.32). Related lures also were more likely to be recognized when presented in the same language as was used during the presentation of the corresponding list (.41) than in the opposite language (.32). This finding should not be surprising, given that subjects often believe that the related lure was studied in the same format as had been used to present the corresponding list (see the source attribution data in Chapter 4). The fact that the language-shift effect was larger for list words than for related lures might indicate that, because list words were actually presented, a match between study and test benefited them more (via the encoding specificity principle). Such a finding is compatible with any reasonable theory of the false memory effect.

Kawasaki-Miyaji, Inoue, and Yama (2003) conducted a similar study in Japanese–English bilinguals, but unlike Cabeza and Lennartson (2005), subjects were asked to recognize all studied items, regardless of the test language. Consistent with Cabeza and Lennartson, and the encoding specificity principle, recognition of list items was greater when the study and test languages matched than when they did not match. Unlike Cabeza and Lennartson, testing related lures in Japanese led to greater levels of false recognition regardless of the language used to present the corresponding list at study. These data suggest that the false recognition findings in Cabeza and Lennartson might have been due to the instructions used (i.e., accept only those words that were studied and tested in the same language), although direct comparison between the studies is difficult because of the difference in materials and subjects (subjects in Kawasaki-Miyaji et al. had Japanese as their first language). The importance of this last consideration is highlighted by more recent findings by Anastasi, Rhodes, Marquez, and Velino (2005). These researchers found that DRM false memories were most likely when the study lists were presented in the primary language of monolingual subjects, compared to a secondary language with which they had little or no experience. Not surprisingly, subjects were most likely to activate the related lure or extract the gist from lists in their primary language.

☐ MULTIPLE TESTS

Recall before Recognition

As mentioned in Chapter 2, Roediger and McDermott (1995) found that immediately recalling each list led to increases in subsequent recognition of list words and related lures, relative to lists that were not immediately recalled, and these differences were found in "remember" judgments as well. These testing effects are not surprising, in the sense that retrieving information at one time serves as an additional encoding opportunity, as well as an opportunity to practice or "prime" subsequent retrieval. When information is correctly recalled, subsequent true memory is boosted, and when information is incorrectly recalled, subsequent false memory is boosted. In an earlier review of research using the DRM task, Roediger et al.

(1998) concluded that evidence for the testing effect on true recognition was solid, whereas the effect on false recognition of related lures was at best inconclusive, having been found in a few studies but not in others. This is not to say that other testing effects have not been found on false remembering (discussed below), but rather that the specific effects of prior recall on subsequent false recognition in the typical DRM task have been considered somewhat unreliable. Because this is an important theoretical and methodological issue, it is scrutinized a bit more here.

Table 6.1 summarizes the results from 14 published studies that have included conditions similar to those of Roediger and McDermott (1995, Experiment 2): Several DRM lists were studied for either immediate recall or math (or other unrelated tasks), and then a final recognition test was administered. Unless otherwise noted, results are only presented for younger adults or control groups, collapsing across other variables. For those studies that reported no difference between prior recall and math, and hence only reported recognition data collapsed across this variable (Melo, Winocur, & Moscovitch, 1999; Norman & Schacter, 1997), this collapsed mean was substituted for both the recall and the math conditions (i.e., to minimize Type I error, null effects were included in the statistical analysis). As can be seen from the table, true recognition (averaged across studies) was greater following prior recall (.75) than prior math (.68), t (19) = 5.94, SEM = .012, $p < .01$. A smaller (but significant) testing effect was found in false recognition (means = .75 and .73, respectively), t (19)= 2.42, $SEM = .01, p < .05$. Analogous effects also were found in "remember" judgments for correctly recognized list words (.55 and .43, t [9] = 5.04, SEM = .025, $p < .01$) and for falsely recognized related lures (.50 and .43, t [9] = 2.27, SEM = .028, $p = .05$), and these latter effects were evident when "remember" judgments instead were expressed as a proportion of the overall probability of false recognition within an experiment (.73 and .64 for true recognition, and .66 and .59 for false recognition, both $ps < .05$).

These findings demonstrate the reliability of the testing effects originally reported by Roediger and McDermott (1995), for both true and false recognition. If so, then why have some studies failed to replicate this finding? One clue comes from looking at overall levels of initial true and false recall across studies. If prior recall leads to greater recognition by boosting memory for the recalled item (be it a list word or a related lure), then higher levels of initial recall should yield larger testing effects. To investigate this issue, the size of the testing effect on false recognition (prior recall minus prior math) was correlated with initial levels of immediate false recall across the 19 data points in Table 6.1 (one study did not report initial levels of false recall). Consistent with the prediction, the correlation between false recall and testing effects on false recognition was quite high (+.60, $p < .01$). This correlation suggests that prior false recall enhances

TABLE 6.1 Effects of Prior Task (Unrelated Task [U] or Immediate Free Recall [R]) on True and False Recognition and Corresponding "Remember" Judgments

| Study | Proportion Recognized | | | | "Remember" Judgments | | | |
| | List Words | | Related Lures | | List Words | | Related Lures | |
	U	R	U	R	U	R	U	R
Brainerd et al. (2001, Exp. 2)	.54	.65	.74	.86	na	na	na	na
Brainerd et al. (2002, Exp. 3)	.67	.72	.61	.66	na	na	na	na
Gallo et al. (2001a, Exp. 1)	.56	.68	.67	.70	.33	.51	.38	.45
Intons-Peterson et al. (1999, Exp. 1)	.67	.74	.74	.80	.41	.52	.43	.53
Intons-Peterson et al. (1999, Exp. 2)	.69	.84	.78	.80	.43	.63	.39	.53
Johansson and Stenberg (2002, Exp. 1)	.65	.72	.72	.76	.32	.45	.34	.43
Lampinen et al. (1999, Exp. 1)	.83	.86	.80	.77	na	na	na	na
Lampinen et al. (1999, Exp. 2)	.76	.82	.77	.80	na	na	na	na
Melo et al. (1999)	.65	.65	.72	.72	na	na	na	na
Norman and Schacter (1997, Exp. 1)	.79	.79	.71	.71	.54	.54	.36	.36
Norman and Schacter (1997, Exp. 2)	.71	.71	.59	.59	na	na	na	na
Payne et al. (1996, Exp. 2)	.55	.69	.66	.71	.37	.52	.42	.51
Roediger and McDermott (1995, Exp. 2)	.65	.79	.72	.81	.41	.57	.38	.58
Roediger et al. (2004, Exp. 1)	.70	.74	.75	.67	na	na	na	na
Roediger et al. (2004, Exp. 2)	.70	.77	.78	.81	na	na	na	na
Roediger et al. (2004, Exp. 3)	.68	.75	.73	.78	na	na	na	na
Roediger et al. (2004, Exp. 4)	.70	.76	.76	.79	na	na	na	na
Schacter et al. (1996c)	.83	.85	.89	.83	.71	.71	.83	.70
Winograd et al. (1998)	.67	.73	.76	.80	.40	.49	.40	.46
Zoellner, Foa, Brigidi, and Przeworski (2000)	.55	.75	.63	.66	.36	.60	.42	.44
Mean	.68	.75	.73	.75	.43	.55	.43	.50
Effect	.07**		.02**		.12**		.07*	

Notes: All data are from college undergraduates or control groups, except those from Intons-Peterson et al. (1999, Exp. 1), which were collapsed across younger and older adults. Results from Brainerd et al. (2001) are from the standard (verbatim) test. $^{**}p < .05$; $^{*}p = .05$; na = not applicable.

false recognition by providing an additional source of confusion, and that some studies did not find this effect simply because initial levels of false recall were too low to have much of an influence.

Another important point is that, in addition to prior false recall enhancing false recognition, prior true recall might enhance recollective distinctiveness, and thereby enhance diagnostic monitoring processes that can *reduce* false recognition. Gallo and Roediger (2002) discussed such a possibility to explain an otherwise puzzling pattern of results. In Experiment 2, subjects studied several DRM lists, each for immediate free recall, and then took a final recognition test. Experiment 3 was designed to be similar, but the prior recall tests were replaced with math problems, so recognition was no longer confounded with prior recall. As expected, true recognition was greater when the lists were previously recalled, but false recognition of related lures was *lower* when prior recall tests were given (especially when a slow presentation rate was used). Further, in all 12 experimental cells of their design, false alarms to unrelated lures were significantly lower with prior recall than without (overall means = .08 and .25, respectively, all $ps < .05$). To explain these effects, Gallo and Roediger argued that prior recall enhanced the recollective distinctiveness of the list words. As a result, subjects were more likely to use a diagnostic monitoring process to suppress false recognition on the final test. As additional confirmation of this effect, consider the unrelated false alarms across several studies that either had recall testing or did not (these studies are listed, for a different purpose, in Chapter 8, Table 8.2). The same finding (no prior recall > prior recall) was obtained with these data (.17 vs. .08, $p = .01$). These findings suggest that prior recall might serve as yet another variable that can enhance recollective distinctiveness, and thus enhance diagnostic monitoring processes.

Repeated Recall or Recognition

As discussed in Chapter 5, several studies have shown that repeating the study/test trials can reduce false recall and recognition. One explanation is that, with repeated opportunities to study the lists, subjects are better able to realize that the related lure was not presented. Other studies have investigated the effect of repeated testing on false remembering, without repeating the study trial. Subjects in Payne et al. (1996) studied several DRM lists, and then took three consecutive free recall tests (i.e., subjects recalled all of the list words they could remember for 7 min, then their recall sheets were removed, and they then recalled the words another two times). In their third experiment, they found that true recall increased by about 3% across the repeated tests, demonstrating a small hypermnesia effect (e.g., Erdelyi,

1996; Roediger & Payne, 1982). There also was a significant increase in false recall across repeated tests (6%), and this effect was significantly greater than that for list words. Brainerd et al. (2003a) reported similar results. One interpretation of these "false hypermnesia" effects is that, after repeated tests, subjects strengthen their idea of the theme or gist of the list, and this boosts false recall. Alternatively, repeated recall could facilitate associative organization and resulting activation processes.

A related set of findings indicate that, even though false memories can be successfully monitored (or avoided) on one test, this does not guarantee that the same false memory will not "resurface" at a later point in time. Marsh and Hicks (2001) showed that, even when subjects failed to recall the related lure on an immediate test, on a final output-monitoring test they often were willing to claim to have previously recalled this same item. Seamon, Berko, Sahlin, Yu, Colker, and Gottfried (in press) found a related effect with study/test repetitions (see also McDermott, 1996). In this study, subjects were able to use repeated study/test trials to suppress false recognition, as in other studies. However, on a final speeded or delayed test, these previously edited lures showed a "rebound" effect, in that they were now *more* likely to be falsely recognized. Apparently, these lures were highly familiar (because they were previously processed and rejected), but subjects had forgotten that they had earlier rejected these items. As a result, false recognition was enhanced.

Free versus Forced Recall

Another testing manipulation is to force subjects to recall a certain number of test words, guessing if necessary. Payne et al. (1996, Experiment 2) presented subjects with six 10-item DRM lists, followed by a final 7 min recall test. One group was given free recall instructions, whereas the other group took a forced recall test, in which they were instructed to recall all 60 words, even if they had to guess. Forcing subjects to recall items increased true recall (means = .44 for free recall and .53 for forced recall), but had a larger effect on false recall of related lures (means = .27 and .46, respectively). These findings suggest that forcing subjects to recall additional items can do more harm than good. McKelvie (2001, see also McKelvie, 1999) reported similar results using recall tests immediately after each list, with forced recall increasing false recall of the related lure much more than true recall of list words (if at all), and also increasing false recall of noncritical lures. Not surprisingly, confidence ratings of falsely recalled items (both related lures and noncritical intrusion) tended to be lower in the forced recall conditions than in the free recall conditions of that study, because subjects were instructed to recall words even if they had to guess in the forced condition. More interesting, confidence ratings under forced recall instructions were still greater for related lures than for noncritical intrusions, demonstrating that even forced false recalls were more compelling for related lures. Meade and Roediger (in press) also found that forcing subjects to recall items led to more false recall, using a categorized list task. Further, forcing subjects to recall words led to increases in false recognition on a subsequent test, because they had confused previously generated items with presented items.

☐ SOCIAL RETRIEVAL

One final line of work to be discussed here is "social retrieval," or the recall of information in a group setting. Using his serial reproduction task (subsequently known as the "telephone game"), Bartlett (1932) found that a story became distorted as one person told it to another from memory. Evidence from these sorts of tasks was later used in the study of rumor transmission or how misinformation propagates through a society. Of relevance to present concerns, Deese (1961) conducted a serial reproduction experiment using his associatively related lists (i.e., those subsequently used in the DRM task). The goal was to understand the role of associative processes in the schematic distortion effects that Bartlett had popularized. Deese had one group of subjects study and recall the associative lists, and then a second group of subjects studied the words recalled from members of the first group, and so on. Not surprisingly, Deese found that the later groups recalled fewer words from the original lists than the first group, an outcome that was necessarily obtained (i.e., because they had only studied the prior group's recall, the subsequent groups could not recall more list words than the first group, and with forgetting, they recalled fewer). The largest drop in true recall was from the first group to the second, suggesting that after the list had been recalled once, the remaining items were more memorable for subsequent subjects (probably owing to item-selection artifacts, as well as having a shorter list to study). Deese also showed that the associative structure of the original list (i.e., inter-item associative strength, or connectivity) strongly predicted which list words would be recalled in each group, suggesting that associative processes strongly influenced what was recalled across the groups.

More interesting for present purposes, Deese (1961) found that recall intrusions tended to increase across the recall groups (critical, related lures were not analyzed separately from other intrusions). Roediger, Meade, Wong, Olson, and Gallo (2003) obtained similar results. In this study, the first person of a group of four individuals studied several DRM lists for immediate free recall, and these recalled items were then studied by the second person for recall, and so on. Like Deese, it was found that true recall of list words significantly decreased across the recall groups, when scored against the original lists (means = .52, .35, .28, and .23). In contrast, false recall of related lures increased across the recall groups (means = .31, .40, .45, and .43), although this effect was not statistically significant. Because these words were so highly associated to the original lists, once the first subject falsely recalled them, the subsequent subjects (who actually studied them) were unlikely to forget them.

A different social analysis of memory involves the effects of group recall (i.e., the recall of information in a social setting). Basden et al. (1998, Experiment 1) compared recall from individual subjects to that of groups of three subjects that studied and recalled the same material (a collaborative group). (Data from the individual subjects were pooled into groups of three after the experiment, to create nominal groups for comparison to the collaborative groups.) Subjects studied several DRM lists for a final recall test. Subjects in collaborative groups studied the lists together, and then alternated recalling words (one word per person in a cycle). Replicating prior work with other materials, the collaborative groups recalled significantly fewer list words (.40) than the nominal groups (.46), and associative clustering analyses indicated that this collaborative interference effect corresponded to disrupted retrieval organization. By comparison, false recall of related lures did not differ between conditions (.44 and .43), although there was evidence for enhanced noncritical intrusions in the collaborative group. In a second experiment, using categorized lists, false recall of nonstudied exemplars was significantly greater in the collaborative group (.19 and .12). The authors argued that, with categorized materials, the collaborative groups relied more heavily on category knowledge during recall. Because of social pressure to participate in group recall, if a subject could not recall a list word on their turn they would be more likely to generate a likely (but false) item from one of the categories. In both experiments a final recognition test was given. The most interesting result was that, for list words, subjects were more likely to claim to "remember" items that they themselves had previously recalled compared to other subjects. In contrast, for related lures, there were no differences in "remember" judgments for self-recalled and other-recalled lures. Thus, if one subject suggested a lure during recall, this lure was likely to be falsely "remembered" by other subjects.

Basden, Reysen, and Basden (2002) had subjects participate in "perceived" social recall of DRM lists. Subjects in this study thought that the computer was providing them with recalls of other subjects (in different rooms), when in fact the computer was providing them with prespecified words (including related lures). Basden et al. found that subjects were likely to incorporate falsely provided related lures into their own recall of the lists, and they were subsequently more likely to falsely recognize and give "remember" judgments to these words. In a second experiment, this social conformity effect in recall was replicated, but it was shown that subjects were less likely to be influenced by the misleading words when they thought that they had come from other subjects, as opposed to a computer program that was designed to provide words to "cue" their memory. That is, presentation of the misleading words influenced subjects under each condition, but subjects were more skeptical of words purportedly recalled by other subjects.

Roediger, Meade, and Bergman (2001b) used an actual person to spread misinformation. Subjects studied schematic scenes (e.g., a kitchen) and subsequently recalled items from that scene. Unbeknown to the other subjects, a confederate subject was instructed to falsely recall misleading items (e.g., oven mitts) that had not actually occurred in the scene. Consistent with the idea that social recall can increase false memories, the misleading item was more likely to be falsely recalled when it had been suggested by the confederate (see Wright, Mathews, & Skagerberg, 2005a, for analogous results with different types of materials). Meade and Roediger (2002) further showed that, like DRM errors, the memory errors elicited by their social contagion task were difficult for subjects to avoid, even after they were warned against them. Further, in both experiments, it was found that subjects were more likely to incorporate into their memory those suggested items that were high in expectancy (i.e., very likely to be found in a kitchen) compared to those that were lower in expectancy, which is analogous to the effects of associative strength on DRM errors. Collectively, these social recall experiments demonstrate that subjects are prone to source memory errors, whereby the presentation of related lures by other subjects is incorporated into one's own memory. These errors can be difficult to avoid, can elicit illusory judgments of "remembering," and show generality across materials (i.e., related words or pictures of related items).

APPLICATIONS AND DATA

CHAPTER

Individual Differences and Generalizability

This chapter reviews research into why some people are more prone to false memories than others, and also research comparing false memories created in the laboratory to those created outside the laboratory (e.g., autobiographical memory distortions). These two areas of inquiry are tightly coupled. Laboratory tasks are sensitive to a core set of mental capabilities that characterize each individual, and as such, performance on one task could be used to predict memory accuracy in other situations (e.g., eyewitness memory). The identification and measurement of individual differences in memory distortion has important practical applications, most notably in legal, medical, and clinical settings. The key is in determining the degree to which task performance is determined by stable individual differences in information processing, as opposed to more transient strategies or task-specific processes.

Most of the earlier literature on individual differences in memory errors was concerned with source errors in misinformation or suggestibility tasks (for reviews see Eisen, Winograd, & Qin, 2002; Schooler & Loftus, 1993). These studies have identified several variables that can correlate with memory errors, such as age, hypnotizability, dissociative experiences, and mental imagery. Many of the aforementioned variables also have been investigated in DRM and related tasks, in addition to a variety of other factors that might potentially contribute to individual differences. These variables include cognitive differences (e.g., working memory span, processing speed), personality characteristics (e.g., dissociative experiences, self-esteem, suggestibility), and group differences (e.g., people with a history of abuse, trauma, or beliefs of alien abduction). Research in these areas is reviewed in the following sections. Other individual difference variables, such as development, aging, and neuropsychological disorders, are reviewed in subsequent chapters. Before reviewing research on these variables, the issue of stable individual differences within the DRM task is discussed, as well as correlations between DRM false memories and other types of false memories.

☐ WITHIN-TASK STABILITY

There are stable individual differences in the likelihood of creating false memories in the DRM task. In normative studies with dozens of undergraduates, Stadler et al. (1999) and Gallo and Roediger (2002) found that, across subjects, false recall and recognition of related lures were positively correlated (the correlation was +.65 in Stadler et al., and +.61 in Gallo & Roediger; see also Platt, Lacey, Iobst, & Finkelman, 1998; Wilkinson & Hyman, 1998; Winograd et al. 1998). Of course, because the recognition test was administered after all the lists had been studied and recalled in these studies, these correlations were driven, in part, by the influence of prior recall on subsequent recognition (see Chapter 6). A reanalysis of the results of Gallo and Roediger, though, indicates that this testing effect cannot be the entire story. When false recall of noncritical lures (i.e., other recall intrusions) was correlated with subsequent false recognition of unrelated lures (i.e., those which came from nonstudied lists, and hence would not be confounded with prior recall), a significant positive correlation was still found across subjects (+.37). These findings suggest that, within a single experimental session, those subjects who were more likely to make recall errors also were more likely to make recognition errors.

Is this variability due to fundamental cognitive differences that make some people more prone to false memories, across measures, or is it instead due to situational factors (e.g., having a bad day)? Blair, Lenton, and Hastie (2002) investigated this question by studying the reliability of individual differences in the DRM task across two testing situations (separated by 2 weeks). In each session, subjects studied several DRM lists for a final recognition test (the same materials and procedures were used in each session). Across subjects, the overall level of false recognition to related lures at Time 1 was correlated with false recognition to related lures at Time 2 ($r = +.76$). This relationship persisted even when false recognition was corrected with false alarms to unrelated lures, suggesting that this correlation was not driven by variable tendencies to respond positively to all items (i.e., response bias), although certainly such bias could contribute to individual differences. A significant cross-list relationship also was found, indicating that the propensity to falsely recognize a related lure from one list at Time 1 predicted whether a subject would falsely recognize a different related lure at Time 2. Thus, these reliable correlations were not due to the fact that the same materials were used across the two sessions. Instead, these data indicate that some people were more prone to false recognition than others, and this difference was stable across testing situations. Individual differences also were found in true recognition, although this relationship was not as great as for false recognition.

☐ CROSS-TASK STABILITY

Laboratory Memories

Several studies indicate that individual differences in the propensity to make DRM false memories generalize across other types of false memories. Lövdén (2003) found significant correlations, across subjects, with false recall in the DRM task and false memory in two other tasks—category cued recall, $r = +.30$; and recognition of similar pictures (e.g., Koutstaal & Schacter, 1997), $r = +.21$. Using a different type of false memory task, Eisen and colleagues (cited in Eisen et al., 2002) reported a relationship between DRM false recognition and the susceptibility to misleading information. These findings demonstrate that a variety of false memory tasks, although different in many ways, tap into a common set of cognitive processes. Given the importance of these types of findings, additional studies of cross-task correlations would greatly add to the literature.

Autobiographical Memories

Two studies have investigated whether false recall in the DRM task correlates with false autobiographical memories. Platt et al. (1998) tested undergraduates' memory for when they heard the verdict of a highly publicized court case (the criminal trial of O. J. Simpson). The evening of the verdict, subjects completed a questionnaire regarding the circumstances in which they heard the verdict (e.g., location, activity, source, etc.), and their memory for these same circumstances was tested several months later. There was considerable distortion in people's autobiographical memories across sessions (measured by the difference between the initial questionnaire and subsequent memory), demonstrating false autobiographical memories. Approximately a year and a half after the verdict, these same subjects participated in a typical DRM false memory task. The critical finding from this study was a significant correlation between false recall in the DRM task and memory accuracy for the auto-biographical event ($r = -.30$). (A similar correlation was found for false recognition, but this test was confounded with prior recall.) These correlations indicate that subjects who were more likely to falsely recall related lures also were more likely to have distorted autobiographical memories. Thus, individual differences in laboratory-induced false memories generalized to false measures of nonlaboratory events.

Wilkinson and Hyman (1998) used a different method to measure false autobiographical memories. Undergraduates were first asked to write a brief description of an event from their early childhood (between ages of 2 and 10) that they could not recollect themselves, but that they knew from other sources (e.g., family stories, pictures, etc.). They then were asked to imagine the event and answer a few elaborating questions. Finally, they were asked to rate their memory on a 7-point scale from (1) "only know" to (7) "explicitly remember." Higher ratings on this 7-point scale were interpreted as greater amounts of autobiographical memory distortion. Unlike Platt et al. (1998), no relationship between DRM false recall and autobiographical memory distortion was found in this study. The inconsistency with these findings and Platt et al. might reflect differences in power (only 5 DRM lists were used in Wilkinson and Hyman, whereas 12 were used in Platt et al.) or differences in the ways of eliciting autobiographical memory errors. Whereas Platt et al. directly measured autobiographical memory distortions, Wilkinson and Hyman indirectly inferred that false autobiographical memories had been created. Subjects may have interpreted the 7-point rating scale differently, and because a control condition was not included (in which no imagery session took place), it cannot be determined if differences in this scale truly reflected false autobiographical memories. As was the case with cross-task correlations, additional comparisons of autobiographical false memories and laboratory-induced false memories would greatly add to the literature, especially given that some positive relationships have been documented.

☐ COGNITIVE DIFFERENCES

Working Memory

Watson, Bunting, Poole, and Conway (2005) compared false recall across high and low working memory subjects (measured by a memory span task).

As expected, high span subjects were more likely to recall list words than were low span subjects. There were no false memory differences across groups in an unwarned condition, but when the groups were warned (before study) to avoid false recall the high span subjects were better able than low span subjects to suppress false recall. These findings are consistent with the idea that warning subjects before study reduces false recall via an identify-and-reject strategy (see Chapter 5). The ability to figure out the related lure of a list, and to keep this word in mind while that list is being presented, relies on working memory. Lövdén (2003) also reported relevant findings, with significant negative correlations between DRM false recall and a variety of cognitive tasks, including those thought to reflect processing speed, inhibition, true recall, and recognition. It is unknown how these various measures map onto false recall, but they likely tap into some of the same frontally mediated strategic processes that guide false memory monitoring. Of course, it is difficult to make firm conclusions on the basis of correlational analyses alone. Additional evidence linking frontal lobe function and memory monitoring is discussed in Chapters 8 and 9.

Imagery

Winograd et al. (1998) reported a significant positive correlation between DRM false recognition and mental imagery (the Vividness of Visual Imagery Questionnaire [VVIQ]), indicating that more vivid mental imagers were more likely to claim to "remember" falsely recognized related and unrelated lures. Winograd et al. noted, however, that the VVIQ also was positively correlated with a measure of social desirability (i.e., a willingness to please others). This relationship suggests that the correlation between VVIQ and false "remember" judgments may have been influenced by demand characteristics. Wilkinson and Hyman (1998) also reported that some measures of mental imagery correlated with false recognition.

☐ PERSONALITY DIFFERENCES

Dissociative Experiences

One of the most extensively researched personality characteristics in the false memory literature is a tendency towards dissociative experiences. The DSM-IV defines dissociation as "a disruption in the usually integrated functions of consciousness, memory, identity, or perception of the environment" (p. 477). This tendency can be measured by self-report questionnaire (i.e., the Dissociative Experiences Scale, or DES; Bernstein & Putnam, 1986), which estimates the frequency of various experiences such as finding oneself in a room without knowing why, confusing dreams with reality, etc. (see Table 7.1 for a sample of items from the DES). Everyone has had at least some of these experiences, but there is considerable individual variability in the likelihood of having these experiences on a daily basis. The propensity towards dissociative experiences, as measured by DES scores, has correlated with false memories in several tasks. These tasks include those involving repeated imaginations, or misleading questions regarding autobiographical memories (e.g., Hyman & Billings, 1998; see Eisen & Lynn, 2001, for a theoretical review). Ostensibly, the DES provides an index of one's ability to effectively engage in reality monitoring. The more prone one is to dissociative tendencies, the less likely they are to correctly monitor the accuracy of their memories.

Several studies have reported a relationship between DRM false memories and DES scores, although this relationship was not always obtained. In Winograd et al. (1998), undergraduates were tested in a typical DRM task in one session, and a variety of personality measures were obtained on separate testing occasions. The correlation between the DES and false recall of related lures was not significant, but there was a significant positive correlation between DES scores and noncritical recall intrusions ($r = +.37$). This finding indicates that people with more dissociative experiences also were more likely to make recall intrusions. No measures correlated with true recall of list words. Considering only the recognition data

TABLE 7.1   A Sample of Items from the DES (Bernstein & Putnam, 1986)

...finding themselves dressed in clothes that they do not remember putting on.

...finding new things among their belongings that they do not remember buying.

...finding that they are approached by people who they do not know and who call them by another name or insist that they have met them before.

...looking in a mirror and not recognizing themselves.

...feeling that other people, objects, and the world around them are not real.

...being in a familiar place but finding it strange and unfamiliar.

...becoming so involved in a fantasy or daydream that it feels as though it were really happening to them.

...finding that in certain situations they are able to do things with amazing ease and spontaneity that would usually be difficult for them (for example, sports, work, social situations, etc.).

Note: Subjects rate the frequency with which each experience applies to them (on a scale from 0% [never] to 100% [always]).

that were not confounded with prior recall, there was a significant correlation between false recognition of related lures and the DES ($r = +.32$) and also between false recognition of unrelated lures and the DES ($r = +.52$). These positive relationships tended to manifest themselves in "remember" judgments, as opposed to "know" judgments, reflecting a greater degree of illusory recollection in more dissociative personalities.

Wilkinson and Hyman (1998) also found significant correlations between DRM recall intrusions and a few subscales of the DES, but overall DES scores were not correlated with DRM false recall. Several other studies have failed to find significant correlations between DRM false memories and the DES (e.g., Bremner, Shobe, & Kihlstrom, 2000; Geraerts, Smeets, Jelicic, van Heerden, & Merckelbach, 2005; Platt et al., 1998; Wright et al., 2005b; see also Eisen & Lynn, 2001). However, a few studies have reported significant relationships between the DES and DRM false memories when the subject sample included people who had more extreme scores on the DES (as opposed to college undergraduates), such as those with a history of abuse (e.g., Clancy, Schacter, McNally, & Pitman, 2000; Zoellner et al., 2000; see also Clancy et al., 2002). These findings bolster the conclusion that dissociative tendencies are related to DRM false memories, especially in populations where there is sufficient variability in DES scores.

Depression

Several studies have reported positive correlations between depression and DRM false memories. Zoellner et al. (2000) reported a positive correlation ($r = +.68$) between DRM false recall (for noncritical intrusions) and depression (Beck Depression Inventory). Clancy et al. (2002) reported a positive correlation between depression (again using the Beck Depression Inventory) and DRM false recall and recognition of related lures. Using a different measure, Peiffer and Trull (2000) found that false recall was positively correlated with negative affect. Finally, in a more recent study, Moritz, Gläscher, and Brassen (2005) found that a group of clinically depressed patients was more likely than controls to falsely recognize related lures, but only when these lures were emotionally charged. These findings indicate that depressed people were more prone to memory errors in the DRM task, but they need to be interpreted with caution. As discussed below, all of these studies included special populations of subjects (e.g., those with a history of abuse), and other differences in these populations might have driven these correlations. Also, two studies failed to find a relationship between depression and DRM memory errors (Bremner et al., 2000; Clancy et al., 2000). Studies with additional controls of participant characteristics, as well as more elaborate correlational methods (such as multiple regression), are needed to more fully understand the potential relationship between depression and these types of false memories.

Other Traits

A variety of other personality variables have been correlated (or not) with DRM false memories. However, these measures are often correlated with each other, they often correlate with only one aspect of DRM task performance (e.g., false recall of unrelated lures), and sometimes the correlations are not reliable across studies. Because of these and other interpretative limitations, these correlations are simply listed here for the interested reader. Significant positive correlations with DRM false memories have been reported for anxiety (Zoellner et al., 2000), absorption and magical ideation (Clancy et al., 2002), acquiescence (Peiffer & Trull, 2000), and delusional ideation (Laws & Bhatt, 2005). Tests or traits that failed to correlate with DRM false memories include the Creative Imagination Scale, the Group Embedded Figures Test, the Marlowe–Crowne Social Desirability Scale, the Subjective Memory Questionnaire, the Self-Righteousness Scale, verbal fluency, vocabulary, and the verbal Scholastic Aptitude Test (Winograd et al., 1998); absorption and fantasy-proneness (Platt et al., 1998); and suggestibility and self-esteem (Peiffer & Trull, 2000).

☐ GROUP DIFFERENCES

Several studies have compared various groups in their average propensity to make false memories in the DRM task. Much of this work was motivated by the recovered/false memory debate that peaked in the 1980s and 1990s (for review and debate, see Alpert, Brown, Ceci, Courtois, Loftus, & Ornstein, 1998; Lindsay & Read, 1994; McNally, 2003; Pope, 1996). This debate centers on the legitimacy of the idea that traumatic memories (e.g., memories of childhood sexual abuse) can be "repressed" into a nonconscious state, so that they are unavailable to conscious awareness for many years, until they are recovered after clinical intervention. In the absence of corroborating evidence for these allegedly recovered memories, it is difficult to know whether the traumatic events really occurred (and the memory was repressed), or whether the memories are false, potentially owing to suggestive therapeutic techniques. Schooler, Bendiksen, and Ambadar (1997) argued that each of these phenomena exists, and presented corresponding case studies, but the debate is ongoing.

Not surprisingly, the extent to which laboratory-based false memory tasks can inform this debate is a contentious topic (see Freyd & Gleaves, 1996; Gleaves, Smith, Butler, & Spiegel, 2004; Kihlstrom, 2004; Roediger & McDermott, 1996). Take the example of the correlations between dissociative experiences and DRM false memories. As discussed by Winograd et al. (1998), and reviewed below, people who claim to recover memories of past abuse often score highly on the DES. The correlation between DES and laboratory-based false memories raises the issue as to whether the recovered memories of abuse also are false, or in contrast, whether actual abuse can lead to dissociative personalities that, in turn, can cause memory monitoring problems. These questions obviously need to be addressed on a case-by-case basis, and cannot be answered with laboratory experiments alone. Nonetheless, the research reviewed in the following sections highlights some of the general processes that need to be considered by any perspective, and could potentially inform the debate at a theoretical level.

Continuous Memories of Abuse

Bremner et al. (2000) investigated DRM false memories in women who reported continuous memories of childhood abuse (and whose memories of abuse were judged to be genuine). Subjects were recruited from newspaper advertisements. Women who reported abuse were divided into those with a diagnosis of post-traumatic stress disorder (PTSD, based on DSM IV criteria and a clinical interview) and those without a diagnosis of PTSD. Bremner et al. found that false recall of related lures did not differ between any of the groups. However, abused women with the PTSD diagnosis were significantly less likely to recall list words (.50) than the other groups (.60), which did not differ, and this true recall impairment correlated with severity of PTSD symptoms. Abused women with a diagnosis of PTSD also were significantly more likely to make noncritical recall intrusions (.31 vs. .16). On a final recognition test (confounded with prior recall), abused women with a diagnosis of PTSD were more likely to falsely recognize related and unrelated lures than the other groups. These findings suggest that PTSD can result in impaired true memory and enhanced memory errors. As argued by Bremner et al., PTSD has been found to cause episodic memory problems in other tasks, potentially implicating trauma-induced deficiencies in those processes that are necessary for accurate memory.

Zoellner et al. (2000) also investigated the influence of abuse-related trauma on DRM false memories, again recruiting subjects through newspaper advertisement. One group of subjects were women who received a clinical diagnosis of PTSD, with half the cases being attributed to sexual assault and the other half attributed to nonsexual assault (e.g., robbery). Another group of women also fit the DSM-IV criteria for trauma, based on sexual or nonsexual assault, but were not given a clinical diagnosis of PTSD. The PTSD group differed from the non-PTSD trauma group (and controls without trauma) in severity of PTSD symptoms, depression, anxiety, and dissociative experiences. Results from the immediate recall tests can be found in Figure 7.1. The control group tended to recall more list words than the other two groups, although statistical comparisons for true recall were restricted to items from middle serial positions (which did not differ across groups). Larger effects were found in false recall. Both trauma groups falsely recalled significantly more related lures (.50) than the controls (.26), and the PTSD group made more noncritical recall intrusions than either of the other groups. Further, PTSD and anxiety were both positively correlated with false recall. Like Bremner et al. (2000), these results indicate that trauma can leave people more prone to false memories. There also was evidence of elevated false recognition in the trauma groups, but these results were not always significant (also see

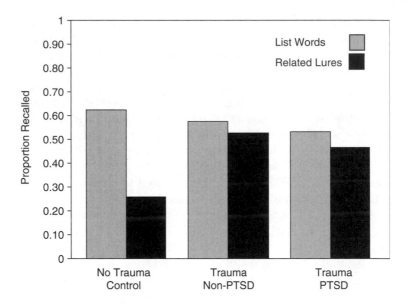

FIGURE 7.1   The effects of trauma and post traumatic stress disorder (PTSD) on true and false recall in Zoellner et al. (2000). True recall was approximated from their Figure 1. The rate of noncritical recall intrusions was greater in the PTSD group (5.5%) than in the non-PTSD group (2%) or the control group (1.4%).

Clancy et al., 2002, for a failure to find a correlation between a PTSD measure and DRM false recognition).

Maltreated Children

Howe, Cicchetti, Toth, and Cerrito (2004) compared DRM performance in maltreated children from low social-economic status (SES) to non-maltreated children from the same SES and non-maltreated children from middle SES. All maltreated children had previously been reported to the Department of Human and Health Services, and had experienced abuse or neglect. All of the groups were evenly mixed with males and females, and the two low SES groups had more children of minority race/ethnicity (85%) than did the control group (mostly Caucasian). Analysis of recall results revealed that, although true and false recall increased with age within each group, neither SES nor history of maltreatment affected true or false recall. (The effects of age are discussed more in Chapter 8.) On the final recognition test, overall levels of true recognition (corrected for false alarms to unrelated lures) were greater in the middle SES children than in the lower SES children, but neither true nor false recognition varied as a function of maltreatment. Thus, maltreated children were not more likely to make false memories than non-maltreated children, although maltreatment may have caused other cognitive difficulties that were not measured in this study.

Recovered Memories of Abuse

Clancy et al. (2000) investigated DRM false recognition effects in four groups of subjects: women who reported recovering memories of childhood sexual abuse (recovered-memory group), women who believed they were abused but had no memories of abuse (repressed-memory group), women who were sexually abused as children and always remembered the abuse (continuous-memory group), and women with no histories of sexual abuse (control group). Subjects were recruited from newspaper advertisements seeking women who fit into the aforementioned categories. Several DRM lists of varying lengths were studied for a subsequent recognition test. For simplicity, the results from the 15- and 8-item lists are collapsed and discussed here (also, note that only corrected-corrected data were reported in the paper). On these lists, true recognition was very high and did not differ across groups (mean corrected true recognition was .86). In contrast, false recognition of related lures was higher in the recovered-memory group (.70) than in the other groups, which did not differ significantly (.51). Using similar procedures, Geraerts et al. (2005) also found that groups reporting recovered memories of abuse were more prone to the DRM illusion than other groups, and further found that some of these effects extended to lists of trauma-related associates (e.g., *rape, police, beating, child*, etc.).

There are two main points to take from these findings. First, the finding that women with continuous memory of abuse were no different than controls suggests that abuse does not necessarily leave one more prone to these types of false memories (consistent with the non-PTSD results of Bremner et al., 2000, and with Howe et al., 2004). The second point centers around the recovered-memory group. As discussed by Clancy et al. (2000), the larger false recognition effect in this group cannot be attributed to cognitive impairments related solely to claims of sexual abuse, because there was no difference in the other groups claiming to have been abused and the control group. Other factors that differentiated the recovered-memory group from these other groups must have been involved. For instance, false recognition correlated with the DES in Clancy et al. (2000), and the largest DES scores were in the recovered-memory group. Clancy et al. offered two alternative interpretations of these results: (1) The recovered memories were true, and the recovery of suppressed memories caused cognitive impairments (e.g., dissociation and reality monitoring problems) that, in turn, caused heightened levels of false recognition in the laboratory task. (2) The recovered memories were false, caused by pre-existing dissociation and reality monitoring problems, and these problems also made this group more likely to falsely recognize items in the laboratory task. This study provided no evidence in favor of one explanation over the other. As noted by Clancy et al., because these data were correlational, casual connections between dissociation, false recognition, or recovered memories could not be made.

Memories of Alien Abduction

One of the limitations of the Clancy et al. (2000) study was that there was no corroborating evidence of abuse in the recovered memory group, and thus it was difficult to determine the accuracy of the memory. Clancy et al. (2002) attempted to avoid this ambiguity by investigating the propensity for DRM false memories in a group of subjects who claimed to have recovered memories of space alien abduction. Clancy et al. (2002) noted that these types of memories tend to be similar across individuals, potentially implicating a shared cultural script that is obtained through common sources such as movies or books. In brief, the typical memory involves waking from sleep and finding that one cannot move. This state likely corresponds to an episode of sleep paralysis, a relatively common phenomenon during which one is briefly "stuck" halfway between sleep and wakefulness. As described by Clancy et al. (2002):

> Many people will experience hypnopompic ('upon awakening') hallucinations during these episodes. Hallucinations vary, but often included electrical tingling sensations throughout the body, feelings of levitation, loud buzzing sounds, flashing lights, and most strikingly, visual hallucinations of figures hovering near one's bed....The modal 'abductee' often assumes that something must have happened after the onset of the sleep episode but prior to full awakening. They seek the aid of a hypnotherapist to help understand their anomalous experiences, and it is during hypnotic regression sessions that they 'recall' memories of having been abducted (i.e., being taken into space ships, sexually experimented on by aliens, etc.). (p. 456)

Of course, other people claim to have been abducted by space aliens without clinical intervention, so hypnotherapy is not necessary for these sorts of memories to occur.

Clancy et al. (2002) assumed that these people were not really abducted by space aliens, and that these memories of abduction represent false memories of a traumatic experience. Three groups of subjects were recruited through newspaper advertisements, and the experimenter established the sincerity of each individual's belief. The first group, described above, claimed to have recovered memories of alien abduction (recovered memories group). The second group also believed that aliens had abducted them, but this group had no detailed memories of the abduction (instead, their beliefs were based on other signs, such as scars, sleep problems, etc.). The third group contained control subjects who did not claim to have been abducted by aliens. All groups had an approximately even mix of women and men. Subjects studied several DRM lists, of varying lengths, for immediate free recall tests.

Analysis of true recall and recognition of list words revealed no significant differences across the groups, but false recall and recognition did differ across groups. False recall of related lures, at each list length, is presented in Figure 7.2. As can be seen from the figure, false recall steadily increased as a function of list length in each group (i.e., studying more associates increased false recall; see Chapter 2). More important, each of the groups that claimed to have been abducted by aliens was more likely to falsely recall related lures than the control group (collapsing across list length, these differences were significant). Similar effects were obtained in false recognition, although this test was confounded with prior recall.

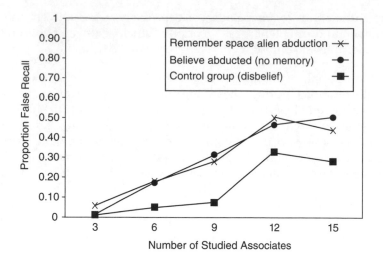

FIGURE 7.2 False recall in subjects who had memories of space alien abduction, subjects who believed they had been abducted with no corresponding memory, and control subjects who denied abduction, in Clancy et al. (2002), as a function of the number of associates studied per list. True recall did not differ across groups, and false recall of noncritical words was not reported.

There was little evidence that false memories differed between the recovered- and repressed-memory groups, suggesting that beliefs in alien abductions correlated with laboratory-based false memories regardless of whether or not there was a detailed memory for the abduction.

The exact cause of these group differences is difficult to ascertain, but group differences in personality traits (e.g., suggestibility) or pre-existing reality monitoring problems may have been involved. The groups did not differ in dissociative experiences (measured by the DES), but a marginal correlation was found between false recall and DES scores across groups ($r = +.29$, $p = .06$), again implicating dissociation as a possible factor. Regardless of the cause of these effects, Clancy et al. (2002) argued that people who are prone to false memories of traumatic experiences also are more prone to laboratory-based false memories.

Sex

Although many of the aforementioned studies involving memories for abuse involved mostly female subjects, it is important to note that Clancy et al. (2002) included both female and male subjects. Thus, the findings applied equally to members of both sexes. Seamon, Guerry, Marsh, and Tracy (2002a) conducted a more extensive investigation of potential sex differences. They compared large groups of female and male undergraduates on false recall in the DRM task. No significant differences were obtained in true recall of list words, false recall or related words, or noncritical intrusions (also see Bauste & Ferraro, 2004; Christman, Propper, & Dion, 2004). Indeed, the means of each group were all within a single percentage point of each other in the Seamon et al. study.

☐ GROUP × MATERIAL INTERACTIONS

Most of the DRM experiments discussed so far in this chapter have used words associated to common concepts (e.g., *sleep, chair, window,* etc.), and have collapsed across the different lists for analyses of memory performance. One exception was the Blair et al. (2002) study, in which it was found that people were more likely to consistently falsely recognize some related lures (e.g., *chair*), across testing sessions, compared to other related lures. This finding led the authors to suggest that people may be "schematic" for certain concepts (i.e., established associative networks vary across individuals), thereby leaving them more prone to false memories that take advantage of these associations. Based on these ideas, some researchers have investigated whether different groups of people are more or less prone to false memories for concepts that are specifically relevant to their group, using the same basic procedures as in the DRM task.

Gender Stereotypes

Lenton et al. (2001) investigated whether lists of stereotypical occupations (e.g., *secretary, nurse, housekeeper, nanny,* etc.) could elicit false memories of nonpresented occupations (e.g., *hairdresser, librarian,* etc.) that fit within the list (e.g., stereotypical female occupations). Subjects (male and female undergraduates) studied several lists for a final recognition test. Four neutral DRM lists and one stereotype list (stereotypical female or male occupations) were presented at study. As expected, subjects were significantly more likely to falsely recognize occupations that were related to the studied stereotype (mean = .44, collapsed across male and female lists) than those occupations that were unrelated to the studied stereotype (i.e., control lures, .16).

Lenton et al. also investigated awareness of stereotype use, and whether individual differences in the strength of the underlying stereotypes would relate to false recognition. To address the awareness issue, subjects were asked to recall the themes of the lists that were studied and also whether they had noticed or used gender information to make memory judgments. Although subjects were very good at recalling the general themes of each list, there was no evidence that subjects had explicitly noticed or used gender information to make their decisions. These findings led the authors to conclude that the influence of stereotype activation on false memories was relatively implicit or automatic (as opposed to controlled or strategic). With respect to individual differences, several measures of the strength of the relevant stereotypes were gathered for each participant (i.e., an implicit priming task of stereotypes, an explicit stereotype association task, and a few sexism questionnaires), but none of these correlated with false recognition of the stereotypical lures.

Food Memories and Eating Disorders

Ferraro and Olson (2003) investigated false memories for food-related words in individuals at risk for eating disorders (indexed by questionnaires such as the Setting Conditions of Anorexia Nervosa Scale). Three food-related DRM lists (those corresponding to the related lures *bread*, *sweet*, and *fruit*) and three non-food-related lists (*king*, *doctor*, and *black*) were used in the study. Although the two groups did not differ in false memory for non-food-related items, individuals at risk for eating disorders were significantly less likely to falsely recall or recognize food-related lures than were control subjects. This pattern suggests that the at-risk individuals may have attended more to the food-related lists at study, thereby enhancing true recall and decreasing false recall via recollection-based monitoring processes. Unfortunately, true memory scores were not reported, and recognition was confounded with prior recall.

Alcohol Expectancies and Heavy Drinkers

Reich, Goldman, and Noll (2004) investigated whether heavy alcohol drinkers would be more likely than light drinkers to falsely remember adjectives related to alcohol expectancies. Undergraduates studied several DRM lists, in addition to a list of adjectives that had previously been identified as expected outcomes of alcohol use (*crazy, loud, wacky, uninhibited, carefree, fun, sociable, mellow, relaxed, dizzy,* and *sick*). None of these words is strongly associated to the word *alcohol*, but it was hypothesized that heavy drinkers would be more likely to make alcohol-related associations to these words than non-heavy drinkers, especially within an alcohol-related testing environment. To test this hypothesis, subjects were tested either in a standard conference room (control context) or a laboratory room equipped to resemble a bar (including a dimly lit wooden bar with stools, bottles of brand-name alcohol, neon signs, music, and a recycling bin with old beer bottles). After studying and recalling each list, a final recognition test was administered. For related lures, three words that were more likely to be attributed to alcohol use by heavy drinkers than light drinkers were included on the recognition test (e.g., *happy*, *silly*, and *confident*). After the test was completed, subjects filled out questionnaires regarding alcohol use so that they could be divided into heavier drinkers (mean = 6.2 drinks/week), lighter drinkers (less than 1 drink/week), and nondrinkers (never drink).

Subjects rarely falsely recalled the alcohol-expectancy lures, and so only false recognition data were reported. (True recognition data were not reported.) False recognition of lures related to the standard DRM lists did not differ between any of the groups or contexts, indicating that drinking status did not exert an influence on one's overall propensity to make false recognition errors, in general. By comparison, false recognition of alcohol-expectancy lures did differ across conditions. For nondrinkers, false recognition of these lures (approximately .30) did not differ as a function of testing context. For lighter and heavier drinkers, though, false recognition of the alcohol-expectancy lures was greater when tested in the bar context than in the control context, and this difference was significant for heavier drinkers (approximate means for heavier drinkers = .45 and .25). These findings indicate that the creation of false memories not only depends on the pre-existing associations of an individual, but also on the context in which those associations are elicited.

In sum, the results in this section demonstrate how different groups can be prone to different types of false memories, depending on their pre-existing knowledge, expectancies, or associations towards the to-be-remembered material. Analogous results were reported by Kim and Ahn (2002), in which it was found that trained clinicians were more likely than control subjects to falsely recognize clinical symptoms if these symptoms were consistent with hypothetical patients that they had earlier categorized. These sorts of findings are a natural consequence of the idea that pre-existing associations and knowledge, which can vary across individuals due to differences in experiences, heavily influence true and false memory. Researchers have begun to take advantage of these findings to study various clinical populations, as in the Ferraro and Olson (2003) study. Significant findings are not always found, though. Wenzel et al. (2004) failed to find true or false memory differences for blood-related concepts in people with blood phobias, or for spider-related concepts in people with spider phobias. These null results are difficult to interpret, because it always could be argued that the task was not sufficiently sensitive to detect an existing group difference, or that the conditions necessary to elicit the relevant associations were not tapped. In this regard, the results of Reich et al. (2004) are particularly intriguing, because they suggest that environmental context might play a powerful role in the priming of relevant associations and concepts, and hence relevant false memories.

CHAPTER

Development and Aging

Episodic memory improves with early development (e.g., from birth to late childhood), and then declines with advanced aging (e.g., from early to late adulthood). These changes are linked to the development and decline, respectively, of brain mechanisms and cognitive strategies that are critical for memory. This chapter reviews research on how development and aging affect true and false memories in converging associates tasks (for broader reviews of developmental effects on memory errors, see Ceci & Bruck, 1993; Reyna & Lloyd, 1997; Reyna, Mills, Estrada, & Brainerd, in press; and for a review of aging effects see Pierce, Simons, & Schacter, 2004). The general consensus from these and other areas of research is that children and older adults are more susceptible to false memories than healthy young adults. However, the extent of these effects is not without debate. Whether or not they are found can depend on the type of measurement, individual differences, and important situational factors. To more fully understand these issues one needs to carefully look at how development and aging can differentially affect the various cognitive processes that contribute to true and false memories.

☐ DEVELOPMENT AND THE DRM TASK

Predicting how children will perform on false memory tasks is difficult, because there are potentially opposing influences of cognitive development on performance (for an excellent discussion see Ghetti et al., 2002). Children have less experience with language and the world, and so their associative and conceptual networks should not be as elaborate as those in adults (or, even if they are, the ability to strategically process associative relationships might be underdeveloped). Children also might be less likely to strategical-ly encode relational information and hence capture the overall thematic structure or gist of the studied materials (see Reyna et al., in press). These factors would decrease the propensity to falsely remember nonstudied events on the basis of association or thematic consistency. Some early research using Underwood's (1965) continuous-recognition task (discussed in Chapter 1) is consistent with this general prediction. Felzen and Ansifeld (1970) found that third-graders were less likely than sixth-graders to falsely recognize a lure that was semantically related to a studied word. Unfortunately, the developmental findings with the continuous-recognition task have been somewhat difficult to interpret (see Cramer, 1974; Lindauer & Paris, 1976). More recent work using converging associates tasks also highlights developmental changes in different types of associative and/or gist-based processes. Dewhurst and Robinson (2004) found that false recall from phonologically related lists was greater than that to semantically relat-ed lists in 5-year olds, but the reverse was true in 11-year olds. Thus, although children may be less likely to process the relationships between words, the type of relationship and the level of development of the corre-sponding processes need to be considered.

Another major consideration is that retrieval monitoring processes might not be fully developed in children. Children have limited exposure to memory tasks (and resulting strategies), their true memory for the studied materials is not as great as older individuals, and prefrontal mechanisms that are critical for strategic monitoring processes (as dis-cussed in Chapters 9 and 10) are not fully developed. All of these factors could limit monitoring processes in children, making them more prone to false memory effects. Consistent with this idea, young children are more susceptible to some types of source memory errors than are older children (e.g., Foley, Johnson, & Raye, 1983), and these effects have been linked to measures of frontal lobe functioning (e.g., Rybash & Colilla, 1994). Brainerd et al. (1995b) reported a series of experiments that also are con-sistent with this prediction. Young children (5 years in Experiment 1) were more likely than older children (8 years) to falsely recognize lures that were categorically related to a studied word, and these differences were especially pronounced in those conditions where monitoring processes might have been used to suppress false recognition (the details of this task were discussed in Chapter 6).

Only a few studies have investigated developmental effects in the DRM task. Brainerd, Reyna, and Forrest (2002) reported a series of relevant experiments in young children. Their third experiment was the most comprehensive. Using typical DRM procedures, performance was compared between young children (5 years), young adolescents (11 years), and young adults (college undergraduates). All subjects studied several 15-word lists, which were read to them at a rate of 2 s per word. Half of the lists were followed by immediate free recall (recall was spoken to avoid age differences in writing proficiency), and half were followed by an unrelated task (repeating random letters). A final recognition test was administered after all lists had been presented.

Results from the immediate recall test are provided in Figure 8.1, presented separately for those lists with the strongest associative connections to their related lure (strong lists) and for those with the weakest connections (weak lists). True recall followed the expected pattern (adults > 11 years > 5 years), with minimal differences between strong and weak lists. False recall showed a very similar pattern to true recall (adults > 11 years > 5 years), with the exception that age-related differences were most pronounced in the strongly associated lists. These findings are consistent with an attenuated memory signal for related lures in children, either because associative networks were less developed, or because they had difficulty processing the theme or gist of the lists. As a result, children were less prone to false recall (for analogous results comparing similar age groups, see Dewhurst & Robinson, 2004; Howe et al., 2004). The fact that associative strength greatly influenced false recall in adults (.53 > .21) but not in the youngest children (.10 vs. .12) also is consistent with the idea that associative networks and/or gist-based processes were less developed in children.

Brainerd et al. (2002) found that false recall of related lures was lower in children, but this is not to say that children were less susceptible to memory errors overall. In fact, noncritical intrusions (i.e., related words other than the prespecified related lure, or words from other lists) tended to be greater in children. These effects demonstrate the underdevelopment of monitoring processes in children. The recognition results also suggested that the youngest children had monitoring difficulties. Considering only those lists that were not confounded with prior recall, true recognition of list words and false recognition of related lures did not differ systematically across groups, but false alarms to unrelated lures were greater in young children. This last effect might have been due to an underdeveloped use of gist to inform diagnostic monitoring processes (e.g., "I do not remember studying any lists related to this word, so it is probably new."). When recognition was adjusted for these base rate false alarm differences, the recognition results were similar to the recall results. The relatedness effect on false recognition was lower in children, and associative strength influenced false recognition only in adults.

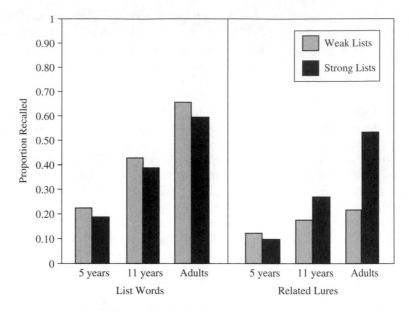

FIGURE 8.1 The effect of development on true and false recall, as a function of associative strength, in Brainerd et al. (2002, Experiment 3). The rate of noncritical intrusions was .11 (5 years), .11 (11 years), and .03 (adults), and the rate of cross-list intrusions was .22, .02, and 0, respectively. Extralist intrusions did not vary as a function of list strength.

There are few studies of the subjective experience of these types of false memories in children, probably because subjective judgments are difficult to interpret in young children (who might not understand the instructions in the same way as adults). One notable exception is a study by Brainerd, Holliday, and Reyna (2004), in which the conjoint recognition technique was used to estimate the subjective phenomenology in children (see Chapter 4 for discussion of this technique). Comparing children 5 to 14 years old, they found that age-related increases in true recognition mostly corresponded to increases in recollection, as opposed to more general familiarity-based responding (which was not affected, or was affected less, by development). There also was some evidence that age-related increases in false recognition were accompanied with an increase in vivid illusory recollection (i.e., phantom recollection), but these false recognition findings were not found in every condition of their experiments.

Collectively, these DRM results suggest that children are less prone to semantically based false recall and recognition, potentially due to under-developed semantic networks or abilities to extract the themes or gist of the lists (for more recent evidence that also is consistent with these proposals, see Brainerd, Forrest, & Karibian, in press; Lampinen, Leding, Reed, & Odegard, 2006). In contrast, memory errors for unrelated lures tended to be enhanced in children (e.g., Brainerd et al., 2002, 2004), pointing to underdeveloped monitoring processes.

It should be noted that associative norms were based on data from younger adults in the studies reviewed above, as opposed to children, and so the relevant associations might not have been available to children. The results from a study using drawings of categorized pictures are relevant to this idea. Seamon et al. (2000) compared first-graders (6–7 years), fifth-graders (10–12 years), and undergraduates (17–22 years) on false recognition in a categorized pictures task. Subjects studied six lists of nine category exemplars each, with each exemplar presented as a picture (e.g., line drawings of a *guitar, piano, drum*, etc. for the category *musical instruments*), and so it should have been easy to grasp the theme of each list. They then took a final recognition test, with targets and lures presented pictorially. The data from a 3-day delayed test were the most informative. On this test, first-graders were less likely to recognize studied pictures (.73) than were undergraduates (.83), but were more likely to falsely recognize related lures (.32 vs. .23) and unrelated lures (.15 vs. .06). (Not surprisingly, the fifth-graders performance was in-between that of the other two groups.) Younger children were more susceptible to errors overall, potentially due to underdeveloped monitoring processes, but they displayed similar relatedness effects on false recognition as the adult group with these materials.

This last result suggests that children were just as likely as adults to grasp the themes of each list when categorized pictures were used, but two caveats must be drawn. First, the overall low level of false recognition with these picture materials (compared to DRM lists) raises the issue of floor effects, especially in adults (see also Ghetti et al., 2002, discussed in the next section). Second, a few unpublished DRM experiments that used age-appropriate lists have been cited as replicating the developmental differences reported above (i.e., smaller relatedness effects in children), suggesting that those differences cannot be attributed to the materials, per se (see Reyna et al., in press). Additional studies that directly compare false memory for different types of materials in children would help to resolve this interpretative issue.

☐ DEVELOPMENT AND MONITORING MANIPULATIONS

As discussed, enhanced false recognition of unrelated lures in children suggests that children have underdeveloped monitoring processes, as do the corresponding estimates of recollection rejection obtained via the conjoint recognition procedure (Brainerd et al., 2004). A few other results from the DRM task bolster this idea, and further suggest that different types of monitoring may emerge at different stages of development.

Exclusions and Warnings

Rybash and Hrubi-Bopp (2000) compared children (first-graders) to younger adults (college students). In the control condition, after studying each list, subjects were instructed to take 20 s to mentally generate words from unrelated categories, and then to recall the list. Like Brainerd et al. (2002), children in this condition were less likely to recall list words and related lures than were undergraduates, potentially owing to impaired associative or gist-based processes. In another condition, subjects were instructed, after each list, to think of words that were related to the study list but that were not presented. These instructions probably served as a warning against false recall of related words, and because a repeated study/test design was used the warning could have affected both study and test phases. Younger adults benefited from such instructions, as false recall was lower in this condition (.10) than in the control condition (.37), but children were not affected much (means = .13 and .17, respectively). If this warning interpretation is correct, then these results suggest a monitoring deficit in young children (i.e., difficulties with an identify-and-reject strategy).

Distinctiveness

Ghetti et al. (2002) investigated a more diagnostic type of monitoring, whether children could use the distinctive heuristic to reduce false recall and recognition. Subjects were 5-year olds, 7-year olds, and college undergraduates (mean age = 21 years). For all groups, the DRM task was modified in an effort to make it more age-appropriate for children. Shorter word lists were used (7 words/lists), including only words that were within the vocabulary of 5-year olds, and the presentation rate was slower than typical (5 s per word). Subjects studied 10-word lists, each followed by a free recall test (delayed by a 25 s mathematics task, to prevent rehearsal). Two speakers presented the lists via videotape (each presenting half of the lists). To manipulate the level of distinctiveness at study, the speakers presented a line-drawing picture that corresponded to each studied word for half the subjects (the picture condition), whereas the other subjects did not see a corresponding picture (the no-picture condition). A final recognition test was administered after all of the lists had been studied and recalled.

Consider first the results from the no-picture condition. As expected, true recall increased with age, from .46 (5 years) to .61 (7 years) to .88 (undergraduates). However, false recall of related lures was more likely in young children (means = .32, .25, and .15, respectively). A similar pattern was obtained in recognition, although those results may have been influenced by the prior recall tests. These DRM results were different than those reported by Brainerd et al. (2002) and others, probably owing to methodological differences between the studies. The use of shorter lists and visually spoken words in Ghetti et al. (2002) would have maximized monitoring processes, especially in older subjects. The fact that true recall was extremely high (.88) and false recall was very low (.15) in the undergraduates confirms that they had less difficulty discriminating list words from related lures in this version of the task than under more standard DRM conditions. This factor would have reduced false recall in younger adults, making it more likely that children would show relatively greater levels of false recall. Additionally, the use of modified lists might have made it easier for children to grasp the gist of each list, relative to the more typical DRM procedure, thereby enhancing false recall.

Consider next the results from the picture condition. As expected, true recall increased with age, from .41 (5 years) to .70 (7 years) to .90 (undergraduates). In contrast, false recall was not influenced by age (.18, .13, and .15, respectively). This failure to find age differences was due to the fact that studying pictures reduced false recall in children, ostensibly due to the distinctiveness heuristic. This distinctiveness effect (no-picture > picture) was evident in 5 year olds (.32 vs. .18) and 7 year olds (.25 vs. .13), but not in younger adults (.15 vs. .15), probably owing to floor effects. The predicted format effect (no-picture > picture) was evident in all three groups on false recognition (which was not at floor levels in any group), and this effect was evident for both related and unrelated lures.

The finding that even young children could use picture encoding to suppress false recognition suggests that diagnostic monitoring processes develop very early in life. Because pictures are recalled easily and vividly, the distinctiveness heuristic may place fewer demands on frontally based strategic processing than other monitoring processes, and thus might be more efficient in children. By comparison, some disqualifying monitoring processes (e.g., identify-and-reject, as discussed above in the context of Rybash & Hrubi-Bopp, 2000) might be more dependent on frontal functions, and thus might take more time to develop.

☐ AGING AND THE DRM TASK

Many studies have investigated the effects of aging in later adulthood (typically 65–75 years of age) on false memories in converging associates tasks. The theoretical consensus is that associative processes are intact in older adults (e.g., Balota et al., 1999), and that the use of thematic or gist-consistent information is either intact or enhanced (e.g., Tun, Wingfield, Rosen, & Blanchard, 1998; see also LaVoie & Faulkner, 2000). In contrast, monitoring processes can be impaired in older adults, due to prefrontal and/or medial temporal deficits or to deficits in the spontaneous use of such strategies (e.g., Henkel, Johnson, & De Leonardis, 1998). This cognitive profile makes older adults more prone to memory errors, but it does not imply that false memories are always greater in older adults, or even that they represent a significant aspect of mental life in late adulthood. As reviewed below, researchers are beginning to uncover those situations where aging does, and does not, increase the likelihood of false memories.

Table 8.1 summarizes the results of 18 experimental conditions that compared younger adults (mean age = 21 years) and older adults (73 years) under typical DRM recall conditions. Data are selectively reported from the most standard conditions in these studies, in the sense that several DRM lists were studied, and memory was tested with free recall tests (see the table note for a more thorough description). Averaging across studies (weighing each equally), true recall of list words was significantly lower in older adults (.62 vs. .47), whereas false recall of related lures was significantly greater (.33 vs. .40). The mean number of noncritical intrusions per list also was significantly greater in older adults (.31 vs. .46). As discussed in Chapter 2, these noncritical intrusions tend to be semantic associates to list words, or, less often, phonological associates. If several lists are studied and recalled, then older adults also are more likely to intrude items from one list into the recall of another, although these intrusions are usually rare (i.e., Balota et al., 1999; Watson et al., 2001). Importantly, whereas all 16 comparisons showed an effect in the predicted direction (Y > O) for true recall, about a third of the comparisons showed little or no age-related increase in false recall. Thus, although age-related increases in false recall are well documented, they are not inevitable.

Age differences are even less pronounced in false recognition. Table 8.2 summarizes the results of 21 experimental conditions that compared younger adults (mean age = 20 years) and older adults (72 years) on DRM recognition memory. Again, data are reported from standard conditions, usually with a final recognition test administered after studying several DRM lists (see table note for details). Data are separated for recognition tests that were preceded by recall tests, because, as discussed in Chapter 6, prior recall testing can influence recognition. Consider first the data that

TABLE 8.1   DRM Recall Rates in Healthy Younger (Y) and Older (O) Adults

Experiment	Mean Age		List Words		Related Lures		Other Intrusions	
	Y	O	Y	O	Y	O	Y	O
Balota et al. (1999)[†]	20	77	72	60	29	38	.05	.33
Butler et al. (2004)	19	76	62	53	20	29	.21	.32
Dehon and Brédart (2004, Exp. 1)	23	71	69	51	24	48	.30	.60
Dehon and Brédart (2004, Exp. 2)	23	72	63	40	16	34	.30	.45
Intons-Peterson et al. (1999, Exp. 1)	20	72	56	39	56	52	na	
Intons-Peterson et al. (1999, Exp. 2)	20	74	60	35	55	64	na	
Kensinger and Schacter (1999, Exp 1)	20	67	37	28	38	38	na	
Lövdén (2003)	29	69	55	43	34	46	na	
Norman and Schacter (1997, Exp. 1)	19	68	67	48	38	51	.70	1.27
Norman and Schacter (1997, Exp. 2)	19	67	69	54	34	47	.90	.80
Rybash and Hrubi-Bopp (2000)	20	73	68	54	37	38	na	
Thomas and Sommers (2005, Exp. 1)	20	76	80	65	21	19	na	
Thomas and Sommers (2005, Exp. 2)	20	76	82	62	20	23	na	
Tun et al. (1998, Exp. 1)	20	70	63	53	33	35	.22	.22
Tun et al. (1998, Exp. 2)	19	73	63	47	32	32	.15	.20
Waldie and Kwong See (2003)[†]	21	74	51	45	43	54	.17	.15
Watson et al. (2001)[†]	19	79	60	54	14	31	.09	.23
Watson et al. (2004)	19	73	33	23	41	48	na	
Mean	21	73	62	47	33	40	.31	.46
Effect (O − Y)	+52**		−15**		+7**		+15*	

Notes:[†] means estimated from figure, **$p < .01$; *$p < .05$. "Other intrusions" represents the mean number of extralist intrusions per list (na = not available). Balota et al. and Watson et al. (2001) data are collapsed across young–old and old–old, Butler et al. data are collapsed across frontal groups, Dehon and Bredart data are from Phase 1-unwarned, Intons-Peterson et al. data are collapsed across testing times, Rybash and Hrubi-Bopp data are from control condition, Thomas and Sommers data are from word-only conditions, Watson et al. (2004) data are from Trial 1-unwarned, collapsed across rate.

were unconfounded with prior recall. True recognition of list words was significantly lower in older adults, regardless of whether one considers raw recognition rates (.77 vs. .73) or those that were corrected by subtracting false alarms to unrelated control lures (.63 vs. .58), but these effects were small. False recognition was not significantly different across age groups on either raw data (.68 vs. .71) or adjusted data (.50 vs. .52), with over half of the studies showing little or no difference. False alarms to control lures also did not differ across age groups (see table note). Larger age-related differences in false recognition were found in the data that were confounded with prior recall testing (bottom of Table 8.2), but these differences are probably due to carryover effects from the recall tests. Even in a study by Tun et al. (1998), which is often cited as showing age-related increases in false recognition, significant age differences were not found in all conditions.

In addition to these findings from simple "old"/"new" recognition tests, age differences in measures of illusory recollection also are mixed. Norman and Schacter (1997) found that older adults were more likely to give "remember" judgment to falsely recognized related lures than were younger adults (see Intons-Peterson et al., 1999; Schacter et al., 1999, for similar results), and older adults were more likely to claim to remember how a related lure sounded at study or its position in the list. However, the two groups did not differ (or differed in the opposite prediction) for illusory recollections of reactions, associations, thoughts, or recall of neighboring items from the study phase. Similarly, even though aging impaired source memory accuracy, Gallo and Roediger (2003) failed to find the expected age-related difference (older adults > younger adults) in the overall likelihood to attribute a related lure to one of the studied sources. After adjusting for baseline ratings to unrelated lures, they also failed to find age differences in ratings of illusory recollections of perceptual details, emotional reactions, associations, or trying to remember the related lure during the study phase. In sum, age-related increases in illusory recollection have not been universally obtained, although only a few studies have investigated this issue.

Considered as a whole, these data are consistent with the observation that age-related impairments in memory are more likely to be found in recall tests than in recognition tests (e.g., Craik & McDowd, 1987). Of course, that observation typically refers to true memory, and can be explained by the fact that recognition tests offer better retrieval cues for true memories than do recall tests. The current analysis suggests that recall tests also are more sensitive to aging differences in false memory, compared to recognition tests. This is a somewhat surprising state of affairs, because recognition tests are prone to familiarity-based errors that are thought to be greater in older adults (e.g., Jacoby, 1999; Tun et al., 1998).

TABLE 8.2   DRM Recognition Rates in Healthy Younger (Y) and Older (O) Adults

Experiment	Mean Age		List Words		Related Lures		Adjusted List Wds		Adjusted Rel. Lures	
	Y	O	Y	O	Y	O	Y	O	Y	O
No Prior Recall Testing										
Benjamin (2001)	22	74	83	76	58	61	75	64	50	49
Budson et al. (2000)	19	74	84	73	68	67	81	69	65	63
Budson et al. (2003b)	22	74	83	81	44	67	77	75	38	61
Gallo and Roediger (2003)	21	75	66	62	73	72	42	38	42	41
Gallo et al. (in press)	19	72	75	78	52	48	65	74	36	39
Intons-Peterson et al. (1999, Exp. 1)	20	72	67	66	71	78	57	53	53	55
Intons-Peterson et al. (1999, Exp. 2)	20	74	69	73	78	82	56	54	68	51
Kensinger and Schacter (1999, Exp 2)	19	68	77	70	89	80	60	49	72	59
McCabe and Smith (2002, Exp. 1)	20	71	86	76	78	77	69	60	47	48
McCabe and Smith (2002, Exp. 2)	21	70	86	76	86	83	67	64	65	66
Schacter et al. (1999, Exp. 1)	20	68	79	72	66	72	58	54	38	55
Schacter et al. (1999, Exp. 2)	20	69	79	71	54	76	63	45	30	51
Thomas and Sommers (2005, Exp. 1)	20	76	69	73	61	65	53	48	45	40
Thomas and Sommers (2005, Exp. 2)	20	76	74	77	69	65	52	59	47	47
Mean	20	72	77	73	68	71	63	58	50	52
Effect (O − Y)	+52**		−4*		+3[ns]		−6*		+3[ns]	
Prior Recall Testing										
Balota et al. (1999)	20	77	80	77	58	81	78	71	56	75
Intons-Peterson et al. (1999, Exp. 2)	20	74	84	78	80	89	71	59	70	58
Norman and Schacter (1997, Exp. 1)	19	68	79	73	65	80	71	58	52	59

(Continued)

TABLE 8.2   (*Continued*)

Experiment	Mean Age		List Words		Related Lures		Adjusted List Wds		Adjusted Rel. Lures	
	Y	O	Y	O	Y	O	Y	O	Y	O
Norman and Schacter (1997, Exp. 2)	19	67	74	67	52	67	70	59	44	55
Tun et al. (1998, Exp. 1)	20	70	88	86	85	84	87	83	84	81
Tun et al. (1998, Exp. 2)	19	73	87	86	73	86	86	83	72	83
Waldie and Kwong See (2003)[†]	21	74	90	86	85	92	82	81	77	87
Mean	20	72	83	79	71	83	78	71	65	71
Effect (O − Y)	+52**		−4**		+12**		−7**		+6[ns]	

Notes: [†] means estimated from figure, $**p < .01$, $*p < .05$, ns = not significant. For adjusted data, base rate false alarms to control lures (unrelated to studied lists) were subtracted from list word hits and related lure false alarms (if only one base rate was obtained, this same rate was used for both item types). Across studies, base rate false alarms did not differ between younger and older adults for list word controls (.11 and .13) or related lure controls (.19 and .22), although base rate false alarms were greater for related lures than for list words in each age group (both $ps < .001$, see Chapter 2). Benjamin data are from lists studied once, Budson et al. (2000) and Kensinger and Schacter data are from first trial, Budson et al. (2003b) data are from semantic lists, Gallo and Roediger (2003) are from 15-item lists, Gallo et al. data are from nonstudied lures in the word condition, Intons-Peterson et al. data are collapsed across testing times, McCabe and Smith data are collapsed across rate, Norman and Schacter data are from the standard condition, and Thomas and Sommers (2005) data are from the word-only conditions.

Thus, one might have predicted that age-related differences would be greater in false recognition than in false recall. One potential explanation for the obtained pattern is that the DRM recall task (free responding immediately after each list's presentation) benefits more from the online monitoring of retrieval than does the recognition task (forced responding usually at the conclusion of a considerably longer study phase). This is not to say that attempts to monitor retrieval are less likely on the recognition test, but under typical DRM conditions there might be very little information available for successful recognition monitoring even in younger adults (see Chapter 5). Age-related monitoring impairments might be greater in free recall tests because they require subjects to consciously generate and regulate their own responses immediately after the list's presentation (see Balota et al., 1999; Lövdén, 2003; Sommers & Huff, 2003, for relevant inhibitory theories of false recall and aging).

Frontal Functioning

The previous analysis indicates that age-related increases in DRM false memories are sometimes found, but not always. Two important subject-variables have been identified as critical to these effects. The first variable is frontal lobe functioning. Butler, McDaniel, Dornburg, Price, and Roediger (2004) compared younger and older adults in a typical DRM study/recall procedure. They also administered several tests that are thought to depend heavily on frontal lobe functions (Wisconsin Card Sort, FAS Controlled Word Association, Wechsler Mental Control, Backward Digit Span, and arithmetic), and divided their older adults into high- and low-frontal functioning groups. Not surprisingly, they found that true recall was greater in the high functioning group (.57) than in the low functioning group (.47), whereas false recall was lower in the high functioning group (.23 vs. .35). More interesting was that low-frontal older adults showed the typical age-related increase in false recall compared to high-functioning college students (.35 vs. .20), but high-frontal older adults were not different than younger adults in false recall (.23 vs. .20) or true recall (.57 vs. .62). These data suggest that age-related increases in false recall are not inevitable, but depend critically on whether aging impairs frontally mediated processes within a given individual. Frontal processes have been identified as critical to retrieval monitoring (see Chapters 9 and 10), and these data support the idea that age-related differences in false recall are due to monitoring impairments.

Time of Day

A second subject-variable that is critical to obtaining age effects on false memories is the time of day in which the experiment is conducted. As discussed by Intons-Peterson et al. (1999), aging changes circadian rhythms, with older adults typically performing better on cognitive tasks when tested at optimal times (usually in the morning). Consistent with this idea, in Experiment 1 Intons-Peterson et al. found that nonoptimally tested older adults were more likely to falsely recall related lures than were optimally tested older adults (.66 vs. .38), and this pattern extended to false recognition of both related lures (.86 and .69) and unrelated lures (.30 and .16). These optimality effects also moderated differences in false memory across age groups. When the nonoptimally tested groups were compared, older adults were more likely to falsely recall (.66) and recognize (.86) related lures than were younger adults (.54 and .69). When optimally tested groups were compared, these age-related differences in false recall and recognition were eliminated (Experiment 1) or minimal (Experiment 2).

☐ AGING AND MONITORING MANIPULATIONS

Much of the aging research in the DRM task has focused on whether older adults can reduce false memories via manipulations that encourage recollection-based monitoring. As reviewed in Chapter 5, these manipulations can be divided into those that encourage the use of disqualifying or diagnostic monitoring. Disqualifying monitoring refers to the rejection of false memories due to the recollection of logically inconsistent information ("I did not see this word, because I recall generating it on my own."). Diagnostic monitoring refers to the rejection of false memories based on the failure of these memories to conform to memorability expectations ("I did not see this word, because I do not have a vivid recollection of seeing it on the computer screen."). Comparing results across several tasks in the literature, a general finding is that older adults are impaired in their ability to use disqualifying monitoring processes to reduce source memory errors, potentially owing to reduced recollection of source-specific information, and/or an impaired ability to strategically use this information during the memory decision (e.g., Jacoby, 1999; see Light, Prull, La Voie, & Healy, 2000). Related findings have been observed in the DRM task, as reviewed in the next section. In contrast, older adults seem to be less impaired (if at all) in their use of diagnostic monitoring processes, such as the distinctiveness heuristic.

Exclusion and Warnings

Perhaps the most direct way to investigate a disqualifying recall-to-reject process is to have subjects study the related lure in a list that is different from the study list. At test, if subjects can recall that the related lure was in the nontarget list, and if they know or assume that the lists were mutually exclusive, then they can reject it from having been studied in the study list. As discussed in Chapter 5, Dodhia and Metcalfe (1999) and Smith et al. (2001) found that this sort of procedure reduced false recognition in younger adults. Gallo et al. (in press) used a similar technique to investigate age differences in monitoring. Subjects studied several DRM lists for a subsequent test. Just prior to the test, subjects were warned to avoid false recognition of related lures. To help them avoid false recognition, they were then presented with a "helper" list that contained some of the related lures. Subjects were told that these related lures were not presented in the study phase, and that they should avoid falsely recognizing them on the subsequent recognition test (i.e., they should exclude items from the helper list).

Recognition data for the strongly related lures are presented in Figure 8.2. Younger adults used presentation in the helper list to reduce false recognition. False recognition was greatest for related lures that were never studied (.52); this effect was reduced when related lures were presented in the helper list (.34), and both means were greater than false recognition of unrelated lures that were never presented (.16). In contrast, older adults were unable to use this recall-to-reject strategy to reduce false recognition, with no effect of presentation in the helper list on false recognition of related lures (.48 vs. .49). Pierce, Sullivan, Schacter, and Budson (2005b) reported a similar age-related deficit in this type of source-based exclusion, using false recognition in a categorized list task.

Another way to elicit disqualifying monitoring is to warn subjects about the memory illusion before they study the lists (e.g., Gallo et al., 1997). Warned subjects can determine the related lure for some of the lists during study, and subsequently they can avoid false recognition via a recall-to-reject strategy at test ("I did not hear this word, because I recall that it was the nonstudied lure."). Given their impairments in the use of

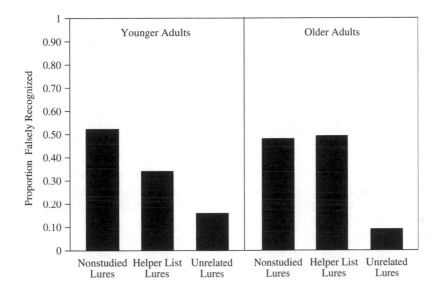

FIGURE 8.2 Impaired use of a disqualifying recall-to-reject strategy in older adults in Gallo et al. (in press). Data are from strong lures, in the condition where only words were presented at study. Nonstudied = nonstudied lures related to studied lists, helper list = lures related to studied lists that were presented in the helper list, unrelated = control lures from nonstudied lists.

other recall-to-reject strategies, as well as potential difficulties "figuring-out" the related lures under the time constraints of the task, older adults should be less successful than younger adults at using study warnings to reduce false recognition.

There is some evidence supporting this prediction, but aging effects in warning studies are mixed. Watson, McDermott, and Balota (2004) had subjects study several DRM lists for a final recall test. Considering only the first study-test trial, and collapsing across study rate, the warning effect on false recall was at least as large in older adults (.23) as it was in younger adults (.14). This finding is inconsistent with the reduced-monitoring hypothesis in aging (see also Rybash & Hrubi-Bopp, 2000). McCabe and Smith (2002) used recognition instead of recall tests. When false recognition was corrected for base rate false alarms, younger and older adults showed similar warning effects in Experiment 1. The data from Experiment 2 were more consistent with a reduced-monitoring hypothesis. Younger adults were more likely than older adults to use warnings to suppress false recognition, but no statistics were reported for this comparison.

One possible reason for these mixed findings is that, without an explicit warning, younger adults are more likely than older adults to spontaneously monitor false memory. Thus, even if younger adults are better at using this type of recall-to-reject strategy, older adults might benefit more from instructions to use such a strategy (relative to an unwarned group) because they are less likely to engage this type of process on their own (cf. Craik, 1986; see Watson et al., 2004). A study by Dehon and Brédart (2004) is consistent with this interpretation. In the first phase of their procedure, subjects studied and recalled several DRM lists, without warnings. As expected, older adults recalled fewer list words but falsely recalled more related lures than younger adults. Results from a post-recall test were more important for present concerns. On this test, subjects were asked to indicate if they had previously thought of a word but decided not to recall it because it was not presented in the study list. Younger adults were twice as likely to indicate that they had previously identified and rejected the related lure (.60) than were older adults (.33). This result suggests that older adults were less likely than younger adults to spontaneously monitor the related lure, without warnings, on free recall tests. Dehon and Brédart replicated this result in a second experiment, and in support of a reduced-monitoring hypothesis they found that warning younger adults before study reduced false recall relative to an unwarned condition (.16 vs. .04), whereas older adults did not benefit from the warning (.34 vs. .39).

As a whole, these studies indicate that aging impairs the use of disqualifying recall-to-reject strategies to reduce false recall and recognition. The clearest data come from exclusion studies, where subjects are explicitly instructed to reject lures that they can recollect from exclusion lists (e.g., Gallo et al., in press; Pierce et al., 2005b). The warning data are more mixed. Although some studies showed the predicted effect in some conditions (greater warning effects in younger adults), these effects were not universally obtained. As discussed, warning studies are more complicated to interpret than exclusion studies, potentially owing to age differences in the spontaneous use of an identify-and-reject strategy in unwarned conditions.

Distinctiveness

In contrast to deficits in disqualifying recall-to-reject processes in older adults, several studies have found that older adults are just as likely as younger adults to use diagnostic monitoring processes (such as the distinctiveness heuristic) to reduce false recognition. Schacter et al. (1999, Experiment 1) presented the first evidence for a distinctiveness heuristic in older adults using the DRM task. Subjects heard several lists at study. In the Word Condition words were simultaneously presented on the computer screen, whereas in the Picture Condition a black and white line drawing that corresponded to the word was presented on the screen. Figure 8.3 presents recognition data from the condition where test words were presented auditorily (note that these younger adult data were discussed in Chapter 5).

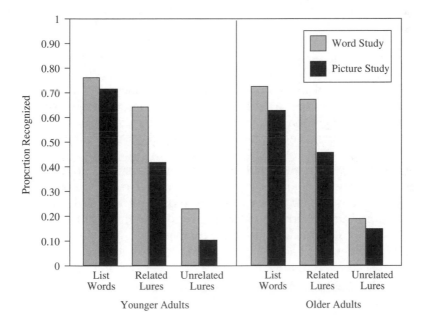

FIGURE 8.3   The distinctiveness heuristic in older adults in Schacter et al. (1999, Experiment 1). False alarms to unrelated lures are collapsed across list word controls and related lure controls.

True recognition of list words was lower in older adults, and study format did not affect true recognition in either group (as is usually the case with this procedure). More importantly, false recognition was reduced in the Picture Condition in both younger and older adults, suggesting that age did not impair the older adults' ability to use the distinctiveness heuristic. Similar effects were found in the condition where pictures were re-presented at test. The finding that older adults can suppress false recognition via a distinctiveness heuristic has been replicated in the DRM task by Budson, Sitarski, Daffner, and Schacter (2002b) and has been demonstrated in other tasks, too (e.g., Dodson & Schacter, 2002a).

One exception to these findings was in the aforementioned study by Gallo et al. (in press), in which younger but not older adults used recollection from an exclusion list to suppress false recognition. In separate conditions, where pictures were presented at study, it was found that only younger adults were able to use a distinctiveness heuristic to suppress false recognition. Given several previous findings that older adults can use the distinctiveness heuristic with these materials, Gallo et al. (in press) proposed that the disqualifying recall-to-reject component of their task had interfered with the use of a distinctiveness heuristic in older adults. Because the test instructions focused subjects on using the helper list to exclude related lures, and because older adults had difficulty with this strategy, it was argued that they were distracted from using a distinctiveness heuristic. Consistent with this argument, Gallo, Cotel, Moore, and Schacter (2006b) found that older adults were just as likely as younger adults to use a distinctiveness heuristic in a source monitoring task that focused retrieval on the to-be-recollected features of words and pictures (i.e., the criterial recollection task). Importantly, this outcome was obtained even in a condition where older adults had used a a disqualifying recall-to-reject strategy to reduce false recognition. Older adults were able to use each type of recollection-based monitoring, as long as the to-be-recollected information was distinctive (i.e., pictures).

Another exception to these findings is that older adults do not show the study modality effect (auditory > visual) on false recall, even under conditions where younger adults show the typical effect (Smith et al., 2005). Smith et al. interpreted this pattern as evidence for impaired distinctive processing in older adults. If this explanation is true, then the sizable study format effect (words > pictures) in older adults might be due to the fact that pictures provide a stronger and more compelling manipulation of distinctiveness, and hence even older adults show the effect. Alternatively, it might be the case that the study modality effect is not caused by the same global distinctiveness heuristic that is thought to cause the picture/word effect (see Chapter 5 for further discussion of this last point).

Emotionality

After studying lists of phonological associates (e.g., "bell", "dell", "fell", etc.), subjects were less likely to false alarm to rhyming words that were emotional (e.g., "hell") compared to those that were neutral (Pesta et al., 2001, see Chapter 5). Even though the two types of lures should have been equally familiar, subjects were better at avoiding false recognition of emotional lures probably by using a diagnostic monitoring process ("I could not have studied 'hell,' because I would remember it if I did."). Kensinger and Corkin (2004) extended these findings to older adults, using both recall and recognition tests. In their first experiment, false recall of neutral and emotional lures was .19 and .07 in younger adults, and .28 and .11 in older adults. Older adults demonstrated greater false recall, overall, but showed a similar reduction in false recall of emotional words (the interaction was not significant). In their second experiment, false recognition of neutral and emotional lures was .75 and .58 in younger adults, and .77 and .57 in older adults (similar results were found on corrected recognition data). Again, younger and older adults showed a similar reduction in false memory of emotional words. Correlational analyses argued against a disqualifying recall-to-reject explanation of these findings, leading the authors instead to propose that subjects had used a distinctiveness heuristic to suppress false memory of the emotional lures. Much like the picture-based distinctiveness heuristic, older adults were able to use emotional distinctiveness to avoid false memories.

Study and Study/Test Repetitions

Benjamin (2001) demonstrated that repeating DRM study lists led to lower levels of false recognition in younger adults, relative to a condition where the lists were only studied once prior to test (.35 vs. .58). As discussed in Chapter 5, these results indicate that some form of recollection-based monitoring became more accurate with study repetitions. In contrast to these effects in younger adults, Benjamin found that repetition increased false recognition relative to the once-presented condition in older adults (.72 and .61), implicating a monitoring deficit with age. It is unclear how study repetitions enhanced monitoring (e.g., by making it easier to "figure-out" the related lure, thereby enhancing an identify-and-reject strategy, or by enhancing the distinctiveness of true recollections and the use of diagnostic monitoring), but the results of a speeded recognition test in younger adults bolstered the idea that monitoring processes at retrieval were critical. On this speeded test, which was thought to minimize monitoring processes, the effect of repetition in younger adults was similar to those found in older adults (under self-paced conditions).

Instead of repeating only the study lists, Kensinger and Schacter (1999) repeated both the study and test phase for several DRM lists. Subjects studied three DRM lists for a final recall test, and this procedure was repeated across five trials on the same set of lists. True and false recall data, across study/test trials, are presented in Figure 8.4. As expected, age impaired true recall of list words across all of the study/test trials, and repeated practice with the lists increased true recall in both groups. False recall followed a different pattern. On the first trial there was no age difference in false recall. Across trials, though, younger adults were able to reduce false recall whereas older adults were not, so that large age differences were obtained on the final trial. This same pattern of results was obtained using a recognition test in a second experiment. As was the case with Benjamin (2001), there are a few possibilities as to how younger adults had used repetitions to reduce memory errors, but some form of recollection-based monitoring likely was involved (see Chapter 5 for a discussion of this task). Older adults were impaired in this monitoring process. Budson et al. (2000) reported similar recognition results. Older

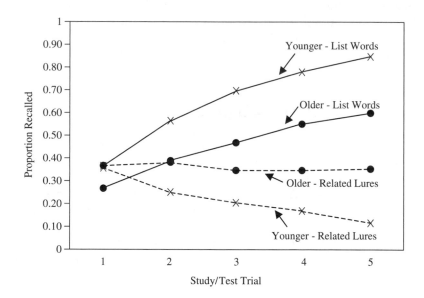

FIGURE 8.4 Effects of study/test repetition on true and false recall in younger and older adults in Kensinger and Schacter (1999, Experiment 1, data approximated from their Figure 1). Noncritical intrusions were rare and so were not reported.

adults were able to reduce false recognition by the fifth trial in that study, but not as much as younger adults. Finally, Watson et al. (2004) replicated Kensinger and Schacter (1999) in false recall, and further showed that older adults were less likely to reduce false recall after repeated study/test trials even when warned against the false memory effect. Thus, these age differences seemed to be due to an inability to monitor memory retrieval, as opposed to a failure to realize that such a strategy would be useful.

Study Rate

Watson et al. (2004) found that slowing study presentation rate (from 1.25 to 2.5 s per item) reduced false recall in older adults (means = .58 and .38, considering only the first unwarned trial). This finding suggests that slower rates encouraged the monitoring of false recall in older adults, and as with study repetitions these rate effects could have operated through diagnostic or disqualifying processes. Surprisingly, the typical effect of rate on false recall was not found in younger adults (.38 and .44). These results represent an exception to the other findings reviewed above, in that there was evidence for successful monitoring in older adults but not in younger adults. As discussed by Watson et al., though, these effects of presentation rate might not be directly comparable across age groups, due to age-related differences in speed of processing. Younger adults already had lower levels of false recall, relative to older adults, even at the fastest rate. McCabe and Smith (2002) also manipulated study presentation rate (2 s vs. 4 s), testing memory with recognition instead of recall tests. Considering their unwarned condition, rate did not affect false recognition in either younger or older adults, probably because recognition is less sensitive to rate effects than recall (see Chapter 5).

Encoding Context

Thomas and Sommers (2005) investigated whether presenting DRM list words in the context of sentences could reduce false recall and recognition in younger and older adults. Presenting each list word within a sentence reduced false recall and recognition in younger adults, relative to a condition where only words were studied. Theoretical interpretation is tricky in this situation, because the sentence manipulation could have reduced false recognition by decreasing associative or gist encoding (at study) or by enhancing diagnostic monitoring (at test). As discussed in Chapter 6, though, sentence presentation probably reduced associative or gist processing at study. More important for present purposes, sentence encoding also reduced false recognition in older adults, but only when the sentences biased the meaning of each list word away from the meaning shared with the related lures. When the sentences biased meaning towards the related lure, only younger adults showed reductions in false memories of related lures. These results might reflect an over-reliance on associative or gist processing in older adults—whereas both types of sentences reduced relational encoding in younger adults, only those sentences that forced subjects to focus on the divergent meaning were effective at reducing relational encoding in older adults.

☐ AGING AND OTHER TASKS

Phonological Associates

Several studies have investigated aging effects on true and false memory of phonologically related materials. Watson et al. (2001) compared aging effects on false recall from phonological, semantic (DRM), and hybrid lists (containing both phonological and semantic associates). Age impaired true recall of list words from all three types of lists, and increased false recall of related lures. In fact, one of the largest false recall effects ever reported in the literature was found with hybrid lists in the oldest group (mean age 86 years)—true recall was around 35%, whereas false recall was greater than 70%! Interestingly, these amazingly high levels of false recall have not extended to false recognition. Using materials from Watson et al., Budson, Sullivan, Daffner, and Schacter (2003b) investigated aging effects on false recognition from semantic, phonological, and hybrid lists. Although there were no age or list differences in true recognition, older adults demonstrated more false recognition than younger adults for all of the lists (mean = .66 and .46), with minimal differences in false recognition across lists (see also Watson et al., 2003). Sommers and Huff (2003) also found age-related increases in false recall and recognition with phonological lists, although the age differences in false recognition were minimal in the condition that was not confounded with prior recall (after correcting for base rate false alarms, see their Experiment 1). Similarly, considering only the neutral lures in Kensinger and Corkin (2004), age increased false recall but the two groups showed the same level of false recognition. Taken as a whole, the results from phonological lists are very similar to those from semantic (DRM) lists. Older adults showed elevated levels of false recall, and sometimes (but not always) showed elevated levels of false recognition.

Similar Pictures

Koutstaal and colleagues developed a similar-pictures (or categorized pictures) task to study gist-based false recognition. In the typical experiment, subjects studied different colored pictures of the same type of object (e.g., several exemplars of teapots). At test, administered a few days later, subjects discriminated these studied exemplars from nonstudied exemplars from the same category (e.g., a new teapot picture from the same set) or from nonstudied categories (e.g., a picture of a teddy bear). The results from Koutstaal and Schacter (1997, Experiment 1) are found in Table 8.3. When only one picture per category was studied, true recognition was lower in older adults than in younger adults (.68 vs. .82). When more than one picture was studied per category, there was no age difference in true recognition (mean = .76 and .78, collapsed across set sizes). This pattern suggests that studying more than one picture per category allowed subjects to encode the gist or theme of the list, and this gist processing boosted recognition performance in the older adults. The false recognition results also indicated that older adults were more likely to rely on the general gist of the studied categories. Overall false recognition was greater in older than in younger adults (mean = .51 and .27), and this difference was greatest for the largest categories (i.e., those that had the strongest gist). Koutstaal and Schacter replicated these results in two other experiments.

Koutstaal, Schacter, Galluccio, and Stofer (1999a) investigated whether subjects could reduce false recognition in the similar-pictures task via encoding or retrieval manipulations. In their first experiment, subjects either took a recognition test with typical "old"/"new" instructions, or they were warned that some test lures were related to studied items, and told to use an additional response option ("old"/"new-related"/"new-unrelated"). Both true and false recognition were reduced with this warning, but, especially in older adults, false recognition was reduced more than true recognition. These findings suggest that the unwarned older

TABLE 8.3   Recognition from the Categorized Picture Task as a Function of Study Set Size in Younger and Older Adults (Koutstaal & Schacter, 1997, Experiment 1)

Group	Studied Pictures				Related Pictures			Unrelated
	1	6	9	18	6	9	18	
Younger	.82	.75	.78	.81	.21	.25	.35	.03
Older	.68	.73	.72	.83	.43	.40	.70	.11

Note: False alarms to unrelated pictures are collapsed across category size.

adults were more likely to rely on gist-based responding than younger adults, so that the warning had a larger effect in older adults (although age-related increases in false recognition were still found in the warning condition). In a second experiment, some subjects were encouraged to focus on distinctive item-specific information during the encoding of each picture (e.g., "Notice the smooth black hair and big gold eyes of this cat."). Much like the retrieval manipulation, providing subjects with this distinctive item-specific information reduced false recognition. Again, the effect was larger in older adults, but age-related increases in false recognition were still found. Providing subjects with more distinctive item-specific information could have reduced false recognition by reducing gist encoding, or by enhancing diagnostic monitoring at retrieval. In a third experiment both the encoding and retrieval manipulations were combined, but an age-related increase in false recognition still was obtained.

Considered as a whole, these studies indicate that when the studied materials are extremely similar (i.e., different pictures of the same object), older adults are more likely than younger adults to rely on the general gist of the category, as opposed to the recollection of item-specific information, in order to make their response. As discussed by Koutstaal et al. (2001a), even when older adults were equated to younger adults on the true recollection of studied details, older adults were less likely to use this information at retrieval than younger adults. Unlike the DRM task, in which age differences in false recognition are minimal (under typical conditions), age differences in this type of gist-based false recognition were more pronounced. It is important to note, though, that a retention interval of at least 3 days was used in all of these studies, whereas the study and test phase of the DRM task are usually administered in the same experimental session. This difference raises the possibility that age-related increases in false recognition are more pronounced after long retention intervals. When the study and test phases were administered in the same experimental session, Lövdén (2003) found that false recognition in the similar-pictures task was very low in both younger and older adults (discussed next).

Cross-Task Comparisons

Lövdén (2003; also see Lövdén & Wahlin, 2005) conducted a very large aging study, comparing groups of individuals aged from 20 to 80 years on three false memory tasks: false recall from DRM lists (e.g., recalling *sleep* after studying *bed, rest,* etc.), false cued recall from categorized word lists (e.g., recalling *robin* after studying *sparrow, blue jay,* etc.; Smith et al., 2000), and false recognition from similar-picture lists (e.g., false recognition of a new teapot picture after studying several different pictures of teapots;

Koutstaal & Schacter, 1997). Considering only the extreme age groups, the DRM task showed the typical pattern: true recall decreased with age (.55 vs. .43) and false recall increased with age (.34 vs. .46). A similar pattern was found in false cued recall from categorized lists, with a marginal decrease in true recall (.57 vs. 51) and a significant increase in false recall (.06 vs. .13). Note that false recall was considerably lower with categorized lists than with DRM lists, consistent with the idea that the stronger associations within DRM lists considerably enhance false recall (see Chapter 3). Finally, true recognition of similar pictures did not differ across age groups (.61 vs. .58), but false recognition was greater in older adults (.07 vs. .19). These results are consistent with Koutstaal and Schacter (1997), although the false recognition effects were much lower in Lövdén (2003), probably because they used immediate tests.

☐ INDIVIDUAL AGING DIFFERENCES

The effects of aging on cognitive abilities are highly variable, with some older adults performing at least as well as younger adults on a variety of tasks, and others performing considerably worse. As discussed in a previous section, Butler et al. (2004) found no age differences in DRM false recall with high-frontal older adults, but found a significant difference with low-frontal older adults. Other types of individual differences on false memories in aging also have been investigated. For instance, McCabe and Smith (2002) found that, in some conditions, false recognition was negatively correlated with a working memory task (Stroop-span) that is thought to be sensitive to frontally mediated processes. This finding is consistent with the idea that frontally mediated processes are involved in false memory monitoring. Sommers and Huff (2003) found a similar pattern of results using phonologically related materials. Across younger and older adults, they found that both false recall and recognition correlated negatively with performance on the Stroop task.

In an extensive correlational study, Lövdén (2003) provided additional evidence that age-related impairments in recollection-based monitoring can cause increased false memories. In that analysis, DRM false recall was correlated with age ($r = +.28$), various measures of processing speed (mean $r = -.24$), various measures of inhibition (mean $r = -.22$), and various measures of true recall or recognition (mean $r = -.22$). Using structural equation modeling, Lövdén concluded that age-related impairments in true recall/recognition were the most direct links to age-related increases in false memory, potentially because true recall/recognition provides a measure of recollection (and hence recollection-based monitoring processes).

As a whole, these studies demonstrate that a variety of measures of cognitive function correlate with false memory creation in younger and older adults, and most of these correlations can be explained by differences in recollection-based monitoring efficacy.

9
CHAPTER

Neuropsychology and Drugs

False memory research in neuropsychological populations and other special populations, as well as drug-induced amnesias, is critical for at least two reasons. First, especially in neuropsychological studies where brain damage is well defined, this research provides insights into the neuronal mechanisms that subserve memory processes. This approach necessarily is constrained, due to the logical limitations of inferring normal mechanisms from abnormal function, but it can provide some of the strongest evidence that a brain structure or region is involved in a certain cognitive function, such as false memory creation or monitoring. Second, delineating how specific types of brain damage or psychological states affect different cognitive processes has practical implications for diagnosis, understanding, and treatment.

This chapter is focused on results from typical DRM task conditions and other tasks (similar pictures, abstract shapes, phonological associates, etc.) that have been used to elicit relatively high levels of false recall and recognition. Most of the neuropsychological research to date has been centered on medial temporal amnesics, frontal lobe patients, and Alzheimer's patients, and these studies are the first to be reviewed below. A few studies have investigated these types of false memories in semantic dementia, schizophrenia, Asperger's syndrome, and alcoholics, and have explored more general brain hemisphere effects, and these are discussed later in the chapter. Finally, studies investigating the influence of various pharmacological agents on false memory will be reviewed.

Based on the general framework that has been discussed throughout this review, two potentially opposing sets of processes can contribute to false memories in neuropsychological populations (and the same logic extends to drug studies). If brain damage causes profound deficits in true memory, as is the case in amnesia, then one might expect that some of the processes giving rise to false memories also would be impaired. If one has difficulty remembering studied events, then one also should be less likely to falsely remember an event that is related to those events. For example, in the DRM task, one might be less likely to falsely recall a related lure that was mentally generated during study, or they might have difficulty recollecting the theme or gist of the list. On the other hand, with many types of brain insult, implicit memory tends to be less affected than recollection. If the processes that can activate the related lure in the DRM task are relatively more automatic than recollection, then a strong memory signal for the related lure might exist even when true memory (and corresponding recollection-based monitoring processes) is impaired. With intact activation processes, but impaired monitoring processes, one could reasonably predict increases in false recall or recognition.

Due to the complexity of the processes involved, several interpretative assumptions are made below (and in the literature, in general). The first is that reduced levels of true recall or recognition—which are often obtained in abnormal populations—reflect impaired recollection. As discussed above, impaired recollection not only could decrease the memory signal for the related lures (thereby decreasing false memories) but also could decrease recollection-based monitoring processes (thereby increasing false memories). Because of this ambiguity, interpretation of the results is often post hoc. If false recall or recognition of related lures is increased in a population (relative to controls), then this is interpreted as monitoring processes being more impaired than activation processes, and vice versa if false recall or recognition is decreased in a population. Interpretation of recognition results is further complicated by the fact that different processes can affect related and unrelated lures. Some diagnostic monitoring processes can selectively affect unrelated lures (e.g., rejecting an unrelated lure because it does not fit the gist of studied items), and some disqualifying monitoring processes can selectively affect related lures (e.g., rejecting a related lure because one recalls identifying it as nonstudied during study). As a result, interpreting the relatedness effect on false recognition (i.e., the difference between related and unrelated false alarms) as a "pure" measure of activation of related lures is problematic. Given all of these considerations, a complete understanding requires the use of experimental manipulations that selectively target specific processes, as well as converging evidence from different memory tasks.

☐ MEDIAL TEMPORAL AMNESIA

Ever since famous case studies such as H.M., it has been well known that damage to the medial temporal lobes (MTL) and structures—including the hippocampus and surrounding areas—results in an impaired ability to consciously recall and recognize subsequently studied information (anterograde amnesia). By comparison, other cognitive abilities (such as language, attention, or even implicit/procedural memory) can be relatively unaffected, suggesting a unique role of MTL structures in the formation and retrieval of new associations that are necessary for recollection (see Eichenbaum & Cohen, 2001, for a theoretical synthesis). As discussed above, such impairments could increase or decrease false memories. Using tasks that do not rely on converging associations to elicit false memories, a few early studies found evidence for increased false recognition in various amnesic groups, consistent with recollection-based monitoring impairments (see Schacter et al., 1996c, for discussion). However, using the DRM task and other converging associates tasks, results from several recent studies indicate that damage to medial temporal regions can reduce false recognition of related lures. These and other findings suggest that MTL damage impairs the memory signal for related lures, ostensibly through the forgetting of overlapping semantic features, gist, or lures that were mentally generated at study. There have been fewer studies investigating false recall in these amnesics, and these results have not been as definitive as the recognition results.

False Recall and Recognition

Schacter et al. (1996c) conducted one of the first studies of amnesia in the typical DRM task, comparing amnesics of various etiologies (e.g., alcoholic Korsakoff's syndrome, anoxia, and encephalitis) to control subjects without clinical memory impairments. As expected, the amnesic group recalled fewer list words than the control group (means = .27 and .52). There were no group differences in false recall of related lures (.29 and .33), but amnesics were significantly less likely than controls to intrude other items that were related to the list, providing some evidence for impaired associative or gist-based processes. In contrast, amnesics were significantly more likely to make cross-list intrusions, demonstrating source monitoring difficulties. Melo et al. (1999) also investigated the effects of MTL amnesia on DRM false recall, and again false recall of related lures was not statistically different in amnesics and controls (although there were only four MTL amnesics). The failure to find a difference in false recall to related lures across groups might reflect a trade-off between an impaired memory signal for the related lures (which would decrease false recall) and impaired monitoring processes (which would increase false recall).

Results from the final recognition test in Schacter et al. (1996c) are reported in Figure 9.1. Both true and false recognition were lower in amnesics than in controls, and these results were obtained regardless of whether or not recognition was confounded with prior recall (and whether or not one corrects for false alarms to unrelated lures). These results are consistent with the idea that amnesia impaired a memory signal for the related lures. Subjective judgments (i.e., "remember"/"know," see Chapter 4) indicated that these deficits in both true and false recognition were accompanied with fewer claims of remembering (or recollection) in the amnesic group (see also Schacter et al., 1997b). In contrast, false alarms to unrelated lures were greater in amnesics, implicating a monitoring impairment. As discussed by Schacter et al. (1996c), decreased levels of gist-based memory in amnesic patients might have made them less able to reject unrelated lures that were inconsistent with the gist of the lists (using present terminology, this would be a type of diagnostic monitoring—"I don't remember studying anything related to this word, so it is probably new").

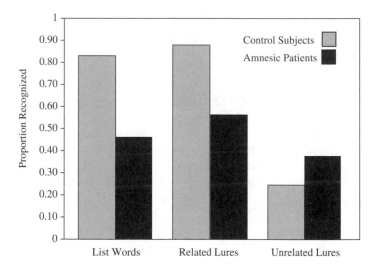

FIGURE 9.1 Effect of amnesia (via medial temporal damage or alcoholic Korsakoff syndrome) on true and false recognition in Schacter et al. (1996c). Data shown are from those lists that were not confounded with prior recall. False alarms to unrelated lures are collapsed across list word controls and related lure controls.

Subsequent studies investigating DRM false recognition effects in MTL amnesics provide converging evidence that gist-based memory is impaired. Several studies have replicated the finding that false recognition of related lures was lower in amnesics than in controls (Schacter et al., 1997b, 1998b), or at least that a smaller relatedness effect on false recognition was observed in amnesics relative to controls (e.g., Melo et al., 1999; Schacter et al., 1997b, 1998b; Verfaellie, Schacter, & Cook, 2002). Verfaellie et al. (2002) directly tested the idea that MTL amnesics have impaired gist-based memory by having subjects study several DRM lists and then take a meaning test, in which subjects must respond positively to any item that appears to be related in meaning to a studied item, regardless of whether the test item itself was studied. Consistent with the reduced-gist hypothesis, amnesics were less likely than controls to judge both list words and related lures to be meaningfully related to studied lists, and were more likely than controls to erroneously judge unrelated items as related to the lists.

In a more recent study, Verfaellie, Page, Orlando, and Schacter (2005) found that MTL amnesics showed intact priming of DRM studied words on an implicit word-stem completion test (see Chapter 3), relative to control subjects, but impaired priming of related lures. This finding further demonstrates a reduced memory signal for related lures in MTL amnesics. Importantly, because the implicit test did not require intentional retrieval (episodic memory), this effect was not attributed to impaired episodic memory (e.g., an inability to recollect the gist). Verfaellie et al. instead argued that MTL amnesics had difficulty extracting the gist during study (i.e., processing the relations between list items), and so there was less gist-based priming at test. It further was argued that these findings could not be easily explained by associative activation, which was assumed to be intact in MTL amnesics. Note, though, that this interpretation presupposes that the retrieval of gist caused priming of related lures at test. This assumption is at odds with studies suggesting that priming of related lures is caused by associative activation (see Chapter 3), in which case impaired priming of related lures in amnesics would implicate reduced associative activation. Under either interpretation, these findings suggest that reduced episodic memory might not be the sole reason for reduced false recognition of related lures in MTL amnesics.

Other Convergence Tasks

Additional evidence that MTL amnesia impairs gist-based processing (at encoding and/or retrieval) comes from false recognition in other tasks. Schacter et al. (1997b) found reduced relatedness effects on false recognition of both semantic (DRM-type) and phonological lists in MTL amnesics, relative to controls. Koutstaal et al. (1999b) found evidence for reduced relatedness effects on false recognition of abstract shapes (i.e., amnesics were less likely to falsely recognize a nonstudied prototype from which all of the studied shapes were derived). Koutstaal, Verfaellie, and Schacter (2001b) found that amnesics were less likely to show relatedness effects on false recognition of pictures of objects that were perceptually similar to studied pictures. Finally, Verfaellie, Rapcsak, Keane, and Alexander (2004) found reduced relatedness effects on false recognition in amnesics using categorized words as stimuli.

Monitoring Manipulations

In the studies reviewed so far, the distinction between alcoholic Korsakoff and non-Korsakoff amnesics has had little difference on overall levels of behavioral performance. However, because of the difference in etiology of brain damage in these populations, more subtle behavioral differences sometimes can emerge (see Koutstaal et al., 1999b; Verfaellie et al., 2002). Schacter et al. (1998b) noted that Korsakoff's patients are characterized by cognitive deficits not seen in non-Korsakoff amnesics, likely due to concurrent frontal lobe damage in the Korsakoff's group. Based on this cognitive profile, they reasoned that Korsakoff's patients would be particularly impaired on the ability to engage in frontally mediated monitoring processes to suppress false recognition. Of course, non-Korsakoff amnesics would be impaired in their ability to use some monitoring processes, due to reduced recollection, but Korsakoff's patients would be even more impaired, potentially because they suffer from both a recollective deficit and a deficit in strategic control.

In order to investigate this issue, Schacter et al. (1998b) compared Korsakoff amnesics, non-Korsakoff amnesics, and control subjects on a repeated study/test task. Subjects studied six DRM lists for a final recognition test, and this cycle was repeated (for the same lists) across five study/test trials. As discussed in Chapter 5, after repeated study/test cycles, healthy subjects have been found to increase true recognition of list words and decrease false recognition of related lures, due to the enhancement of some form of recollection-based monitoring (although the exact type of monitoring is unclear). Consistent with these other results, both groups of control subjects in Schacter et al. increased true recognition and decreased false recognition after repeated study/test cycles. Also consistent with prior results, collapsing across the study/test trials, both amnesic groups demonstrated lower levels of true recognition and higher levels of false recognition of unrelated lures relative to controls. However, the two amnesic groups were affected differently by the study/test repetitions. The

Korsakoff's amnesics showed large increases in false recognition across study/test trials, both before and after correction for false alarms to unrelated lures, demonstrating an inability to use monitoring processes to counter the increase in lure activation across the trials. In contrast, false recognition of related lures in the non-Korsakoff's amnesics was not affected reliably by study/test trials. Unlike the Korsakoff's patients, these patients apparently were able to use monitoring processes to counter increases in activation of the related lures across trials, although they still were not as effective at such monitoring as the control subjects.

In sum, medial temporal damage impairs true recall and recognition of studied items. False recall of related lures has not been found to differ in these groups, but only two relevant studies (using immediate tests) have been reported. Several studies have found reduced false recognition of related lures in amnesics. These reductions implicate a reduced memory signal for related lures, most likely owing to reduced memory for overlapping features or the gist of the study lists, although impaired associative activation and/or memory for activated lures also might be involved in the DRM task. These reduced levels of false recognition persisted even though false recognition of unrelated lures tended to increase with this type of brain damage, due to impaired recollection-based monitoring processes.

☐ FRONTAL LESIONS

By many accounts, the frontal lobes play a critical role in the strategies involved in the encoding and retrieval of information, working with medial temporal systems that may be involved in the actual storage (or binding) of information into memory traces (e.g., Moscovitch, 1995). A striking memory deficit that can result from frontal damage, particularly in ventralmedial prefrontal cortex, is confabulation. Patients who confabulate not only make memory errors (e.g., misremembering when or where they did something), but they also generate fanciful stories to explain inconsistencies in their memory without awareness of the improbability of these events (e.g., Burgess & Shallice, 1996). Not all frontal patients confabulate, but the existence of the phenomenon implicates a critical role for the prefrontal lobes in the strategic monitoring of memory retrieval (a point that is bolstered by the neuroimaging data in Chapter 10). Damage to prefrontal regions can impair retrieval monitoring processes, and thus leave frontal patients more prone to false recall and recognition. Consistent with these ideas, case studies of patients with frontal lesions have documented increased false recognition for a variety of materials relative to controls (e.g., Parkin, Bindschaedler, Harsent, & Metzler, 1996; Schacter et al., 1996a).

False Recall and Recognition

Using the typical DRM task, Melo et al. (1999) compared two groups of frontal patients to two groups of control subjects (medial temporal patients also were tested, as discussed in the previous section). Six patients had lesions restricted to the frontal lobes, and did not show signs of confabulation or severe true memory deficits (non-amnesic frontal patients). The other group of frontal patients had damage to both frontal regions (likely spanning ventralmedial prefrontal cortex) and medial temporal regions, with three of the four patients classified as confabulators (amnesic frontal patients). On immediate free recall, Melo et al. found that the non-amnesic frontal patients recalled as many list words as controls (.41 vs. .47), whereas the amnesic frontal patients recalled significantly fewer list words than controls (.24 vs. .52). False recall of related lures also differed across groups. Consistent with the idea that frontal damage impairs monitoring processes, the non-amnesic frontal patients falsely recalled more related lures than controls (.46 vs. .31). In contrast, the amnesic frontal patients recalled fewer related lures than controls (.19 vs. .41), suggesting that additional damage to MTL regions impaired the memory signal for the related lure (as in MTL amnesics). Neither of these effects was significant relative to controls (potentially because of small sample sizes), but the very large difference in false recall of related lures between the two groups of frontal patients was significant. Noncritical recall intrusions did not differ across the groups.

Results from the final recognition test, presented in Figure 9.2, were consistent with these interpretations. As expected, both groups of frontal patients tended to make more false alarms to unrelated lures, relative to controls, and these effects were largest in the amnesic frontal group. This pattern suggests that monitoring processes were impaired in both groups of frontal patients, especially in the patients with more widespread damage. The amnesic frontal patients were less likely to recognize both list words and related lures than were controls, consistent with the MTL damage in this group (these effects were significant on corrected recognition scores). The frontal patients without MTL damage showed a different pattern. True recognition was not significantly different from that of controls, but false recognition of related lures was significantly greater than that in controls, again suggesting a monitoring deficit (because both related and unrelated false alarms were greater in patients; the relatedness effect on false recognition was not significantly different between patients and controls). For other demonstrations of elevated DRM false recognition in patients with focal frontal lesions, see Budson et al. (2002c) and Umeda, Akine, and Kato (2001).

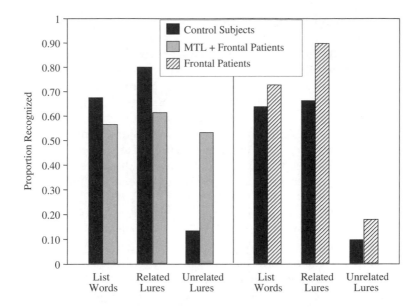

FIGURE 9.2   The effects of frontal lobe damage on true and false recall in Melo et al. (1999). MTL + frontal patients are those with damage to both medial temporal regions and frontal regions. Frontal patients had damage restricted to the frontal lobes. False alarms to unrelated lures are collapsed across list word controls and related lure controls.

Verfaellie et al. (2004) also found evidence for enhanced false recognition in frontal patients, using categorized words as materials. However, not all frontal patients differed in memory performance relative to controls, ostensibly because the location and extent of damage can vary widely across patients and can cause considerable variability in performance. A case study reported by Belleville, Caza, and Peretz (2003) nicely illustrates this basic point. Due to a ruptured aneurysm and subsequent surgery, patient I.R. suffered large frontal lesions, including precentral and inferior frontal regions, as well as lesions in the left superior temporal gyrus and other areas (but not including MTL structures). Despite relatively normal intellectual functioning and recognition memory, I.R. exhibited a selective deficit in the processing of phonological information. Consistent with this cognitive profile, Belleville et al. found that I.R. showed unusually high levels of false recognition of lures related to lists of phonological associates, relative to controls, whereas false recognition of related lures from semantic lists was more similar to that of controls.

Monitoring Manipulations

Budson et al. (2002c) compared frontal patients and controls in a repeated DRM study/recognition test analogous to that used with MTL amnesics by Schacter et al. (1998b). The frontal patients were selected because they all had damage including dorsolateral prefrontal cortex (near BA 9/46), a region that has been implicated in retrieval monitoring processes (see Chapter 10). On the first study/test trial, patients and controls had similar levels of true recognition of list words, and the patients had significantly greater false recognition of related lures. Of greater interest here was the finding that control subjects reduced false recognition across the study/test trials (from .65 in Trial 1 to .41 in Trial 5), but frontal patients did not (.83 to .76). As was the case with the MTL amnesics in Schacter et al., this pattern suggests that frontal patients were less likely to use recollection-based monitoring processes to reduce false recognition across the trials. Using a similar group of patients, Budson, Dodson, Daffner, and Schacter (2005) have shown that frontal patients were less likely than controls to reduce false recognition following the study of pictures (relative to words). The authors took this as evidence for an impaired distinctiveness heuristic in the frontal patients (i.e., a diagnostic decision process), although the task that they used (repetition lag) also had a strong recall-to-reject component (i.e., a disqualifying decision process), so that impairment in either of these recollection-based monitoring processes could have yielded the obtained pattern of results.

In sum, selective damage to prefrontal cortex does not necessarily impair true recall or recognition, but it does seem to increase false recall and recognition. In the study that investigated DRM false recall, frontal patients (without MTL damage) were more likely to falsely recall related lures than were controls, although the effect was not statistically significant. Several studies have demonstrated significantly higher levels of false recognition in frontal patients than in controls. These effects have been found for both related and unrelated lures, suggesting a general retrieval monitoring deficit in patients. Unlike MTL patients, frontal patients show similar relatedness effects on false recognition (related false alarms minus unrelated false alarms) as do controls, suggesting that frontal damage did not impair the processing of the associations or themes of the lists.

☐ ALZHEIMER'S DISEASE

Alzheimer's disease is the most common type of dementia. Onset typically occurs in old age, and is characterized by an initial loss of episodic memory (mostly anterograde amnesia), followed by other cognitive functions such as language, attention, and working memory as the disease progresses (see Hodges, 2000, for an overview). These cognitive declines are linked to damage in the hippocampus and inferior temporal systems during the early stages of the disease, and eventually the frontal lobes and other cortical areas. Based on this etiology, one might expect that patients in the early stages of the disease would show reduced levels of false recall and recognition, much like medial temporal amnesics. That is, damage to this memory system would impair the ability to recall a related lure that was generated at study, and/or impair the ability to retrieve the features or gist of a list, resulting in a weaker memory signal for related lures (of course, these impairments also could arise at encoding). On the other hand, impaired frontally mediated processes, such as retrieval monitoring, might increase the likelihood of Alzheimer's patients to make memory errors, much like frontal lobe patients. These competing influences, as well as differences in disease severity across studies, make it difficult for definitive predictions in memory performance. In general, for both semantically related materials (DRM lists) and for other converging associates tasks, false recall and recognition of related lures tend to be unaffected or reduced in Alzheimer's disease.

Unless otherwise noted, all studies reviewed here tested patients that were clinically diagnosed with probable Alzheimer's disease using standardized criteria (McKhann, Drachman, Folstein, Katzman, Price, & Stadlan, 1984). These methods generally involve a clinical interview, neurological exam, and a variety of cognitive tests (especially recall and recognition). All participants were screened for depression and other cognitive disorders that otherwise might have affected performance, and control subjects were matched on age, and usually on other dimensions as well (e.g., gender or years of education).

False Recall

At least four studies have investigated the effects of Alzheimer's disease on false recall in the DRM task. Balota et al. (1999) compared healthy controls to two groups of patients, differing in their severity of disease (very mild and mild). Collapsing across the two healthy older adult groups, true recall (approximately .60) was greater than that for very mild patients (.46) and mild patients (.31). There were no significant differences across groups in false recall of related lures (.38 across groups). In contrast, the patients were more likely than controls to make noncritical intrusions, and most of this difference was driven by greater source confusions from one list to the next (i.e., impaired source monitoring; for similar results see

Sommers & Huff, 2003; Waldie & Kwong See, 2003). As in MTL amnesics, the null effect on related lures might reflect a trade-off between impaired activation and monitoring processes.

Using a similar patient population, Watson et al. (2001) replicated these patterns of true and false recall with semantic lists (DRM). True recall was lower in Alzheimer's patients than in controls, and false recall was roughly the same (comparing the two control groups to the two patient populations). Interestingly, if one compares the two groups of patients, there was a large drop in DRM false recall as severity of the disease progressed from very mild (approximately .42) to mild (.18), although no statistics were reported on this comparison. A smaller decrease in this direction also can be seen in the results of Balota et al. (1999). Such decreases in false recall might reflect impaired associative and/or gist-based processes in patients in the advanced stages of Alzheimer's disease. Waldie and Kwong See (2003) found even larger decreases in DRM false recall in Alzheimer's patients relative to controls. In their study, patients had profound deficits in true recall relative to controls (approximate means = .45 and .10) and also showed extremely reduced false recall of related lures (.58 and .05). Because these researchers used different criteria for diagnosis of probable Alzheimer's disease than Balota et al. and Watson et al., direct comparisons across studies are difficult. However, given the very large deficits in true recall in the patients of Waldie and Kwong See, it is reasonable to conclude that their patients were more severely affected by the disease than in these other studies, and hence were more likely to show decreases in false recall of related lures.

False Recognition

As expected, true recognition of studied words usually is impaired in Alzheimer's disease (relative to age-matched controls). Findings for false recognition of related lures are more complicated. Sometimes false recognition for related lures is the same for patients and controls, but because patients are almost always more likely to falsely recognize unrelated lures (i.e., they have higher base rate false alarms), the relatedness effect on false recognition (i.e., related false alarms minus unrelated false alarms) is usually lower in patients. Budson et al. (2000) reported relevant results. Subjects studied several DRM lists for a final recognition test. On the first study/recognition trial, true recognition was lower in patients (.66) than in controls (.73). False recognition of related lures was equivalent across these groups (.69 and .67), but, because false alarms to unrelated lures were greater in patients (.28 and .04), adjusted false recognition of related lures was 22% lower in patients. Budson and colleagues have replicated these patterns in Alzheimer's patients several times, considering only the typical DRM conditions of each study (e.g., Budson et al. 2002b, 2002c, 2003b; see also Balota et al., 1999 and Waldie & Kwong See, 2003, although recognition was confounded with prior recall in these last two studies). In fact, even uncorrected false recognition of related lures was lower in patients in some of these conditions (see Budson et al., 2002b, 2002c). Whereas the greater levels of false recognition of unrelated lures in Alzheimer's disease are often attributed to monitoring deficits, reduced false recognition of related lures indicates impaired memory for associations and/or the gist of the lists.

Other Convergence Tasks

Like MTL amnesics, there are several explanations for reduced relatedness effects on false memory in Alzheimer's patients. They could be less likely to spontaneously use relational processing at encoding, and so less likely to engage in associative processes or to extract the gist of the lists. Further, due to episodic memory deficits, they would be less likely to recall thoughts of the related lure (from study), or to remember the features or gist of the study lists. Semantic memory deficits in Alzheimer's disease also must be considered. Semantic memory impairments would reduce the relatedness effect on false memory, independent of episodic memory impairments, due to the semantic nature of the DRM illusion (i.e., using meaningfully related associates). Some have questioned the claim that Alzheimer's disease impairs semantic processes, based on evidence from implicit tests such as semantic priming (e.g., Balota & Duchek, 1991), but evidence from more explicit tests such as the generation of category exemplars indicates that the online processing of meaning and semantic memory can be impaired by Alzheimer's disease (see Nebes, 1989, for review). If Alzheimer's patients have difficulty explicitly processing the shared meanings and associations of DRM lists, then one would expect that a memory signal for related lures also would be reduced. A critical question, then, is the degree to which the effects of Alzheimer's disease on false memory are due to the use of semantically related materials.

If Alzheimer's patients were less likely to spontaneously use relational processes during study, in general, or if episodic memory impairments were the critical factor, then one would expect that they would show reduced relatedness effects on false memory for materials that do not rely on semantic associations (e.g., phonological lures, perceptually similar objects, etc.). In contrast, if semantic memory problems were critical, then one would not predict reduced false memory effects for nonsemantic materials relative to controls (or at least there would be a smaller reduction).

The results from nonsemantic tasks support the idea that Alzheimer's patients are impaired in their ability to extract and/or remember the features or gist of the studied lists, regardless of whether the content is semantic or not. Budson et al. (2001) compared Alzheimer's patients and controls on memory for categories of abstract shapes that were generated by deviations in a prototype (e.g., Koutstaal et al., 1999b). After correcting for unrelated false alarms, true recognition of list words and false recognition of related lures both were impaired in the patients, consistent with recognition results from the DRM task. Budson, Michalska, Sullivan, Rentz, Daffner, and Schacter (2003a) found a similar Alzheimer's-related impairment in true and false recognition (corrected for unrelated false alarms) using the similar-pictures task (Koutstaal & Schacter, 1997). Thus, at least for abstract shapes and pictures of similar objects, it appears that memory for the similarities between studied items (or gist) is impaired in Alzheimer's patients, leading to reduced relatedness effects on false recognition.

Lists of phonological associates also have been used to investigate false memory in Alzheimer's patients. In Watson et al. (2001), true recall from phonological lists was impaired in patients relative to controls, but false recall of related lures was similar or even slightly greater in patients. Sommers and Huff (2003) also investigated the effects of Alzheimer's disease on phonological false recall, using subjects drawn from the same population as Watson et al. Sommers and Huff found that the patients were impaired in true recall relative to controls, but were more likely to falsely recall phonological associates (means = .41 for controls, .49 for very mild patients, and .61 for mild patients). Thus, unlike the false recall results from the DRM task, false recall from phonological lists tended to be greater in Alzheimer's patients in these studies. Reasons for this discrepancy in false recall are unclear, but recognition results for phonological lists tended to be similar to those for DRM lists. Budson et al. (2003b) found reduced false recognition of both phonological lures and DRM lures in Alzheimer's patients, relative to controls, after false alarms to unrelated lures were taken into account. These results are consistent with a reduced gist-based processing account. The recognition results from Sommers and Huff were more ambiguous, potentially because they were confounded with prior recall. For very mild patients, false recognition of phonological lures was slightly greater than controls, but for mild patients false recognition was the same as controls, or even slightly lower if one corrects for unrelated false alarms.

Monitoring Manipulations

Although Alzheimer's patients show smaller relatedness effects on false recognition than controls, they can show considerably greater levels of false recognition of related lures in those situations that allow control subjects to monitor retrieval. For instance, in the aforementioned study by Budson et al. (2000), healthy older adults reduced false recognition of related lures after repeated study/test trials. As discussed, a reduction in false recognition with repeated trials indicates that some form of recollection-based monitoring was enhanced. In contrast, false recognition to related lures increased across study/test trials in patients, indicating impaired monitoring processes. Note that, as in Schacter et al. (1998b) and Budson et al. (2002c), these increases may have reflected source confusion from having seen the related lures on prior tests. Budson et al. (2002c) avoided this possibility by repeating only the study phase before a final recognition test (as in Benjamin, 2001). Repetitions reduced false recognition to related lures in control subjects, demonstrating the use of some type of recollection-based monitoring process (e.g., repeated study made memories of list words more distinctive and/or made it easier to "figure-out" the related lures). In contrast, like Budson et al. (2000), repetitions increased false recognition in the patients. These results cannot be attributed to source confusions from prior tests, but instead implicate other types of recollection-based monitoring deficits.

A few studies have targeted specific recollection-based monitoring processes in Alzheimer's disease. Pierce et al. (2005b) compared younger adults, healthy older adults, and Alzheimer's patients on a variant of a categorized list task that has been used to demonstrate an exclusion-based recall-to-reject strategy (e.g., Smith et al., 2001, see Chapter 5). After studying several categorized lists, younger adults reduced false recognition of a nonstudied category exemplar by recalling that it earlier had been presented in an exclusion list. In contrast, in the condition where recollection should have been the greatest (i.e., to-be-excluded lures were deeply processed in the exclusion list), healthy older adults were less likely to suppress false recognition of these lures than were younger adults, and the patients were even more impaired than the healthy older adults. In fact, the patients were more likely to falsely recognize the related lures if they had been presented in the exclusion list than if they had not, suggesting that presentation in the exclusion list simply increased the familiarity or source confusions for these lures, without enhancing a recall-to-reject strategy. Alzheimer's-related impairments in the use of a recall-to-reject strategy also have been found in other types of exclusion tasks (see Gallo, Sullivan, Daffner, Schacter, & Budson, 2004a).

Turning to diagnostic monitoring processes, Budson et al. (2002b) found that Alzheimer's patients were impaired in their ability to use the distinctiveness heuristic to reduce false recognition. Using methods similar to Schacter et al. (1999), subjects studied several DRM lists for a final recognition test. Half the subjects studied only words, whereas the other half studied a picture corresponding to each word. At test, half of the items were presented auditorily, and the other half were presented auditorily and visually (i.e., a visual word in the word condition or a picture in the picture condition). Data from those items that were auditorily presented at test are presented in Figure 9.3. As expected, the patients were less likely to recognize list words than control subjects. Also as expected, the patients were less likely to falsely recognize related lures and were more likely to falsely recognize unrelated lures. More important for present concerns, the control subjects reduced false recognition of related lures following the study of pictures, whereas the patients did not, suggesting that their use of the distinctiveness heuristic was impaired. Impaired use of the distinctiveness heuristic in Alzheimer's patients has subsequently been replicated in other false memory tasks (e.g., Budson et al., 2005; Gallo, Chen, Wiseman, Schacter, & Budson, 2006a).

In sum, in addition to true memory deficits, Alzheimer's patients show equivalent or reduced levels of false recall in the DRM task, relative to controls. They also show reduced relatedness effects on false recognition in the DRM task and other tasks, much like MTL amnesics. These findings suggest

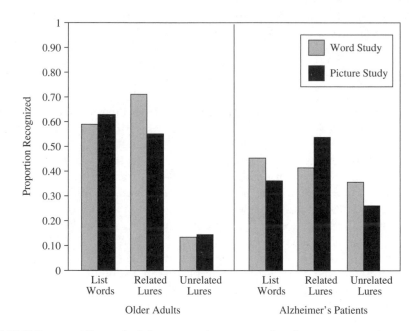

FIGURE 9.3 Effect of Alzheimer's disease on the distinctiveness heuristic in Budson et al. (2002b). Data are from those items that were tested auditorily. False alarms to unrelated lures are collapsed across list word controls and related lure controls.

that Alzheimer's disease impairs memory for the features or gist of a list due to problems with episodic encoding and retrieval and potentially reduces associative processing (at least in the DRM task). In contrast, false alarms to unrelated lures are usually greater in Alzheimer's patients, indicating monitoring deficiencies. With respect to these monitoring problems, both disqualifying monitoring (exclusion-based recall-to-reject) and diagnostic monitoring (the distinctiveness heuristic) can be impaired in Alzheimer's disease, further demonstrating the severe memory problems associated with this disease.

☐ SEMANTIC DEMENTIA

Although deficits in semantic memory are not necessary to explain false recognition effects in Alzheimer's disease, such deficits are central in patients with semantic dementia. This type of dementia typically is caused by focal atrophy of anterolateral temporal regions, resulting in severely impaired semantic memory (e.g., factual knowledge, concepts, vocabulary, object identification, etc.) while leaving episodic memory for nonverbal or abstract materials relatively spared (see Hodges, 2000, for an overview). Given this profile, one might expect that these patients would have difficulty processing the associations or gist in a DRM list, but not necessarily in a list of perceptually related objects or shapes.

Simons et al. (2005) investigated this issue in two experiments, testing patients with a neurological diagnosis of semantic dementia and controls. The first experiment used the similar-pictures task developed by Koutstaal and Schacter (1997), in which lists containing different pictures of the same object (e.g., teapots, cars, etc.) were studied for a final recognition test. Because all of the pictures in this experiment referred to real objects, it was predicted that patients would have difficulty processing the conceptual similarity (or gist) of the lists. Consistent with this idea, both true recognition of studied pictures and false recognition of related lures were lower in patients than in controls. By comparison, false recognition of lures that were only related to one studied item, or that were unrelated to studied items, did not differ across groups (and tended to be greater in the patients). The second experiment used an abstract shapes task in which lists containing perceptually similar shapes to a nonstudied prototype were studied for a final recognition test (e.g., Koutstaal et al., 1999b). Because these abstract shapes had no pre-existing conceptual referents, they did not involve semantic memory. False recognition of these perceptually related lures was not significantly different across the groups, and a direct comparison across experiments revealed a significantly larger deficit in false recognition for conceptually related materials than for perceptually related materials. Thus, unlike Alzheimer's patients, semantic dementia patients showed a selective deficit in gist-based processing of semantically related materials.

□ SCHIZOPHRENIA

A handful of studies have investigated false recognition in schizophrenia. One of the most common symptoms of schizophrenia is a distorted sense of reality (e.g., delusions, hallucinations, and/or paranoia), but episodic memory deficits also have been documented (e.g., lower recall and recognition, and greater source memory errors; see Aleman, Hijman, de Haan, & Kahn, 1999, for review). In comparison to the other neurological disorders discussed above, the causes of schizophrenia are not well known, potentially due to a combination of neurochemical and structural abnormalities in the brain. With respect to those brain systems that are particularly critical for memory function, both frontal and medial temporal regions can be affected (see Antonova, Sharma, Morris, & Kumari, 2004, for review of brain imaging data). In the studies reviewed below, all patients were clinically diagnosed using established criteria (DSM-IV; American Psychiatric Association, 1994), and in most cases patients were taking psychoactive medications for their symptoms. Age-matched controls were used for all comparisons, but note that controls were not matched with subjects on psychoactive medications, and this factor could have influenced group differences.

Elvevåg, Fisher, Weickert, Weinberger, and Goldberg (2004) investigated the influences of schizophrenia on DRM false recall and recognition. On the recall test, patients recalled significantly fewer list words and related lures than controls. Noncritical intrusions did not differ across groups. Similarly, on the recognition test, patients recognized significantly fewer list words and related lures than controls, with little difference in false recognition of unrelated lures. Huron and Danion (2002) also found that patients were less likely to recognize list words and related lures than controls, and further found that these differences were accompanied with fewer "remember" judgments. In contrast to these two studies, Moritz, Woodward, Cuttler, Whitman, and Watson (2004) found that schizophrenics were impaired in true recognition of list words, but found no differences between groups on false recognition of related or unrelated lures. It is unclear why Moritz et al. failed to replicate the reduced false memory effects found in other studies.

These results suggest that schizophrenia can impair the recollection of associations or gist of the lists, perhaps due to reduced attention at encoding (as suggested by Moritz et al., 2004). Unlike other populations reviewed here, though, there was little evidence in these studies for impaired retrieval monitoring in schizophrenia (i.e., noncritical intrusions and unrelated false alarms were not increased by schizophrenia). Few studies have investigated different types of recollection-based monitoring processes in schizophrenia, but using the repetition-lag task, Weiss, Dodson, Goff, Schacter, and Heckers (2002) found some evidence that schizophrenia impaired source memory (i.e., patients were less likely to use a recall-to-reject strategy to suppress false alarms to repeated lures) but did not impair the use of a distinctiveness heuristic (i.e., lower false recognition following picture study than word study).

☐ ASPERGER'S SYNDROME

Asperger's syndrome is thought by some to be a developmental disorder like autism, characterized by abnormal social interactions and communication skills. Unlike other forms of autism, adults with Asperger's syndrome have normal language and intellectual abilities (e.g., Volkmar et al., 1996). Adults with Asperger's syndrome do not typically have profound memory problems, and indeed, sometimes retain unusually large amounts of specialized information of personal interest (e.g., train schedules). However, some deficits in episodic memory have been reported, such as an increased tendency to make intrusions on a cued recall test (e.g., Gardiner, Bowler, & Grice, 2003). In the two studies discussed next, Asperger's syndrome was diagnosed in adults primarily through clinical interview and personal histories of development.

Bowler, Gardiner, Grice, and Saavalainen (2000) investigated the influence of Asperger's syndrome on DRM false recall and recognition. In their first experiment, adults with Asperger's syndrome were significantly impaired in their recall of list words, relative to controls. False recall of related lures was the same in the Asperger's group (.18) and the control group (.23), but noncritical intrusions were significantly greater in the Asperger's group. In the second experiment, recognition performance was not significantly different across groups, but the Asperger's group showed numerically lower levels of both true and false recognition. Using immediate recognition tests after each DRM list, Beversdorf et al. (2000) found that adults with autism spectrum disorder were significantly less likely to falsely recognize related lures relative to control subjects, with no difference in true recognition. False alarms to unrelated lures were numerically greater in the autistic group, but no statistics were reported. Overall, these results suggest that high functioning adults with autistic symptoms might be impaired in their ability to process the gist or associations of semantically related lists, although more extensive work is needed to draw any firm conclusions.

□ ALCOHOLICS

Harbluk and Weingartner (1997) investigated DRM performance in a group of detoxified alcoholics (mean age = 40 years). Alcoholics were detoxified for a minimum of 3 weeks, met clinical criteria for alcohol dependence, and were otherwise medically healthy. Subjects studied several lists for immediate free recall, followed by a final recognition test. Alcoholics recalled significantly fewer list words than controls (means = .59 and .68). False recall of related lures was the same across the two groups (.46 and .48), but noncritical recall intrusions were significantly greater in the alcoholics (.57) than in the controls (.19), with the majority of these intrusions being from other lists. There were no significant differences on the final recognition tests (which was confounded with prior recall). These results indicate that alcoholics had impaired true recollection, and correspondingly, impaired source memory (as evident from greater cross-list intrusions).

□ DRUG-INDUCED AMNESIA

A few studies have investigated the influence of drug-induced amnesic states on the DRM false memory effect. Because healthy subjects serve as their own controls in these experiments, drug studies complement studies of brain-damaged populations by helping to isolate the effects of amnesia, per se, from other confounding factors that are inherent to patient/control comparisons (e.g., subject-specific compensatory strategies). The most heavily investigated agents have been benzodiazepines, such as diazepam (Valium), triazolam (Halcion), and lorazepam. These drugs are sedatives, and are commonly used to treat anxiety and sleep disorders. They act by facilitating inhibitory neurotransmitters (GABA) at receptor sites throughout the cortex, especially in limbic structures that are critical to episodic memory (e.g., the hippocampus). Studies have demonstrated that benzodiazepines can impair episodic memory and induce transient amnesic states (see Mintzer & Griffiths, 2000, for discussion), and of interest here is how these drugs affect memory distortion. A few studies also have investigated the effects of alcohol in the DRM task. However, these studies have yielded null results (Milani & Curran, 2000; Mintzer & Griffiths, 2001b) or alcohol-related increases in false recognition that are difficult to interpret due to prior recall testing (Milani & Curran, 2000), and so are not discussed further.

Mintzer and Griffiths (2000) investigated the effects of triazolam on DRM false recognition. Subjects completed three testing sessions (administered on separate days), during which one of two doses of triazolam (.125 mg/70 kg or .25 mg/70 kg) or placebo was administered via pill. During each session, several lists were studied 1.5 hr after drug administration (during peak drug effects), and a final recognition test was administered 1 hr after the study phase. As a check of the effectiveness of the drug, it was found that the drug produced significant effects on participant-rated measures of the drugged state (e.g., sleepiness, lightheadedness) and also on various psychomotor/cognitive tasks.

Recognition data from Mintzer and Griffiths (2000) are presented in Figure 9.4. Triazolam caused significant reductions in true recognition of list words and false recognition of related lures, relative to placebo. Further, false recognition of unrelated lures was significantly greater in

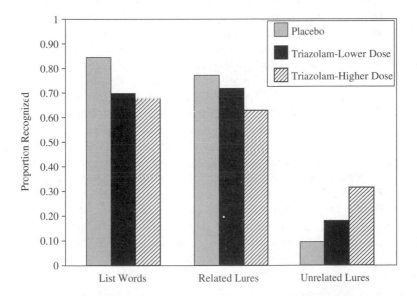

FIGURE 9.4   Effect of a benzodiazepine sedative (triazolam, administered before encoding) on true and false recognition in Mintzer and Griffiths (2000). False alarms to unrelated lures are collapsed across list word controls and related lure controls.

the triazolam groups than in the placebo group. A similar pattern of results was observed in "remember" judgments (on both absolute scores and proportions of overall recognition rates). Huron et al. (2001) failed to find effects of benzodiazepines (diazepam and lorazepam) on DRM false recognition, but given that Mintzer and Griffiths (2001c) replicated the effects of the original Mintzer and Griffiths study, the Huron et al. results were probably due to insufficient power. Using procedures similar to Mintzer and Griffiths (2000), Mintzer and Griffiths (2001a) found that scopolamine (a drug that inhibits acetylcholine and causes memory impairments) also reduced true and false recognition. Considering only the strongest dose, scopolamine decreased true recognition (.85 and .67) and false recognition (.61 and .41) relative to placebo, and similar effects were found in "remember" judgments (although only for raw scores). False recognition of unrelated lures was enhanced in the drug condition relative to placebo (.05 and .16, collapsing across control lures), but this effect was not significant.

Mintzer and Griffiths (2001c) further explored the influence of triazolam on memory performance. In their first experiment, subjects studied several DRM lists for final recognition test. The critical difference between this experiment and that of Mintzer and Griffiths (2000) was that some lists were presented once during study, whereas others were presented twice. In the once-presented condition, false recognition of related lures was lower in the drug condition (.53) than in the placebo condition (.65), and this difference was greater when differences in false alarms to unrelated lures (drug > placebo) were taken into consideration (this pattern was replicated in a second experiment). These findings replicate the effects of Mintzer and Griffiths (2000), providing additional evidence that the drug impaired a memory signal for the related lure. Consider next the effects of repetition on false recognition. As discussed in Chapter 5, repeating list words at study can decrease false recognition (e.g., Benjamin, 2001), owing to some type of recollection-based monitoring process. This outcome was replicated in the placebo condition of Mintzer and Griffiths (2001c). Whereas true recognition increased with repetitions (.87 and .95), false recognition of related lures decreased (.65 and .54). True recognition also increased with repetition in the drug condition (.72 and .91), but, in contrast to the control condition, false recognition increased with repetitions (.53 and .65). This last finding suggests that triazolam impaired recollection-based monitoring processes (much like the effects of speeded responding or aging in Benjamin, 2001).

As discussed by Mintzer and Griffiths (2000), many of these drug effects resemble the effects of organic amnesias on memory performance. The overall effect of the drugs in these studies was to reduce false recognition of related lures, by impairing the encoding of semantic features, associations, or gist. (Retrieval difficulties could have been involved in some of the studies, too, if the effect of the drug had not worn off by the time of test.) In addition, the drugs often led to enhanced false recognition of unrelated lures, owing to impaired recollection-based monitoring processes. The repetition effects reported by Mintzer and Griffiths (2001c) bolstered the idea that these sorts of drugs can impair both activation and monitoring processes.

Neuroimaging and Localization

Whereas the cognitive revolution of the mid-1900s gave rise to information processing accounts of memory, the recent advance of neuroimaging technologies has spurned a new revolution—the mapping of cognitive processes onto patterns of neural activity. This chapter reviews research aimed at measuring brain activity during true and false memory in converging associates tasks. Some exciting and intriguing findings have been made with these tasks, and many of them complement the findings from brain-damaged populations that were reviewed in the previous chapter (see Schacter & Slotnick, 2004, for additional review). However, it is important to keep in mind that the neuroimaging enterprise is still relatively young. New data acquisition and analyses methods are continually being developed, and the large number of technical assumptions force one to tread carefully. The interpretation of neuroimaging results depends heavily on an understanding of neuroanatomy and function, and, equally important, on an understanding of the information processing that occurs during the cognitive task.

Studies using EEG (electroencephalography), PET (positron emission tomography), and fMRI (functional magnetic resonance imaging) are reviewed separately below. EEG measures the electrical activity of the brain using electrodes placed on the scalp. As applied to a cognitive task, the resulting event-related potentials (ERPs) are characterized by excellent temporal resolution (on the order of milliseconds) but poor spatial resolution (typically offering only broad regions from which a signal may have originated). PET and fMRI measures are sensitive to blood flow (directly or indirectly, respectively), which is thought to reflect neural activity within nearby brain tissue. These techniques achieve greater spatial resolution than ERPs (on the order of millimeters), but relatively poor temporal resolution (on the order of seconds for the fMRI studies reviewed here, although these techniques continue to be refined).

Most neuroimaging studies of memory use recognition instead of recall tests. Recognition tests are preferred because they allow more experimental control over factors such as the time-locking of test stimuli to image acquisitions, the exact specification of the type and number of test items, and simplified responding (i.e., a button press). The experimental logic in these studies is similar to that used in purely behavioral studies. The neural signal that corresponds to one sort of response (e.g., falsely recognizing a related lure) is compared to that corresponding to another sort of response (e.g., correctly rejecting an unrelated lure). The resulting difference in brain activity reflects those processes that differ between the two responses (e.g., enhanced familiarity of the related lure, making an "old" vs. a "new" decision, etc.). The interpretation of these data hinges on assumptions about the underlying cognitive processes, as well as the assumption that the mapping between neural signals and cognitive processes does not interact with different response types. However, similar assumptions also apply to the interpretation of behavioral data (e.g., subtracting the false alarm rate to unrelated lures from that to related lures, as a measure of the effects of relatedness on familiarity-based responding), and in many cases the logic of the interpretation is straightforward.

Most of the studies reviewed below used some variant of the DRM recognition task, and were primarily aimed at comparing brain activity for true and false recognition. Typically, subjects intentionally studied several lists, blocked by theme, and then took a final "old"/"new" recognition test, in which list words, related lures, and unrelated lures were randomly mixed. Relevant findings from other converging associates tasks (e.g., categorized word or picture lists) also are discussed. These studies are less frequent, but the main findings are consistent with those from the DRM task. For organizational purposes, the ERP studies are divided into those emphasizing similarities between true and false recognition and those emphasizing differences, whereas the PET and fMRI studies are arranged more chronologically (reflecting methodological advances with each new study).

☐ ERP FINDINGS

True and False Memory Similarities

Düzel et al. (1997) was one of the first ERP studies of DRM false memories and reported several effects that are relevant to subsequent research.

Subjects visually studied several lists, and EEGs were recorded while subjects completed a recognition test (with "remember"/"know" judgments). Four related lures were chosen for each list, so that the targets, related lures, and unrelated lures were equated for length and word frequency. Recognition results followed a reasonable pattern. True recognition (.63) was greater than false recognition of related lures (.50), which in turn was greater than false recognition of unrelated lures (.21). "Remember" judgments followed a similar pattern, whereas "know" judgments were similar for list words and related lures. Response latencies to the initial old/new decision did not differ significantly across item types.

The main results of this experiment were that "remember" and "know" judgments elicited different patterns of activity, but these patterns mostly were similar for list words and related lures, relative to correct rejections of unrelated lures. List words and related lures both elicited a posterior waveform positivity for "remember" and "know" judgments within the 300–600 ms time window (post-stimulus onset). The authors suggested that these effects might reflect a modulation of the N400 effect that has been observed under conditions of repetition or semantic priming. Others have argued that a more frontocentral positivity in this same time window can reflect familiarity of the test stimulus (the so-called FN400, see Curran, 2000), but the effects reported by Düzel et al. (1997) were most evident from posterior recording sites.

Other similarities between true and false recognition were found in later time windows. In the 600–1000 ms window, for both list words and related lures, "remember" judgments elicited a left lateralized temporoparietal positivity, whereas "know" judgments tended to elicit a frontocentral negativity (again, relative to unrelated lures). Of particular interest was the left-lateralized temporoparietal effect for "remember" judgments. This effect is analogous to a parietal "old"/"new" effect observed in other ERP studies, and is thought to correlate with the retrieval of subjectively detailed information, potentially via MTL activity or cortical-hippocampal interactions (for review see Rugg & Allan, 2000). Finally, in the latest window (1300–1900 ms), both "remember" and "know" judgments elicited a frontal positivity for list words and related lures (mostly on the left). Similar effects have been observed in other ERP studies of source memory tasks, and are thought to reflect post-retrieval monitoring or decision processes (see Johnson, Kounios, & Nolde, 1996; Wilding, 1999). Overall, these results suggest that the subjective state of recollection (corresponding to "remember" judgments) and familiarity (corresponding to "know" judgments) elicited different ERP patterns, but these patterns mostly were similar for list words and related lures.

Johnson et al. (1997) also found that ERPs were very similar for true recognition of list words and false recognition of related lures in the DRM task. In fact, in the condition where different types of items were mixed at test, as in Düzel et al. (1997), Johnson et al. reported no ERP differences between list words and related lures (with waveforms that were more positive-going than those for rejections of unrelated lures, across a broad range of time windows and recording sites). However, when test items were blocked (i.e., 12 list words were tested, followed by 12 related lures, etc.), there was greater positivity for list words than related lures across a variety of sites. The reason for this difference between blocked and mixed tests is unclear, given that behavioral performance was the same, but these differences are important to keep in mind when reviewing the PET and fMRI studies.

Curran et al. (2001) subsequently conducted a more powerful study, reporting ERP data in a typical DRM task (with a mixed test) from a large number of subjects (n = 46). These subjects were divided into those with "good" and those with "poor" discrimination between list words and related lures. For Good subjects, true recognition (.70) was greater than false recognition of related lures (.49) and unrelated lures (.20), whereas for Poor subjects, true recognition (.56) was equal to false recognition of related lures (.57), which was greater than false recognition of unrelated lures (.26). Response latencies also differed across groups. For Good subjects, true recognition of list words was significantly faster than false recognition of related lures, suggesting that these subjects had engaged additional monitoring processes to decide whether a related lure had been studied. For Poor subjects, there were no differences in response latencies across item types, suggesting that these subjects may have relied only on gist-based similarity to make their decisions.

Results focused on a comparison of Good and Poor subjects, with three ERP effects of special interest. The first was the FN400 that was predicted to correlate with familiarity-based responding. This effect was not observed in either group of subjects. The second was the left-parietal positivity, occurring within a 400–800 ms window, observed for both list words and related lures (relative to unrelated lures) in Düzel et al. (1997). This effect was replicated in Curran et al. (2001), and was similar for both list words and related lures in the Good group. The effect also was present in the Poor group, but was (unexpectedly) larger for list words than for related lures. Finally, the two groups of subjects differed in terms of a late (1000–1500 ms) frontal old/new effect. For Good subjects, right-frontal ERPs were more positive for true recognition of list words and false recognition of related lures relative to correct rejections of unrelated lures. This effect replicates a similar frontal pattern observed in Düzel et al. (although on the left), and suggests that Good subjects had engaged in additional monitoring or decision processes when responding to list words and related lures. These effects were not observed in Poor subjects, suggesting that they were less likely to engage in such monitoring processes, as might be expected from their behavioral performance.

True and False Memory Differences

Fabiani et al. (2000) had subjects visually study several DRM lists, followed by a mixed recognition test. The critical manipulation was that, at study, words from a given list were presented either to the right or to the left of a fixation cross, while subjects' eyes remained fixated at the center. In this way, study words were preferentially processed by one of the brain hemispheres (at least initially), so that ERPs for these words at test might show laterality effects (test words were presented centrally). Of particular interest was whether related lures would elicit these same laterality effects, even though they were never studied. The behavioral results were comparable to prior studies, with true recognition of list words (.73) about the same as false recognition of related lures (.71), which was greater than false recognition of unrelated lures (.20). Response latencies were similar for list words and related lures, except for those lists presented to the left hemifield (i.e., those processed first by the right hemisphere), from which true recognition was faster.

As expected, there was lateralized brain activity for true recognition of list words, which occurred at central and posterior sites within 210–700 ms of test stimulus onset. This pattern is represented in the top half of Figure 10.1, which presents activity for recognized list words at a left-hemisphere site (T5) and a right-hemisphere site (T6), as a function of whether the corresponding list word was presented to the right or left hemifields at study. Remember that test words were presented centrally, so that these laterality effects ostensibly were due to memory for the side of presentation at study. Systematic laterality effects were not found for falsely recognized related lures (bottom half of the figure), indicating that only studied words revealed this type of memory or sensory signature. Some differences also were obtained between true and false recognition in the P300 (a posterior positivity occurring within 300–700 ms), an effect that was of more central concern in the study reviewed next.

Miller, Baratta, Wynveen, and Rosenfeld (2001) investigated the P300 effect in the DRM task. This effect often is found in "oddball" paradigms, in which an infrequent event (e.g., a target, or oddball) occurs within the context of more probable events (e.g., distracters). In each experiment, subjects visually studied several DRM-type lists (rating each word for pleasantness). ERPs were recorded during the final recognition test, which contained 50 list words, 50 related lures, and 233 unrelated lures, all equated on length and word frequency. The greater number of unrelated lures at test was aimed at

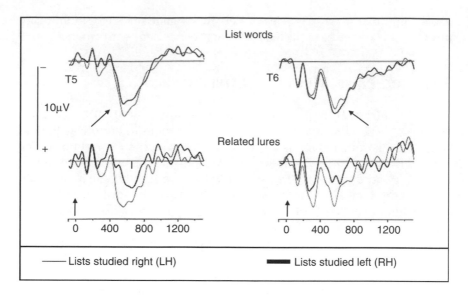

FIGURE 10.1 Grand average ERP waveforms from two posterior sites in Fabiani et al. (2000). Results for true recognition of list words (top panel) and false recognition of related lures (bottom panel) are presented separately for items corresponding to lists presented to the right hemifield (light line), and hence processed first by the left hemisphere (LH), and those presented to the left hemifield (dark line). T5 = left, T6 = right. (Reproduced from Fabiani et al. (2000), *Journal of Cognitive Neuroscience*, with permission from MIT press.)

eliciting an oddball effect for the list words and related lures. Behavioral results were comparable to prior studies using visual presentation (and more weakly related lures), with list word recognition (.89) greater than false recognition of related lures (.51), which in turn was greater than false recognition of unrelated lures (.15). Because subjects were prompted to make their recognition decisions (via button press) 2 s after the test word had been on the computer screen, response latencies were the same for all item types.

Like other studies, true recognition of list words and false recognition of related lures elicited very similar ERP activity. Analyses were focused on the P300 effect from a central–posterior recording site. Both list words and related lures demonstrated a significant P300 effect, of comparable amplitudes and topographies, relative to correctly rejected unrelated lures. However, the P300 peaked much earlier and was shorter for related lures than for list words, demonstrating a reliable ERP difference between false recognition of related lures and true recognition of list words. The reason for this difference is not known, and the authors suggested that it might reflect subjective differences in the recollected details that accompany true and false recognition. The authors also noted that shorter P300 latencies have been found to occur for semantically primed words, relative to unprimed words, and such a priming effect for related lures might have played some role in the effect observed here. In a related study, Merritt and DeLosh (2003) also found differences in the P300 between true and false recognition. They further found larger P300 amplitudes at test in a visual study condition, relative to an auditory study condition, and also larger late-frontal amplitudes. These effects may have corresponded to enhanced recollection-based monitoring processes following visual study conditions (see the study modality effect, reviewed in Chapter 5).

The final ERP study reviewed in this section was aimed at shedding some light on the conditions in which activity is similar or different for true and false recognition. Nessler, Mecklinger, and Penney (2001) compared ERPs to true and false recognition from categorized lists instead of DRM lists. Subjects auditorily studied several five-word categories, with words blocked by category and preceded by a category label, for a final visual recognition test. This test contained all of the studied words, an equal number of nonstudied exemplars from studied categories, and unrelated lures from nonstudied categories. As is typical for categorized materials, true recognition (.78) was greater than false recognition of related lures (.26), which in turn was greater than false recognition of unrelated lures (.05). Response latencies also differed, with true recognition of list words and correct rejections of unrelated lures being faster than false recognition of related lures.

As was the case in ERP studies of the DRM task, true recognition of list words and false recognition of related lures yielded very similar activity relative to correctly rejected unrelated lures. Both list words and related lures yielded an early (300–500 ms) frontomedial positivity, reminiscent of the FN400 effect that is thought to reflect familiarity. Both types of items also elicited the parietal old/new effect (500–700 ms) that was obtained by both Düzel et al. (1997) and Curran et al. (2001), but this effect was smaller for related lures than list words in the Nessler et al. (2001) study (perhaps because the false recognition effect was weaker). Finally, list words and related lures both elicited a late (1200–1600 ms) right-frontal positivity, potentially reflecting additional monitoring for these items (as in Curran et al., 2001 and Düzel et al., 1997). Nessler and Mecklinger (2003) replicated many of these effects, using similar materials but shorter study lists and minimal delays between study and test.

In a second experiment, Nessler et al. (2001) tested the idea that similarities in ERP waveforms for true and false recognition reflected the use of categorical information to make a recognition decision (e.g., the recollection of the gist of a list, which could drive true and false recognition). The task was similar to that used in their first experiment, except words were mixed across categories at study. One group of subjects organized the words into categories, whereas the other group simply decided whether each word referred to a living entity (thereby discouraging categorical organization). Behavioral results indicated that focusing subjects on categorical organization made them more likely to correctly and confidently reject unrelated lures at test, suggesting that they were more likely to base their recognition decisions on categorical information (although this was not reflected in a group difference in false recognition of related lures). The ERP results were consistent with the idea that category or gist-based processing at test can drive similarities between true and false memory. ERPs for true recognition of list words and false recognition of related lures were more similar for those subjects who had categorized words at study (and ostensibly were more likely to use categorical information at test) than for those subjects who had not focused on categorical organization.

Encoding Effects

Whereas all of the aforementioned studies compared true and false recognition at the time of retrieval, Urbach, Windmann, Payne, and Kutas (2005) provided an encoding analysis. In two separate experiments, ERPs were recorded while subjects studied several DRM lists for a subsequent recognition memory test (although there were methodological differences between the experiments, the overall pattern of results was the same). Only waveforms elicited during the encoding of subsequently recognized list words were analyzed. The critical result was that waveforms from list words that subsequently led to false recognition of related lures were less positive-going than waveforms from list words that subsequently led to correct rejections. These differences emerged around 500 ms after stimulus onset and lasted for the duration of the recording epoch (around 1300 ms), and were found from several recording sites. Based on prior research, the authors argued that this activity difference might have represented the quality of the encoding of the list words. Those list words that elicited more positive-going waveforms may have been encoded more thoroughly (i.e., more item-specific features were encoded). If true, then this deeper or more elaborate encoding might have promoted more distinctive recollections at test, thereby facilitating recollection-based monitoring processes that reduced false recognition.

ERP Summary

In regard to similarities between true and false recognition, two ERP effects have been found across studies. The first is a parietal old/new effect (a positivity, often left lateralized, roughly occurring between 400 and 900 ms after stimulus onset). This effect has been linked to recollection, potentially originating from cortico–hippocampal interactions. Curran et al. (2001) and Düzel et al. (1997) reported this type of effect in the DRM task, and Nessler et al. (2001) and Nessler and Mecklinger (2003) observed the effect in the categorized list task. Goldmann et al. (2003) reported an analogous effect for true and false recognition in a similar-pictures task (e.g., Koutstaal et al., 2001b), in which subjects falsely recognized a lure picture (e.g., a dog) after studying pictures of other variants from the same category (i.e., other dogs). Thus, the parietal old/new effect for both true and false recognition appears to generalize across materials and conditions, suggesting that both true and false recognition are accompanied with some type of recollection.

The second ERP similarity between true and false recognition is a late right-frontal positivity (e.g., Curran et al., 2001; Düzel et al., 1997; Johnson et al., 1997; Nessler et al., 2001; see also Summerfield & Mangels, 2005) often thought to reflect monitoring or decision processes. The excellent temporal resolution of ERPs is useful in interpreting this effect, because one would expect that monitoring or decision processes would occur relatively late in a response, as the subject monitors the products of retrieval and/or searches for more relevant information. A third ERP similarity, the old/new "familiarity" effect (around 400 ms, and usually frontocentrally located), has been observed for true and false recognition in some experiments (e.g., Nessler et al., 2001), but not in others (e.g., Curran et al., 2001).

Differences between true and false recognition also have been found in several studies (e.g., Fabiani et al., 2000; Johnson et al., 1997; Merritt & DeLosh, 2003; Miller et al., 2001; Summerfield & Mangels, 2005). These differences potentially reflect qualitative differences in the types of retrieved information for list words and related lures, as in the case of the laterality effects observed by Fabiani et al. (2000). However, due to the poor spatial resolution of ERP effects, the interpretation of more widespread differences is subject to speculation.

☐ PET AND fMRI FINDINGS

Schacter et al. (1996b) conducted the first neuroimaging study of the DRM task. This study used PET, so that different test items were presented in different recording blocks (i.e., test items were not mixed). Subjects auditorily studied several lists for a final visual recognition test, during which PET scans were acquired. Typical behavioral results were obtained. True recognition of list words (.68) was marginally greater than false recognition of related lures (.58), which in turn was greater than false recognition of unrelated lures (.33 for both list word and related lure controls). Response latencies were not reported.

Similar brain activity was observed when responding to list words and related lures. First, relative to a baseline condition (viewing a fixation cross), list words and related lures elicited activity in left medial temporal lobes (near parahippocampal gyrus). This pattern was not observed when responding to unrelated lures, suggesting that MTL activation for list words and related lures may have reflected some form of recollection. Increased activity for each item type also was in a few other regions, including bilateral occipital cortex, ostensibly reflecting enhanced visual stimulation from word presentation, and anterior prefrontal regions, ostensibly reflecting monitoring or decision making processes. More interesting was that list words were more likely to elicit activity in sever- al regions of auditory cortex (e.g., superior temporal gyrus, temporal plan, and supramarginal gyrus), relative to the other items. Prior PET studies suggested that activity in these regions corresponds to auditory or phonological processing (e.g., Petersen, Fox, Posner, Mintun, & Raichle, 1989), leading Schacter et al. to interpret their findings as greater recollec- tion of auditory details for list words than for related lures. This interpre- tation also meshes well with subsequent studies that have demonstrated that regions of auditory cortex can be reactivated when recollecting audi- tory information (e.g., Wheeler, Petersen, & Buckner, 2000).

These early findings anticipated many subsequent findings, but sever- al caveats apply. First, direct contrasts between list words or related lures and their relative control lures did not reveal significant activity in MTL regions, so that a memory-related interpretation of the MTL activations (relative to fixation) is questionable. Second, the PET study required the blocking of test items and the averaging of activity for all items regardless of the subject's response. As discussed in the Johnson et al. (1997) study, ERP waveforms for true and false recognition were found to differ in a blocked-test design but not in the more typical mixed-test design. Blocked designs are not ideal, because grouping test items by type might influence response strategy or other response characteristics.

Schacter et al. (1997a) conducted an fMRI study of the DRM task, test- ing items with both blocked and mixed designs. This study was one of the first event-related fMRI studies of episodic memory, meaning that the neural signal for different types of items (and subject responses) could be separately estimated in the mixed condition. Subjects auditorily studied several lists for a series of final visual recognition tests. In the blocked con- dition, list words or related lures were tested in blocks of six items at a time, whereas these items were intermixed in the mixed condition. Unrelated lures were not tested in the fMRI experiment, although they were included in a pilot experiment to ensure that the standard DRM behavioral effects could be replicated (they were). In the fMRI experiment, during blocked trials, true recognition of list words (.73) was significantly greater than false recognition of related lures (.54). A similar pattern was observed in the mixed trials, but true recognition (.77) was not significantly different than false recognition (.67). Response latencies did not differ between these four types of responses.

In both the blocked and mixed designs, several regions were active for both true and false recognition relative to the baseline (viewing a fixation cross). Active regions included medial and lateral parietal cortex, bilateral anterior prefrontal cortex, hippocampal/parahippocampal regions, and visual cortex. Unfortunately, because unrelated lures were not included, it is unclear which of these effects were memory-specific. A direct contrast between true and false recognition revealed few differences in activation for the two types of responses, indicating that true and false recognition elicited very similar patterns of activity (and failing to replicate the differences obtained by Schacter et al., 1996b). The only reliable difference between true and false recognition was that related lures in the blocked condition elicited more activation in a right anterior prefrontal area than did list words. This difference might indicate that in the blocked condition subjects were more likely to monitor false recognition responses, which would be consistent with the behavioral data (greater discrimination between list words and related lures in this condition) and also with the conclusions of Johnson et al. (1997). Critically, for both list words and related lures, activity in anterior prefrontal regions peaked relatively later than that observed in more posterior regions (see Figure 10.2, top). The time-course of activity in these anterior prefrontal regions is reminiscent of the late-frontal ERP effects that have been observed for both true and false recognition, and this activity likewise was thought to be due to relatively late monitoring or decision processes. The bottom of Figure 10.2 illustrates that activity in this region was similar for list words and related lures in the mixed design, suggesting that these items were equally likely to elicit retrieval monitoring when the test was mixed.

Building on these prior studies, Cabeza, Rao, Wagner, Mayer, and Schacter (2001) conducted a more powerful event-related fMRI experiment. The experiment consisted of six study/test sessions, with subjects studying several lists in each session (half the lists were DRM lists, whereas half were categorized lists, but all analyses were collapsed across this variable). At study, subjects watched a videotape of two speakers reading the words, and were instructed to remember who said each word, in an effort to elicit more detailed recollections than would result from simply listening to the words (as in prior studies). They then took a final visual recognition test, containing a list word and a related lure from each study list, as well as unrelated lures. Typical DRM behavioral effects were

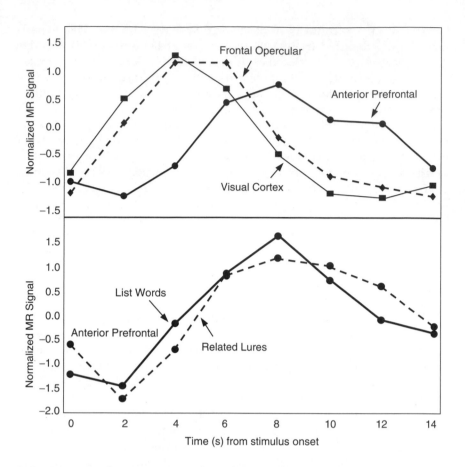

FIGURE 10.2   fMRI activations from the mixed-test conditions of Schacter et al. (1997a). Top: Time course of activity in three brain regions, in the same axial plane, averaging across list words and related lures (and response). Bottom: Activity within anterior prefrontal regions only (left peak Talairach coordinates = −28, 56, 12, right = −37, 50, 9; near Brodmann's area [BA] 10), separated for list words and related lures. (Reprinted with permission from Elsevier.)

obtained, with true recognition (.88) only marginally greater than false recognition of related lures (.80), which in turn was greater than false recognition of unrelated lures (.12). Response latencies also differed, with latencies corresponding to list words (1419 ms) being significantly faster than those to related lures (1576 ms), which were faster than those to unrelated lures (1709 ms).

The main neuroimaging results included a region-of-interest analysis in medial temporal regions. The results of this analysis are presented in

Figure 10.3. The left panel of the figure shows an equivalent activation of anterior hippocampus for both list words and related lures, relative to unrelated lures. It was argued that this activity may have reflected the retrieval of semantic information that could support both true and false recognition. In contrast, a region in posterior MTL near left parahippocampal gyrus (right panel) was more active for list words than either related lures or unrelated lures (which showed similar activity). It was argued that this pattern might have reflected the retrieval of more detailed sensory or contextual information for list words than for related or unrelated lures. Concerning other regions, a whole-brain analysis revealed that several regions were active for both list words and related lures, relative to unrelated lures, including bilateral parietal cortex (near Brodmann's area [BA] 40) which tended to be greater for list words than related lures on the left. This parietal old/new effect is often observed in fMRI studies of recognition memory, and

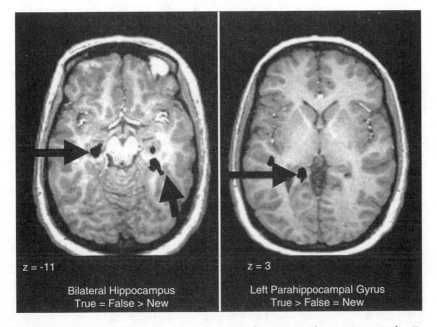

z = -11

Bilateral Hippocampus
True = False > New

z = 3

Left Parahippocampal Gyrus
True > False = New

FIGURE 10.3 fMRI activations from Cabeza et al. (2001). Left: True recognition of list words and false recognition of related lures both elicited more activity in bilateral hippocampus compared to the correct rejection of unrelated (new) lures. Right: True recognition of list words elicited more activity in left parahippocampal gyrus compared to false recognition of related lures or correct rejection of new lures. (Reproduced from *Proceedings of the National Academy of Sciences* with permission. Copyright 2001, National Academy of Sciences, USA.)

may correspond to the left-parietal ERP effect that also has been observed for both true and false recognition. Bilateral dorsolateral prefrontal cortex (e.g., near BA 46) also was active for both true recognition of list words and false recognition of related lures, and like the effects reported by Schacter et al. (1996b, 1997a), this activity may have reflected monitoring processes. By comparison, activity in more ventrolateral PFC regions was greater for unrelated lures than for the other items, indicating that not all prefrontal regions were more active for list words and related lures.

The final fMRI study reviewed here investigated a potential sensory signal that could differentiate true and false recognition. Slotnick and Schacter (2004) conducted an event-related fMRI study to compare true and false recognition of perceptually related abstract shapes (i.e., shapes generated by alterations of a prototype, analogous to Posner & Keele, 1968, 1970). In each of three study/test blocks, subjects visually studied several lists, with items from a given list either presented to the right or left of fixation. The test contained two studied items, two perceptually related lures (nonstudied exemplars derived from the same prototype), and two perceptually unrelated lures, all presented at the center of fixation. Subjects made old-left, old-right, or new judgments, and then rated their confidence for the judgment. Behavioral results followed a typical pattern, with true recognition of list items (.64) greater than false recognition of related lures (.56), which in turn was greater than false recognition of unrelated lures (.26). Subjects were better than chance at identifying the side of the screen that a list item had been presented (.74), and related lures were similarly attributed to the side of the screen that their list had been presented (.73). Response latencies were equivalent across items.

Like prior work in the DRM task, many common regions were active for both true recognition of list items and false recognition of related lures (relative to correct rejections of unrelated lures). Within some of these regions, though, direct comparisons between true and false recognition revealed differences in the magnitude of activation. Regions that were more active for true than false recognition included several parietal regions (e.g., left BA 40), replicating a similar difference obtained by Cabeza et al. (2001), as well as several prefrontal regions (e.g., left BA 10, right BA 46). However, reverse contrasts revealed a similar parietal activation (left BA 40) and other prefrontal activations (right BA 10, left BA 45) that were greater for false than for true recognition. Thus, at a general level, both true and false recognition elicited parietal and prefrontal activations, but more precise differences within subregions of these areas may have unknown functional significance. The hippocampus was found to be active for both true and false recognition, relative to the correct rejection of unrelated lures.

Of more central interest was that visual processing regions (e.g., BA 17, 18, 19, and 37, including striate, lingual gyrus, occipital gyrus, and fusiform) showed activity for both true and false recognition, relative to unrelated lures. Further, early visual processing regions (e.g., BA 17, 18) showed greater activity for true than for false recognition, but later regions (e.g., BA 19, 37) did not. This difference led the authors to hypothesize that the early visual regions may be sensitive to sensory differences that can differentiate true from false recognition, whereas the late visual processing regions might contribute to conscious recognition (true or false). Further, they proposed that early visual activity might have been due either to the recollection of more detailed information for list items, or instead to a nonconscious form of priming that would be greater for items that had actually been studied earlier. In support of the latter hypothesis, activity in the early visual regions was found to be the same for list items regardless of performance (hit or miss), and also regardless of confidence (high-confident misses or low-confidence misses), suggesting that these regions were sensitive to nonconscious memory that did not influence performance, whereas activity in late visual regions tracked behavioral performance (hit activity > miss activity), suggesting that these regions subserved conscious retrieval. This pattern was replicated in a follow-up experiment.

PET and fMRI Summary

As was the case with the ERP studies, a major finding from the PET and fMRI studies was that true and false recognition elicited very similar patterns of neural activity, in both the DRM task and in a perceptually similar shapes task. Three similarities were prominent. (1) Medial temporal regions (including hippocampus) were active to some extent for both true and false recognition in all of the studies reviewed here (Cabeza et al., 2001; Schacter et al., 1996b, 1997a; Slotnick & Schacter, 2004). These activations likely reflected the recollection of information pertaining to the study episode, such as the gist or theme of the list or corresponding associations that could support both true and false recognition. (2) Prefrontal activations also were found for both true and false recognition in all of the studies reviewed here. Of particular interest was activity in right dorsolateral PFC, which was active relatively late in the trial (Schacter et al., 1997b), and had a pattern of activation that could be dissociated from other activations in PFC (Cabeza et al., 2001; see also Umeda et al., 2005). Given the relatively late activity profile, as well as analogous findings in the ERP studies, these regions may underlie monitoring and decision making processes. (3) Several of the studies also showed lateral parietal activity for both true and false recognition (Cabeza et al., 2001; Schacter et al., 1997a; Slotnick & Schacter, 2004), and like the analogous ERP findings, this pattern is thought to reflect the retrieval of information that supports an "old" decision.

Several differences between true and false recognition have been obtained, although here the findings are more disparate across studies. Schacter et al. (1996b) found that true recognition elicited more activity than false recognition in auditory cortex, Cabeza et al. (2001) found this pattern in the parahippocampus, and Slotnick and Schacter (2004) found this pattern in early visual processing regions. These differences may have arose because the experiments differed in the perceptual information that subjects studied (i.e., auditorily heard words, visually spoken words, and abstract visual shapes, respectively), and hence could have recollected for studied items. Again, the idea is that recollection is greater for studied items than nonstudied items, on average, corresponding to a difference in neural activity.

☐ BRAIN HEMISPHERE EFFECTS

Although they have not used neuroimaging techniques, some studies have investigated the potential effects of right- and left-hemisphere processing on false memories and thus are relevant to this chapter. Westerberg and Marsolek (2003a) had subjects auditorily study several DRM lists, and then briefly flashed test words to the left or the right visual field. The general idea behind this type of methodology is that presenting a stimulus to one visual field gives the corresponding brain hemisphere preferential processing of that stimulus (i.e., the contralateral hemisphere, which receives visual input first). Thus, any difference in behavioral performance can be attributed to the preferential processing of that hemisphere. In two experiments, Westerberg and Marsolek found that related lures preferentially processed by the right hemisphere were significantly more likely to be falsely recognized than related lures preferentially processed by the left hemisphere. These effects were small (less than 3%), and also occurred for the correct recognition of list words in some conditions. Nevertheless, the authors concluded that the right hemisphere might provide more diffuse activation of associations than the left hemisphere, thereby enhancing false recognition of associated lures. They did note, though, these effects were at odds with results from Metcalfe, Funnell, and Gazzaniga (1995). In this study, it was found that false recognition for nonstudied exemplars was greater when the left hemisphere in a split-brain patient preferentially processed test stimuli. It is unclear whether this discrepancy was due to differences in materials or the subjects.

Christman et al. (2004) also studied hemispheric effects on false memories, but instead of focusing on lateralization of function, they focused on the effects of interhemispheric communication. In their first experiment, subjects were divided into those that were strongly right-handed and those that were more ambidextrous (mixed-handed), with the assumption that hemispheric communication was greater in mixed-handed people. Although true recall was roughly equal across groups (.61 and .58), mixed-handers falsely recalled considerably fewer related lures (.34) than did strong right-handers (.52). The authors proposed that increased hemispheric communication in mixed-handers increased memory monitoring processes, thereby reducing false recall.

A different approach was used in their second experiment, which only included right-handers. After studying each list, and just prior to recall, half of the subjects tracked a moving circle with their eyes for 30 s, thereby eliciting about two horizontal movements per second. Subjects in the control condition viewed a similar display, with stimuli instead flashed in the center of the screen (to minimize eye movements). Despite only modest differences in true recall (.55 and .52), subjects in the eye movement condition falsely recalled significantly fewer related lures (.38) than did subjects in the control condition (.58). Based on the idea that horizontal eye movements facilitated hemispheric communication, the authors again proposed that increased hemispheric communication facilitated monitoring processes that reduced false recall. These results potentially have broad-reaching implications, but a complete understanding of these effects awaits future replications and extensions, and also could benefit from a neuroimaging approach.

□ CONCLUSIONS AND CAVEATS

In most of the neuroimaging studies reviewed here, both similarities and differences in brain activity for true and false recognition have been emphasized. To the degree that the retrieved information is the same for true and false recognition, the patterns of neural activity also should be the same. This prediction is pertinent to the DRM task, where false recognition of related lures often occurs as quickly, frequently, and with similar confidence as true recognition of list words. Consistent with this prediction, true and false recognition result in mostly similar ERP waveforms, and both activate medial temporal regions (e.g., the hippocampus and surrounding structures), left-parietal regions (e.g., BA 40), and prefrontal regions (e.g., right BA 9/46). The temporal and parietal activations might reflect recollection-based processes that can cause false recognition, such as the retrieval of the theme or associations of a list, whereas some of the frontal activations might reflect post-retrieval monitoring processes that can reduce false recognition. These interpretations sit well with neuropsychological findings (reviewed in Chapter 9), which indicate that medial temporal patients show reduced false recognition, whereas frontal patients show increased false recognition. Several differences also have been observed between brain activity for true and false recognition. These differences are consistent with the behavioral literature, which indicates that true recognition can be more subjectively detailed and compelling than false recognition, at least on average (see Chapter 4).

Although these neuroimaging findings converge well with other findings, some interpretative ambiguities exist. Consider first the similarities between true and false recognition. As reviewed in Chapter 4, subjects often report recalling other associates when falsely recognizing related lures (perhaps due to associative activation, or cuing), and as discussed in Chapter 5, the recall of list words sometimes is used to help monitor false recognition. In these cases one would expect that neural signals elicited by the related lures and list words would share some similarity, not because true and false memories are "caused" by similar brain regions, but rather because the same information (the true recall or recollection of list words) would be retrieved to make both types of decisions. The degree to which true recollection contaminates the neural signal corresponding to false recognition is still unknown, but obviously it is of critical theoretical interest. Questions also remain about the interpretation of the differences between true and false recognition. As argued above, these differences might reflect greater recollection of detailed information for true than false recognition. However, as Slotnick and Schacter (2004) point out, another possibility is that these differences might reflect differences in nonconscious perceptual processes (i.e., enhanced perceptual priming for studied items). This concern might not apply to the DRM task, as priming for verbal materials tends to be exhibited as decreases in neural activity (as opposed to the observed increases), but the difference in neural activity for conscious and nonconscious retrieval is by no means a settled issue. These and other issues await future experimentation.

CHAPTER

Summary and Conclusions

Memory research traditionally has been task-driven, with researchers rallying around an interesting phenomenon long enough to manipulate it, debate it, and otherwise make sense of it. The false memory tasks reviewed here are firmly rooted in this tradition, but they also are somewhat unique, in the sense that they have been used in a variety of research domains. The general acceptance of a common set of task-specific methods and controls has made results comparable across domains, including basic behavioral research, development and aging research, cognitive neuropsychology research (e.g., patient studies or drug studies), cognitive neuroscience research (e.g., neuroimaging studies), and other types of applied research (e.g., individual differences and comparisons with autobiographical memories). Equally important, the widespread adoption of a common set of procedures has fostered a common pool of conceptual terms and ideas, thereby speeding the rate of theoretical advances. No one can deny that we have learned a great deal about associative memory illusions over the past 10 years of intensified research, and that this type of research has fostered a cross-disciplinary approach to understanding the basic processes of human memory.

These gains notwithstanding, history dictates that interest in even the most popular experimental methods and phenomena will eventually wane, if not disappear altogether. The student of memory will no doubt remember Ebbinghaus's studies with nonsense syllables, Sternberg's memory scanning task, and Wickens's release from proactive interference task as good examples of methods that are no longer researched as intensely as they once were. There is no reason to believe that the false memory tasks reviewed here, such as the DRM task, are any different. In fact, such an outcome is inevitable if scientists do their jobs. As researchers gain a fuller understanding of a topic, additional research yields diminishing returns, and studying other topics can make more fruitful gains. Are we at that point yet with associative memory illusions? Judging by the rate at which new studies continue to appear in the literature, probably not. Many important theoretical and practical questions remain, as discussed in previous chapters, and these will keep experimenters busy for some time. We probably are at the point, though, where additional studies either will need to resolve gaping theoretical discrepancies in the literature, or to further advance an applied or cross-disciplinary agenda, in order to make a considerable contribution.

With these considerations in mind a general overview of what we know about these phenomena (or at least, what has been covered in this review) is provided next. Following this summary, a few areas of inquiry that promise to take this sort of research into new and useful directions are discussed. These sections mostly are recapitulations of the research reviewed in previous chapters, so they are intentionally brief. A few comments on the implications of this research enterprise, as a whole, are provided at the end of this chapter.

☐ GENERAL REVIEW

To summarize the most basic behavioral findings (Chapters 3–6), it is clear that people misremember events that are strongly associated or highly similar to studied events. This is true for associated words, similar pictures, abstract shapes, faces, and the like. Especially with materials that are related through pre-existing associations (as in the DRM task), these memory errors can be long lasting and subjectively compelling, and can occur with high confidence and the recollection of specific details (illusory recollection). They also are difficult to avoid, particularly when there is little information in memory to discriminate studied events from nonstudied events. These findings demonstrate the resilience of such relatedness effects, and along with the findings from implicit memory tests and other evidence, they indicate that a memory signal is retrieved for the nonstudied event. As such, it is appropriate to consider these effects to be caused by false memories or memory illusions, as opposed to guessing, criterion shifts, or the like (although these other factors do contribute to performance).

There are several potential causes of these relatedness effects on memory distortion, including associative activation, thematic consistency, and feature overlap, and there is solid evidence for multiple causes of the false memories in the DRM task (discussed in Chapter 3). Associative activation plays a key role in the creation of these errors, as indicated by studies that have controlled or measured both associative strength and semantic similarity. Evidence from overt rehearsal studies, subjective reports, and various experimental manipulations indicates that the related lure can be consciously generated at study, so that part of the DRM false memory effect is due to confusing these thoughts with actual presentation. However, there also is evidence that such generation at study is not necessary for the false memory effect, indicating that associative activation might occur at test, too, or that semantic similarity somehow contributes to the effect (via themes, gist, or feature overlap). The finding that the false memory effect decreases less over time than true memory also cannot be explained through conscious generation at study, and is more consistent with these latter explanations. Other evidence that has been used to support gist-based theories comes from memory-impaired populations (e.g., MTL amnesics, or Alzheimer's patients), and from the effects of test-item context on false recognition. Perhaps the strongest evidence for gist or similarity processes is that they contribute to false recognition of perceptually similar (abstract) materials, for which there can be no associative activation. Given their contribution to these other false recognition phenomena, there is little reason to think that these sorts of similarity processes would not contribute to false memories in the DRM task. In short, there are multiple causes of DRM false memories. The exact cause of any effect will depend on the type of materials used in the memory task, as well as how subjects process this material (e.g., personal associations, encoding and retrieval strategies, etc.).

In addition to those processes that cause a false memory signal, there are several retrieval monitoring processes that help subjects to avoid false memories (discussed in Chapter 5). The specifics of each monitoring process depend on the way the task is designed, but most of these processes can be classified into two major types. Disqualifying monitoring occurs when the subject recollects (or otherwise has access to) information that is inconsistent with the questionable event's presentation in the corresponding context. For instance, the subject might recall that a lure was presented in a different context (i.e., an exclusion list), or they might exhaustively recall all of the words that were presented in the corresponding study list, and thereby reason that the lure could not have been presented. Diagnostic monitoring occurs when the subject's memory for the questionable event does not conform to their expectations, or what they think they should remember if the event had occurred.

For instance, if memories from the to-be-remembered context are perceptually detailed, then the subject might reject the lure as having occurred in that context, or decide that it had been studied in a less distinctive context. Evidence for these monitoring processes is not limited to converging associates tasks, but also can be found in other episodic memory tasks (e.g., exclusion tests, source memory tests, etc.).

Research in subsequent chapters (Chapters 7–10) speaks on the generality of these basic findings. There are individual differences in the propensity to make these sorts of false memories, and these differences can be stable across testing times. Cognitive and personality measures (e.g., working memory; dissociative experiences) are correlated with the propensity to make memory errors, and there are definite effects of development and aging on memory errors in different tasks. Further, one's sensitivity to the DRM effect has been found to correlate positively with one's sensitivity to false memories in other tasks, including false autobiographical memories. These findings indicate that, despite their differences, various types of false memories tap into a core set of psychological processes that transcend individual tasks. Researchers have begun to uncover some of these candidate processes. In many instances, individual differences in susceptibility to memory distortion can be linked to differences in true recollection and the efficacy of retrieval monitoring processes.

Given the complexity of the underlying processes, it should not be surprising that the relationship between true and false memory can be positive or negative. At least three lines of evidence demonstrate the dependence of false memories on true memories. (1) Encoding conditions that impair memory for studied events (e.g., shallow levels of processing or very rapid presentation rates) also lead to reduced false recall or recognition of related events. (2) Damage to regions of the brain that impairs true memory (e.g., the hippocampus, as in MTL amnesics or Alzheimer's patients), or encoding information while under the influence of a drug that impairs true memory, also can lead to reduced false memories of related events. (3) Neuroimaging results indicate that true and false recognition can elicit very similar patterns of neural activity in regions that are linked to episodic remembering, such as medial temporal structures and prefrontal cortex, implicating common underlying processes. In the first two cases, true and false memories probably behave similarly because encoding of the studied events is necessary for a false memory signal for nonstudied events (via associative activation, gist, or feature overlap). Indeed, this idea is embedded in the definition of the relatedness effect on false memory. In the last case, common patterns of brain activity probably reflect the recollection of associative information, and corresponding monitoring processes, for both true and false memories.

True and false memories also can be dissociated. Many dissociations occur with presentation manipulations that enhance true memory (e.g., study repetitions, study distinctiveness, etc.). These dissociations are due to the potentially opposing effects of true memory on false memory. Processing of the studied materials is necessary for relatedness effects on false memories, but it also is necessary for recollection-based monitoring processes that can reduce these errors. Once the related lure is sufficiently activated to lead to a false memory, additional processing of the list words can enhance monitoring processes more than activation processes (as is the case with study repetitions). Dissociations also can be found across populations. For instance, unlike medial temporal damage, damage to prefrontal cortex can enhance false recognition while reducing true recognition (or not affecting it as much). Damage to prefrontal regions apparently can impair monitoring processes more than activation processes, much like speeding recognition decisions (or, sometimes, healthy aging), leading to overall increases in false memories. Finally, differences in neural activity have been found between true and false recognition. These differences often are thought to reflect greater recollective content for true than false memories, as is sometimes indicated in subjective judgments, but they also might reflect more implicit effects of memory on retrieval-related activity (e.g., more priming for studied items, due to prior presentation).

☐ FUTURE DIRECTIONS

Some central theoretical issues within basic false memory research remain unresolved. Perhaps the biggest area for future development is the intersection between nonconscious priming and episodic false memory. A major focus in early implicit memory research was to show, through experimental and neuropsychological dissociations, that priming on implicit tests was different from explicit or episodic memory. However, it also was known that processes influencing performance on an "implicit test" could influence performance on an "explicit test" (e.g., Roediger, 1990). Similarly, one of the ideas emerging from more recent false memory research is that relatively automatic or implicit processes might play a central role in the retrieval of false memories. This link is evident from studies showing that extremely rapid presentation conditions (at study or test) can nevertheless give rise to associative effects on false memory, or that nonstudied associates can be primed on implicit tests (even though the subject is not intentionally trying to remember). The exact relationship between priming and false memory, and implications for the implicit/explicit distinction, has yet to be worked out. A related question is what causes the detailed subjective experience of illusory recollection. One interesting idea that was mentioned in Chapter 4 is that attribution processes that occur nonconsciously can cause the subjective experience of illusory recollection.

In addition to the resolution of outstanding theoretical issues, a direction for more applied research is to use these cognitive tasks (or modified versions of them) as a tool to measure memory accuracy. For instance, Budson and colleagues (Budson et al., 2002a) have used the similar-pictures task in a clinical trial of the efficacy of a drug to treat Alzheimer's disease. The drug did not help memory performance, but the important point here is the idea motivating the study. False memory tasks might be more sensitive to the effects of interventions on memory than more traditional recall or recognition tasks (which focus on true memory), because false memory tasks can involve more complex monitoring processes. These tasks might therefore be used as diagnostic tools of memory accuracy in a variety of situations. Other studies that used these tasks as a tool are Ferraro and Olson (2003); Kim and Ahn (2002); Lenton et al. (2001); and Reich et al. (2004), discussed in Chapter 7. By measuring false memories of words that are related to certain concepts (e.g., food, clinical disorders, stereotypes, and alcohol), one can gain an indirect measure of the activation of these concepts in various populations (e.g., people with eating disorders, psychologists, the prejudiced, and heavy-drinkers, respectively). Based on this logic, these tasks could be developed into useful individual difference measures.

A final research direction is to create new experimental methods to study processes relevant to memory distortion that are difficult to isolate with existing tasks. For example, Koutstaal and colleagues developed the similar-pictures task as a means of investigating gist- or feature-based false recognition, in the absence of the pre-existing associative relationships that influence the DRM task (e.g., Koutstaal & Schacter, 1997). As another example, the criterial recollection was designed to measure diagnostic monitoring processes (e.g., the distinctiveness heuristic) while improving on some of the ambiguities inherent to the DRM task (e.g., Gallo et al., 2004b). No doubt other methods and ideas will become popular in the years to come. As these newer tasks are developed, though, the older tasks should not simply be abandoned. Instead, experimental comparisons with existing tasks should be conducted. Comparisons of different false memory tasks are necessary for the development of basic theories and generalizations. If commonalities can be found across these measures, as was the case between DRM false memories and autobiographical false memories in Platt et al. (1998), then the overall validity of the research is more likely to be understood and appreciated. These comparisons also might generate important research questions. How do psychological constructs such as attention, motivation, stress, or suggestibility predict false memory creation across tasks, situations, or individuals?

☐ BROADER IMPLICATIONS

A frequently asked question is whether false memory research in the sorts of tasks reviewed here applies to false memories in nonlaboratory situations. As discussed in Chapter 7, and in several of the articles cited in that chapter, this topic has been debated extensively. The answer to the question is probably "no" at the specific level, but "yes" at the general level. At the specific level, it is instructive that some of the findings observed in one false memory experiment do not even generalize to other versions of the same task, let alone to memory in nonlaboratory situations. For example, children were *less* prone to false memory than adults when typical DRM procedures were used (Brainerd et al., 2002), but they were *more* prone to false memory when recollection-based monitoring processes were enhanced in adults (Ghetti et al., 2002). Given this variability, findings from one task (e.g., children are less likely to falsely recall associates) obviously cannot be extrapolated directly to other situations (e.g., children make better eyewitnesses). At least in this example, the experimental results and conclusions are too heavily dependent on task-specific parameters to be generalized to more complicated situations.

At the more general level, though, we use the same brain to remember a list of experimental stimuli as we do to remember other events of our lives, so there must be some continuity in the underlying neurocognitive processes. The aforementioned correlations between different types of false memories, as well as the established links between false memories and various neurocognitive functions or personality measures, are all examples of this continuity. To the degree that specific memory processes are isolated in laboratory tasks, their study should further our understanding of memory in nonlaboratory settings (see Banaji & Crowder, 1989). For instance, Brainerd et al.'s (2002) findings suggest that children have difficulty processing semantically related materials, and Ghetti et al.'s (2002) findings implicate underdeveloped retrieval monitoring processes. These theoretical conclusions are not mutually inconsistent, and each has consequences for learning and memory in other situations (see Reyna et al., in press). Specific findings might not generalize, but good theories do.

What are the broader implications of this type of research, as a whole? One obvious implication is that the ease with which false memories can be elicited in cognitive tasks implies that many nonlaboratory memories also might be false. We live in information-rich environments that did not exist in our ancestral past, and so the possibility of making false memories based on associations and similarity to this information might be greater than ever. These points have not been lost in forensic applications of false memory research, or in other nonlaboratory applications. Indeed, Brainerd and Reyna (2005) have written a comprehensive review of basic false memory research and its general applications, with enough material to fill a book of over 500 pages.

All of this is not to imply, though, that false memories occur as frequently as true memories, or even that false memories have a significant negative impact on normal uses of memory. The degree to which false memories occur in nonlaboratory situations is a separate question altogether, and one that has yet to be answered satisfactorily. If it is assumed that episodic memory evolved to be functionally adaptive, then memory should be sufficiently accurate for those events or environmental regularities that are critical to survival (cf. Anderson & Schooler, 1991; Schacter, 1999), at least for healthy individuals under relatively normal situations. Of course, if unusual situations prevail (e.g., brain damage, extremely impoverished learning environments, etc.), then memory for important events might be more susceptible to distortion. Further, a functionally adaptive memory does not necessarily imply a veridical memory. Conway (2005) has proposed that memory distortion might sometimes be beneficial to an individual's mental health, to the extent that the distortion preserves a coherent sense of self.

The research reviewed here does not address the regularity of false memories in nonlaboratory settings, but it does indicate that there is a stubborn regularity to certain types of memory illusions. This regularity suggests that memory illusions are a byproduct of information processing mechanisms that are firmly grounded in the neurocognitive system— mechanisms that otherwise are beneficial to us. Relatedness effects on memory errors result from a natural tendency to mentally activate potentially useful associations, and to simplify useful information into meaningful gist. The large body of research into these sorts of illusions makes a compelling case that pre-existing knowledge of concepts and their associations, as well as retrieval monitoring processes, are some of the basic elements of episodic memory.

References

Alba, J. W., & Hasher, L. (1983). Is memory schematic? *Psychological Bulletin*, *93*, 203–231.

Aleman, A., Hijman, R., de Haan, E. H. F., & Kahn, R. S. (1999). Memory impairment in schizophrenia: A meta-analysis. *American Journal of Psychiatry*, *156*, 1358–1366.

Alpert, J. L., Brown, L. S., Ceci, S. J., Courtois, C. A., Loftus, E. F., & Ornstein, P. A. (1998). Final report of the American Psychological Association working group on investigation of memories of childhood abuse. *Psychology, Public Policy, & Law*, *4*, 931–1078.

American Psychiatric Association. (1994). *Diagnostic and statistical manual of mental disorders* (4th ed.). Washington, DC: American Psychiatric Association.

Anaki, D., Faran, Y., Ben-Shalom, D., & Henik, A. (2005). The false memory and the mirror effects: The role of familiarity and backward association in creating false recollections. *Journal of Memory & Language*, *52*, 87–102.

Anastasi, J. S., Rhodes, M. G., & Burns, M. C. (2000). Distinguishing between memory illusions and actual memories using phenomenological measurements and explicit warnings. *American Journal of Psychology*, *113*, 1–26.

Anastasi, J. S., Rhodes, M. G., Marquez, S., & Velino, V. (2005). The incidence of false memories in native and non-native speakers. *Memory*, *13*, 815–828.

Anderson, J. R. (1983). *The architecture of cognition*. Cambridge, MA: Harvard University Press.

Anderson, J. R., & Bower, G. H. (1973). *Human associative memory*. Washington, DC: Winston.

Anderson, J. R., & Schooler, L. J. (1991). Reflections of the environment in memory. *Psychological Science*, *2*, 396–408.

Anderson, M. C., Bjork, R. A., & Bjork, E. L. (1994). Remembering can cause forgetting: Retrieval dynamics in long-term memory. *Journal of Experimental Psychology: Learning, Memory, & Cognition*, *20*, 1063–1087.

Anisfeld, M., & Knapp, M. (1968). Association, synonymity, and directionality in false recognition. *Journal of Experimental Psychology*, *77*, 171–179.

Antonova, E., Sharma, T., Morris, R., & Kumari, V. (2004). The relationship between brain structure and neurocognition in schizophrenia: A selective review. *Schizophrenia Research*, *70*, 117–145.

Appleby, D. (1987). Producing a déjà vu experience. In V. P. Makosky, L. G. Whittemore, & A. M. Rogers (Eds.), *Activities handbook for the teaching of psychology* (Vol. 2, pp. 78–79). Washington, DC: American Psychological Association.

Arndt, J., & Hirshman, E. (1998). True and false recognition in MINERVA2: Explanations from a global matching perspective. *Journal of Memory & Language*, *39*, 371–391.

Arndt, J., & Reder, L. M. (2003). The effect of distinctive visual information on false recognition. *Journal of Memory & Language*, *48*, 1–15.

Asch, S. (1968). The doctrinal tyranny of associationism: Or what is wrong with rote learning. In T. R. Dixon & D. L. Horton (Eds.), *Verbal behavior and general behavior theory* (pp. 214–228). Englewood Cliffs, NJ: Prentice-Hall.

Atkinson, R. C., & Juola, J. F. (1974). Search and decision processes in recognition memory. In D. H. Krantz, R. C. Atkinson, R. D. Luce, & P. Suppes (Eds.), *Contemporary developments in mathematical psychology: Vol. 1. Learning, memory, and thinking*. San Francisco, CA: Freeman.

Ayers, M. S., & Reder, L. M. (1998). A theoretical review of the misinformation effect: Predictions from an activation-based memory model. *Psychonomic Bulletin & Review, 5*, 1–21.

Bahrick, H. P. (1970). Two-phase model for prompted recall. *Psychological Review, 77*, 215–222.

Balota, D. A., Cortese, M. J., Duchek, J. M., Adams, D., Roediger, H. L. III, McDermott, K. B., & Yerys, B. E. (1999). Veridical and false memories in healthy older adults and in dementia of the Alzheimer's type. *Cognitive Neuropsychology, 16*, 361–384.

Balota, D. A., & Duchek, J. M. (1991). Semantic priming effects, lexical repetition effects, and contextual disambiguation effects in healthy aged individuals and individuals with senile dementia of the Alzheimer type. *Brain & Language, 40*, 181–201.

Balota, D. A., & Lorch, R. F. (1986). Depth of automatic spreading activation: Mediated priming effects in pronunciation but not in lexical decision. *Journal of Experimental Psychology: Learning, Memory, & Cognition, 12*, 336–345.

Banaji, M. R., & Crowder, R. G. (1989). The bankruptcy of everyday memory. *American Psychologist, 44*, 1185–1193.

Bartlett, F. C. (1932). *Remembering: A study in experimental and social psychology*. Cambridge, England: Cambridge University Press.

Basden, B. H., Basden, D. R., Thomas, R. L. III, & Souphasith, S. (1998). Memory distortion in group recall. *Current Psychology: Developmental, Learning, Personality, Social, 16*, 225–246.

Basden, B. H., Reysen, M. B., & Basden, D. R. (2002). Transmitting false memories in social groups. *American Journal of Psychology, 115*, 211–231.

Bäuml, K. & Kuhbandner, C. (2003). Retrieval-induced forgetting and part-list cuing in associatively structured lists. *Memory & Cognition, 31*, 1188–1197.

Bauste, G., & Ferraro, F. R. (2004). Gender differences in false memory production. *Current Psychology, 23*, 238–244.

Belleville, S., Caza, N., & Peretz, I. (2003). A neuropsychological argument for a processing view of memory. *Journal of Memory & Language, 48*, 686–703.

Benjamin, A. S. (2001). On the dual effects of repetition on false recognition. *Journal of Experimental Psychology: Learning, Memory, & Cognition, 27*, 941–947.

Bernstein, E. M., & Putnam, F. W. (1986). Development, reliability, and validity of a dissociation scale. *Journal of Nervous & Mental Disease, 174*, 727–735.

Beversdorf, D. Q., Smith, B. W., Crucian, G. P., Anderson, J. M., Keillor, J. M., Barrett, A. M., Hughes, J. D., Felopulos, G. J., Bauman, M. L., Nadeau, S. E., & Heilman, K. M. (2000). Increased discrimination of "false memories" in autism spectrum disorder. *Proceedings of the National Academy of Sciences, 97*, 8734–8737.

Bjork, R. A. (1970). Positive forgetting: The noninterference of items intentionally forgotten. *Journal of Verbal Learning & Verbal Behavior, 9*, 255–268.

Blair, I. V., Lenton, A. P., & Hastie, R. (2002). The reliability of the DRM paradigm as a measure of individual differences in false memories. *Psychonomic Bulletin & Review, 9*, 590–596.

Boring, E. G. (1950). *A history of experimental psychology*. New York, NY: Appleton-Century-Crofts, Inc.

Bower, G. H. (2000). A brief history of memory research. In E. Tulving and F. I. M. Craik (Eds.), *The Oxford handbook of memory* (pp. 3–32). Oxford, England: Oxford University Press.

Bowler, D. M., Gardiner, J. M., Grice, S., & Saavalainen, P. (2000). Memory illusions: False recall and recognition in adults with Asperger's syndrome. *Journal of Abnormal Psychology, 109*, 663–672.

Brainerd, C. J., Forrest, T. J., & Karibian, D. (in press). Development of the false memory illusion. *Developmental Psychology*.

Brainerd, C. J., Holliday, R. E., & Reyna, V. F. (2004). Behavioral measurement of remembering phenomenologies: So simple a child can do it. *Child Development, 75*, 505–522.

Brainerd, C. J., Payne, D. G., Wright, R., & Reyna, V. F. (2003a). Phantom recall. *Journal of Memory & Language, 48*, 445–467.

Brainerd, C. J., & Reyna, V. F. (1998). When things that were never experienced are easier to "remember" than things that were. *Psychological Science, 9*, 484–489.

Brainerd, C. J., & Reyna, V. F. (2002). Fuzzy trace theory and false memory. *Current Directions in Psychological Science, 11*, 164–169.

Brainerd, C. J., & Reyna, V. F. (2005). *The science of false memory*. Oxford, England: Oxford University Press.

Brainerd, C. J., Reyna, V. F., & Brandse, E. (1995a). Are children's false memories more persistent than their true memories? *Psychological Science, 6*, 359–364.

Brainerd, C. J., Reyna, V. F., & Forrest, T. J. (2002). Are young children susceptible to the false-memory illusion? *Child Development, 73*, 1363–1377.

Brainerd, C. J., Reyna, V. F., & Kneer, R. (1995b). False-recognition reversal: When similarity is distinctive. *Journal of Memory & Language, 34*, 157–185.

Brainerd, C. J., Reyna, V. F., & Mojardin, A. H. (1999). Conjoint recognition. *Psychological Review, 106*, 160–179.

Brainerd, C. J., Reyna, V. F., Wright, R., & Mojardin, A. H. (2003b). Recollection rejection: False-memory editing in children and adults. *Psychological Review, 110*, 762–784.

Brainerd, C. J., & Wright, R. (2005). Forward association, backward association, and the false-memory illusion. *Journal of Experimental Psychology: Learning, Memory, & Cognition, 31*, 554–567.

Brainerd, C. J., Wright, R., Reyna, V. F., & Mojardin, A. H. (2001). Conjoint recognition and phantom recollection. *Journal of Experimental Psychology: Learning, Memory, & Cognition, 27*, 307–327.

Bransford, J. D., Barclay, J. R., & Franks, J. J. (1972). Sentence memory: A constructive versus interpretive approach. *Cognitive Psychology, 3*, 193–209.

Brédart, S. (2000). When false memories do not occur: Not thinking of the lure or remembering that it was not heard? *Memory, 8*, 123–128.

Bremner, J. D., Shobe, K. K., & Kihlstrom, J. F. (2000). False memories in women with self-reported childhood sexual abuse: An empirical study. *Psychological Science, 11*, 333–337.

Brewer, W. F. (1977). Memory for the pragmatic implications of sentences. *Memory & Cognition, 5*, 673–678.

Brown, N. R., Buchanan, L., & Cabeza, R. (2000). Estimating the frequency of nonevents: The role of recollection failure in false recognition. *Psychonomic Bulletin & Review, 7*, 684–691.

Brown, J., Lewis, V. J., & Monk, A. F. (1977). Memorability, word frequency, and negative recognition. *Quarterly Journal of Experimental Psychology, 29*, 461–473.

Bruce, D., Phillips-Grant, K., Conrad, N., & Bona, S. (2004). Encoding context and false recognition memories. *Memory, 12*, 562–570.

Bruce, D., & Winograd, E. (1998). Remembering Deese's 1959 articles: The Zeitgeist, the sociology of science, and false memories. *Psychonomic Bulletin & Review, 5*, 615–624.

Buchanan, L., Brown, N. R., Cabeza, R., & Maitson, C. (1999). False memories and semantic lexicon arrangement. *Brain & Language, 68*, 172–177.

Budson, A. E., Daffner, K. R., Desikan, R., & Schacter, D. L. (2000). When false recognition is unopposed by true recognition: Gist-based memory distortion in Alzheimer's disease. *Neuropsychology, 14*, 277–287.

Budson, A. E., Desikan, R., Daffner, K. R., & Schacter, D. L. (2001). Perceptual false recognition in Alzheimer's disease. *Neuropsychology, 15*, 230–243.

Budson, A. E., Dodson, C. S., Daffner, K. R., & Schacter, D. L. (2005). Metacognition and false recognition in Alzheimer's disease: Further exploration of the distinctiveness heuristic. *Neuropsychology, 19*, 253–258.

Budson, A. E., Michalska, K. J., Rentz, D. M., Joubert, C. C., Daffner, K. R., Schacter, D. L., & Sperling, R. A. (2002a). Use of a false recognition paradigm in an Alzheimer's disease clinical trial: A pilot study. *American Journal of Alzheimer's Disease & Other Dementias, 17,* 93–100.

Budson, A. E., Michalska, K. J., Sullivan, A. L., Rentz, D. M., Daffner, K. R., & Schacter, D. L. (2003a). False recognition in Alzheimer disease: Evidence from categorized pictures. *Cognitive & Behavioral Neurology, 16,* 16–27.

Budson, A. E., Sitarski, J., Daffner, K. R., & Schacter, D. L. (2002b). False recognition of pictures versus words in Alzheimer's disease: The distinctiveness heuristic. *Neuropsychology, 16,* 163–173.

Budson, A. E., Sullivan, A. L., Daffner, K. R., & Schacter, D. L. (2003b). Semantic versus phonological false recognition in aging and Alzheimer's disease. *Brain & Cognition, 51,* 251–261.

Budson, A. E., Sullivan, A. L., Mayer, E., Daffner, K. R., Black, P. M., & Schacter, D. L. (2002c). Suppression of false recognition in Alzheimer's disease and in patients with frontal lobe lesions. *Brain, 125,* 2750–2765.

Burgess, P. W., & Shallice, T. (1996). Confabulation and the control of recollection. *Memory, 4,* 359–411.

Burnham, W. H. (1889). Memory, historically and experimentally considered (III): Paramnesia. *American Journal of Psychology, 2,* 431–464.

Butler, K. M., McDaniel, M. A., Dornburg, C. C., Price, A. L., & Roediger, H. L. III. (2004). Age differences in veridical and false recall are not inevitable: The role of frontal lobe function. *Psychonomic Bulletin & Review, 11,* 921–925.

Cabeza, R., & Lennartson, E. R. (2005). False memory across languages: Implicit associative response vs. fuzzy trace views. *Memory, 13,* 1–5.

Cabeza, R., Rao, S. M., Wagner, A. D., Mayer, A. R., & Schacter, D. L. (2001). Can medial temporal lobe regions distinguish true from false? An event-related functional MRI study of veridical and illusory recognition memory. *Proceedings of the National Academy of Sciences, 98,* 4805–4810.

Calkins, M. W. (1894). Association. *Psychological Review, 1,* 476–483.

Ceci, S. J., & Bruck, M. (1993). Suggestibility of the child witness: A historical review and synthesis. *Psychological Bulletin, 113,* 403–439.

Chan, J. C. K., McDermott, K. B., Watson, J. M., and Gallo, D. A. (2005). The importance of material-processing interactions in inducing false memories. *Memory & Cognition, 33,* 389–395.

Christman, S. D., Propper, R. E., & Dion, A. (2004). Increased interhemispheric interaction is associated with decreased false memories in a verbal converging semantic associates paradigm. *Brain & Cognition, 56,* 313–319.

Clancy, S. A., McNally, R. J., Schacter, D. L., Lenzenweger, M. F., & Pitman, R. K. (2002). Memory distortion in people reporting abduction by aliens. *Journal of Abnormal Psychology, 111,* 455–461.

Clancy, S. A., Schacter, D. L., McNally, R. J., & Pitman, R. K. (2000). False recognition in women reporting recovered memories of sexual abuse. *Psychological Science, 11,* 26–31.

Cleary, A. M., & Greene, R. L. (2002). Paradoxical effects of presentation modality on false memory. *Memory, 10,* 55–61.

Cleary, A. M., & Greene, R. L. (2004). True and false memory in the absence of perceptual identification. *Memory, 12,* 231–236.

Coane, J. H., & McBride, D. M. (in press). The role of test structure in creating false memories. *Memory & Cognition.*

Collins, A. M., & Loftus, E. F. (1975). A spreading-activation theory of semantic processing. *Psychological Review, 82,* 407–428.

Coltheart, V. (1977). Recognition errors after incidental learning as a function of different levels of processing. *Journal of Experimental Psychology: Human Learning & Memory, 3,* 437–444.

Conrad, R. (1964). Acoustic confusions in immediate memory. *British Journal of Psychology*, *55*, 75–84.

Conway, M. A. (2005). Memory and self. *Journal of Memory & Language*, *53*, 594–628.

Cotel, S. C., Gallo, D. A., & Seamon, J. G. (Unpublished, 2006). *Nonconscious activation causes false memories: Experimental control of conscious processes in the Deese, Roediger, and McDermott task*. Wesleyan University, Middletown, CT.

Craik, F. I. M. (1986). A functional account of age differences in memory. In F. Klix & H. Hagendorf (Eds.), *Human memory and cognitive capabilities, mechanisms, and performances* (pp. 409–422). Amsterdam: Elsevier.

Craik, F. I. M., & Lockhart, R. S. (1972). Levels of processing: A framework for memory research. *Journal of Verbal Learning & Verbal Behavior*, *11*, 671–684.

Craik, F. I. M, & McDowd, J. M. (1987). Age differences in recall and recognition. *Journal of Experimental Psychology: Learning, Memory, & Cognition*, *13*, 474–479.

Cramer, P. (1974). Idiodynamic sets as determinants of children's false recognition errors. *Developmental Psychology*, *10*, 86–92.

Cramer, P., & Eagle, M. (1972). Relationship between conditions of CRS presentation and the category of false recognition errors. *Journal of Experimental Psychology*, *94*, 1–5.

Crowder, R. G. (1976). *Principles of learning and memory*. Hillsdale, NJ: Lawrence Erlbaum Associates, Inc.

Curran, T. (2000). Brain potentials of recollection and familiarity. *Memory & Cognition*, *28*, 923–938.

Curran, T., Schacter, D. L., Johnson, M. K., & Spinks, R. (2001). Brain potentials reflect behavioral differences in true and false recognition. *Journal of Cognitive Neuroscience*, *13*, 201–216.

Deese, J. (1959a). Influence of inter-item associative strength upon immediate free recall. *Psychological Reports*, *5*, 305–312.

Deese, J. (1959b). On the prediction of occurrence of particular verbal intrusions in immediate recall. *Journal of Experimental Psychology*, *58*, 17–22.

Deese, J. (1961). Associative structure and the serial reproduction experiment. *Journal of Abnormal Social Psychology*, *63*, 95–100.

Dehon, H., & Brédart, S. (2004). False memories: Young and older adults think of semantic associates at the same rate, but young adults are more successful at source monitoring. *Psychology & Aging*, *19*, 191–197.

Dewhurst, S. A. (2001). Category repetition and false recognition: Effects of instance frequency and category size. *Journal of Memory & Language*, *44*, 153–167.

Dewhurst, S. A., & Anderson, S. J. (1999). Effects of exact and category repetition in true and false recognition memory. *Memory & Cognition*, *27*, 664–673.

Dewhurst, S. A., & Farrand, P. (2004). Investigating the phenomenological characteristics of false recognition for categorized words. *European Journal of Cognitive Psychology*, *16*, 403–416.

Dewhurst, S. A., & Robinson, C. A. (2004). False memories in children: Evidence for a shift from phonological to semantic associations. *Psychological Science*, *15*, 782–786.

Diliberto-Macaluso, K. A. (2005). Priming and false memories from Deese-Roediger-McDermott lists on a fragment completion test with children. *American Journal of Psychology*, *118*, 13–28.

Dodd, M. D., & MacLeod, C. M. (2004). False recognition without intentional learning. *Psychonomic Bulletin & Review*, *11*, 137–142.

Dodhia, R. M., & Metcalfe, J. (1999). False memories and source monitoring. *Cognitive Neuropsychology*, *16*, 489–508.

Dodson, C. S., & Hege, A. C. G. (2005). Speeded retrieval abolishes the false-memory suppression effect: Evidence for the distinctiveness heuristic. *Psychonomic Bulletin & Review*, *12*, 726–731.

Dodson, C. S., & Johnson, M. K. (1993). Rate of false source attributions depends on how questions are asked. *American Journal of Psychology, 106*, 541–557.

Dodson, C. S., & Schacter, D. L. (2001). "If I had said it I would have remembered it": Reducing false memories with a distinctiveness heuristic. *Psychonomic Bulletin & Review, 8*, 155–161.

Dodson, C. S., & Schacter, D. L. (2002a). Aging and strategic retrieval processes: Reducing false memories with a distinctiveness heuristic. *Psychology & Aging, 17*, 405–415.

Dodson, C. S., & Schacter, D. L. (2002b). When false recognition meets metacognition: The distinctiveness heuristic. *Journal of Memory & Language, 46*, 782–803.

Donaldson, W. (1996). The role of decision processes in remembering and knowing. *Memory & Cognition, 24*, 523–533.

Düzel, E., Yonelinas, A. P., Mangun, G. R., Heinze, H. J., & Tulving, E. (1997). Event-related brain potential correlates of two states of conscious awareness in memory. *Proceedings of the National Academy of Sciences, 94*, 5973–5978.

Ebbinghaus, H. (1885). *Memory: A contribution to experimental psychology* (H. A. Ruger & C. E. Bussenius, Trans.). New York, NY: Dover.

Eichenbaum, H., & Cohen, N. J. (2001). *From conditioning to conscious recollection: Memory systems of the brain.* Oxford, England: Oxford University Press.

Einstein, G. O., & Hunt, R. R. (1980). Levels of processing and organization: Additive effects of individual-item and relational processing. *Journal of Experimental Psychology: Human Learning & Memory, 6*, 588–598.

Eisen, M. L., & Lynn, S. J. (2001). Dissociation, memory and suggestibility in adults and children. *Applied Cognitive Psychology, 15*, S49–S73.

Eisen, M. L., Winograd, E., & Qin, J. (2002). Individual differences in adults' suggestibility and memory performance. In M. L. Eisen, J. A. Quas, & G. S. Goodman (Eds.), *Memory and suggestibility in the forensic interview* (pp. 205–233). Mahwah, NJ: Lawrence Erlbaum Associates, Inc.

Elias, C. S., & Perfetti, C. A. (1973). Encoding task and recognition memory: The importance of semantic encoding. *Journal of Experimental Psychology, 99*, 151–156.

Elvevåg, B., Fisher, J. E., Weickert, T. W., Weinberger, D. R., & Goldberg, T. E. (2004). Lack of false recognition in schizophrenia: A consequence of poor memory? *Neuropsychologia, 42*, 546–554.

Endo, M. (2005). Effects of prior warning and response deadline on false memory. *Psychologia, 48*, 54–60.

Erdelyi, M. H. (1996). *The recovery of unconscious memories: Hypermnesia and Reminiscence.* Chicago, IL: University of Chicago Press.

Fabiani, M., Stadler, M. A., & Wessels, P. M. (2000). True but not false memories produce a sensory signature in human lateralized brain potentials. *Journal of Cognitive Neuroscience, 12*, 941–949.

Felzen, E., & Anisfeld, M. (1970). Semantic and phonological relations in the false recognition of words by third and sixth-grade children. *Developmental Psychology, 3*, 163–168.

Ferraro, F. R., & Olson, L. (2003). False memories in individuals at risk for developing an eating disorder. *The Journal of Psychology: Interdisciplinary & Applied, 137*, 476–482.

Fillenbaum, S. (1969). Words as feature complexes: False recognition of antonyms and synonyms. *Journal of Experimental Psychology, 82*, 400–402.

Foley, M. A., Johnson, M. K., & Raye, C. L. (1983). Age-related changes in confusion between memories for thoughts and memories for speech. *Child Development, 54*, 51–60.

Franks, J. J., & Bransford, J. D. (1971). Abstraction of visual patterns. *Journal of Experimental Psychology, 90*, 65–74.

Freyd, J. J., & Gleaves, D. H. (1996). "Remembering" words not presented in lists: Relevance to the current recovered/false memory controversy. *Journal of Experimental Psychology: Learning, Memory, & Cognition, 22*, 811–813.

Gallo, D. A. (2004). Using recall to reduce false recognition: Diagnostic and disqualifying monitoring. *Journal of Experimental Psychology: Learning, Memory, & Cognition, 30*, 120–128.

Gallo, D. A., Bell, D. M., Beier, J. S., & Schacter, D. L. (in press). Two types of recollection-based monitoring in young and older adults: Recall-to-reject and the distinctiveness heuristic. *Memory*.

Gallo, D. A., Chen, J. M., Wiseman, A. L., Schacter, D. L., & Budson, A. E. (Unpublished, 2006a). *Retrieval monitoring and anosognosia in Alzheimer's disease: Evidence from the criterial recollection task*. Harvard University, Cambridge, MA.

Gallo, D. A., Cotel, S. C., Moore, C. D., & Schacter, D. L. (Unpublished, 2006b). *Aging can spare recollection-based retrieval monitoring: Evidence from the criterical recollection Task*. Harvard University, Cambridge, MA.

Gallo, D. A., McDermott, K. B., Percer, J. M., & Roediger, H. L. III. (2001a). Modality effects in false recall and false recognition. *Journal of Experimental Psychology: Learning, Memory, & Cognition, 27*, 339–353.

Gallo, D. A., Roberts, M. J., & Seamon, J. G. (1997). Remembering words not presented in lists: Can we avoid creating false memories? *Psychonomic Bulletin & Review, 4*, 271–276.

Gallo, D. A., & Roediger, H. L. III. (2002). Variability among word lists in eliciting memory illusions: Evidence for associative activation and monitoring. *Journal of Memory & Language, 47*, 469–497.

Gallo, D. A., & Roediger, H. L. III. (2003). The effects of associations and aging on illusory recollection. *Memory & Cognition, 31*, 1036–1044.

Gallo, D. A., Roediger, H. L. III, & McDermott, K. B. (2001b). Association false recognition occurs without strategic criterion shifts. *Psychonomic Bulletin & Review, 8*, 579–586.

Gallo, D. A., & Seamon, J. G. (2004). Are nonconscious processes sufficient to produce false memories? *Consciousness & Cognition, 13*, 158–168.

Gallo, D. A., Sullivan, A. L., Daffner, K. R., Schacter, D. L., & Budson, A. E. (2004a). Associative recognition in Alzheimer's disease: Evidence for impaired recall-to-reject. *Neuropsychology, 18*, 556–563.

Gallo, D. A., Weiss, J. A., & Schacter, D. L. (2004b). Reducing false recognition with criterial recollection tests: Distinctiveness heuristic versus criterion shifts. *Journal of Memory & Language, 51*, 473–493.

Gardiner, J. M., Bowler, D. M., & Grice, S. J. (2003). Further evidence of preserved priming and impaired recall in adults with Asperger's syndrome. *Journal of Autism & Developmental Disorders, 33*, 259-269.

Gardiner, J. M., & Richardson-Klavehn, A. (2000). Remembering and knowing. In E. Tulving & F. I. M. Craik (Eds.), *The Oxford handbook of memory* (pp. 229–244). Oxford, England: Oxford University Press.

Garry, M., Manning, C. G., Loftus, E. F., & Sherman, S. J. (1996). Imagination inflation: Imagining a childhood event inflates confidence that it occurred. *Psychonomic Bulletin & Review, 3*, 208–214.

Geraerts, E., Smeets, E., Jelicic, M., van Heerden, J., & Merckelbach, H. (2005). Fantasy proneness, but not self-reported trauma is related to DRM performance of women reporting recovered memories of childhood sexual abuse. *Consciousness & Cognition, 14*, 602–612.

Ghetti, S. (2003). Memory for nonoccurrences: The role of metacognition. *Journal of Memory & Language, 48*, 722–739.

Ghetti, S., Qin, J. J., & Goodman, G. S. (2002). False memories in children and adults: Age, distinctiveness, and subjective experience. *Developmental Psychology, 38*, 705–718.

Gillund, G., & Shiffrin, R. M. (1984). A retrieval model for both recognition and recall. *Psychological Review, 91*, 1–67.

Glaze, J. A. (1928). The association value of non-sense syllables. *Journal of General Psychology, 35*, 255–269.

Gleaves, D. H., Smith, S. M., Butler, L. D., & Spiegel, D. (2004). False and recovered memories in the laboratory and clinic: A review of experimental and clinical evidence. *Clinical Psychology: Science & Practice, 11*, 3–28.

Goff, L. M., & Roediger, H. L. III. (1998). Imagination inflation for action events: Repeated imaginings lead to illusory recollections. *Memory & Cognition, 26*, 20–33.

Goldmann, R. E., Sullivan, A. L., Droller, D. B. J., Rugg, M. D., Curran, T., Holcomb, P. J., Schacter, D. L., Daffner, K. R., & Budson, A. E. (2003). Late frontal brain potentials distinguish true and false recognition. *NeuroReport, 15*, 1717–1720.

Goodwin, K. A., Meissner, C. A., & Ericsson, K. A. (2001). Toward a model of false recall: Experimental manipulation of encoding context and the collection of verbal reports. *Memory & Cognition, 29*, 806–819.

Grossman, L., & Eagle, M. (1970). Synonymity, antonymity, and association in false recognition responses. *Journal of Experimental Psychology, 83*, 244–248.

Gunter, R. W., Ivanko, S. L., & Bodner, G. E. (2005). Can test list context manipulations improve recognition accuracy in the DRM paradigm? *Memory, 13*, 862–873.

Hall, J. F. (1971). *Verbal learning and retention.* Philadelphia, PA: J. B. Lippincott Co.

Hall, J. W., & Kozloff, E. E. (1970). False recognitions as a function of number of presentations. *American Journal of Psychology, 83*, 272–279.

Hall, J. W., & Kozloff, E. E. (1973). False recognitions of associates of converging versus repeated words. *American Journal of Psychology, 86*, 133–139.

Hancock, T. W., Hicks, J. L., Marsh, R. L., & Ritschel, L. (2003). Measuring the activation level of critical lures in the Deese-Roediger-McDermott paradigm. *American Journal of Psychology, 116*, 1–14.

Harbluk, J. L., & Weingartner, H. J. (1997). Memory distortions in detoxified alcoholics. *Brain & Cognition, 35*, 328–330.

Hege, A. C. G., & Dodson, C. S. (2004). Why distinctive information reduces false memories: Evidence for both impoverished relational-encoding and distinctiveness heuristic accounts. *Journal of Experimental Psychology: Learning, Memory, & Cognition, 30*, 787–795.

Heit, E., Brockdorff, N., & Lamberts, K. (2004). Strategic processes in false recognition memory. *Psychonomic Bulletin & Review, 11*, 380–386.

Henkel, L. A., Johnson, M. K., & De Leonardis, D. M. (1998). Aging and source monitoring: Cognitive processes and neuropsychological correlates. *Journal of Experimental Psychology: General, 127*, 251–268.

Hicks, J. L., & Hancock, T., W. (2002). Backward associative strength determines source attributions given to false memories. *Psychonomic Bulletin & Review, 9*, 807–815.

Hicks, J. L., & Marsh, R. L. (1999). Attempts to reduce the incidence of false recall with source monitoring. *Journal of Experimental Psychology: Learning, Memory, & Cognition, 25*, 1195–1209.

Hicks, J. L., & Marsh, R. L. (2001). False recognition occurs more frequently during source identification than during old-new recognition. *Journal of Experimental Psychology: Learning, Memory & Cognition, 27*, 375–383.

Hicks, J. L., & Starns, J. J. (2005). False memories lack perceptual detail: Evidence from implicit word-stem completion and perceptual identification tests. *Journal of Memory & Language, 52*, 309–321.

Hicks, J. L., & Starns, J. J. (2006). The roles of associative strength and source memorability in the contextualization of false memory. *Journal of Memory & Language, 54*, 39–53.

Higham, P. A., & Vokey, J. R. (2004). Illusory recollection and dual-process models of recognition memory. *Quarterly Journal of Experimental Psychology: Human Experimental Psychology, 57A*, 714–744.

Hintzman, D. L. (1986). "Schema abstraction" in a multiple-trace memory model. *Psychological Review, 93*, 411–428.

Hintzman, D. L. (1988). Judgments of frequency and recognition memory in a multiple-trace memory model. *Psychological Review, 95*, 528–551.

Hintzman, D. L., & Curran, T. (1994). Retrieval dynamics of recognition and frequency judgments: Evidence for separate processes of familiarity and recall. *Journal of Memory & Language, 33*, 1–18.

Hirshman, E., Lanning, K., Master, S., & Henzler, A. (2002). Signal-detection models as tools for interpreting judgments of recollections. *Applied Cognitive Psychology, 16*, 151–156.

Hodges, J. R. (2000). Memory in the dementias. In E. Tulving & F. I. M. Craik (Eds.), *The Oxford handbook of memory* (pp. 441–459). Oxford, England: Oxford University Press.

Homa, D., Smith, C., Macak, C., Johovich, J., & Osorio, D. (2001). Recognition of facial prototypes: The importance of categorical structure and degree of learning. *Journal of Memory & Language, 44*, 443–474.

Howe, M. L. (2005). Children (but not adults) can inhibit false memories. *Psychological Science, 16*, 927–931.

Howe, M. L., Cicchetti, D., Toth, S. L., & Cerrito, B. M. (2004). True and false memories in maltreated children. *Child Development, 75*, 1402–1417.

Hull, C. L. (1933). The meaningfulness of 320 selected nonsense syllables. *American Journal of Psychology, 45*, 730–734.

Hunt, R. R., & McDaniel, M. A. (1993). The enigma of organization and distinctiveness. *Journal of Memory & Language, 32*, 421–445.

Huron, C., & Danion, J. M. (2002). Impairment of constructive memory in schizophrenia. *International Clinical Psychopharmacology, 17*, 127–133.

Huron, C., Servais, C., & Danion, J. M. (2001). Lorazepam and diazepam impair true, but not false, recognition in healthy volunteers. *Psychopharmacology, 155*, 204–209.

Hutchison, K. A. (2003). Is semantic priming due to association strength or feature overlap? A micro-analytic review. *Psychonomic Bulletin & Review, 10*, 785–813.

Hutchison, K. A., & Balota, D. A. (2005). Decoupling semantic and associative information in false memories: Explorations with semantically ambiguous and unambiguous critical lures. *Journal of Memory & Language, 52*, 1–28.

Hyman, I. E. Jr., & Billings, F. J. (1998). Individual differences and the creation of false childhood memories. *Memory, 6*, 1–20.

Hyman, I. E. Jr., Husband, T. H., & Billings, F. J. (1995). False memories of childhood experiences. *Applied Cognitive Psychology, 9*, 181–197.

Intons-Peterson, M. J., Rocchi, P., West, T., McLellan, K., & Hackney, A. (1999). Age, testing at preferred or nonpreferred times (testing optimality), and false memory. *Journal of Experimental Psychology: Learning, Memory, & Cognition, 25*, 23–40.

Israel, L., & Schacter, D. L. (1997). Pictorial encoding reduces false recognition of semantic associates. *Psychonomic Bulletin & Review, 4*, 577–581.

Jacoby, L. L., & Hollingshead, A. (1990). Toward a generate/recognize model of performance on direct and indirect tests of memory. *Journal of Memory and Language, 29*, 433–454.

Jacoby, L. L. (1991). A process dissociation framework: Separating automatic from intentional uses of memory. *Journal of Memory & Language, 30*, 513–541.

Jacoby, L. L. (1999). Ironic effects of repetition: Measuring age-related differences in memory. *Journal of Experimental Psychology: Learning, Memory, & Cognition, 25*, 3–22.

Jacoby, L. L., & Hollingshead, A. (1990). Toward a generate/recognize model of performance on direct and indirect tests of memory. *Journal of Memory and Language, 29*, 433–454.

Jacoby, L. L., Kelley, C. M., & Dywan, J. (1989). Memory attributions. In H. L. Roediger & F. I. M. Craik (Eds.), *Varieties of memory and consciousness: Essays in honour of Endel Tulving* (pp. 391–422). Hillsdale, NJ: Lawrence Erlbaum Associates, Inc.

Jacoby, L. L., Kelley, C. M., & McElree, B. D. (1999). The role of cognitive control: Early selection versus late correction. In S. Chaiken & Y. Trope (Eds.), *Dual-process theories in social psychology* (pp. 383–400). New York, NY: Guilford.

James, W. (1890). *Principles of psychology.* New York, NY: Dover.

Jenkins, J. J. (1974). Can we have a theory of meaningful memory? In R. L. Solso (Ed.), *Theories of cognitive psychology: The Loyola symposium.* Oxford, England: Lawrence Erlbaum Associates Ltd.

Johansson, M., & Stenberg, G. (2002). Inducing and reducing false memories: A Swedish version of the Deese-Roediger-McDermott paradigm. *Scandinavian Journal of Psychology, 43,* 369–383.

Johnson, M. K., Foley, M. A., Suengas, A. G., & Raye, C. L. (1988). Phenomenal characteristics of memories for perceived and imagined autobiographical events. *Journal of Experimental Psychology: General, 117,* 371–376.

Johnson, M. K., Hashtroudi, S., & Lindsay, D. S. (1993). Source monitoring. *Psychological Bulletin, 114,* 3–28.

Johnson, M. K., Kounios, J., & Nolde, S. F. (1996). Electrophysiological brain activity and memory source monitoring. *NeuroReport, 7,* 2929–2932.

Johnson, M. K., Nolde, S. F., Mather, M., Kounios, J., Schacter, D. L., & Curran, T. (1997). The similarity of brain activity associated with true and false recognition memory depends on test format. *Psychological Science, 8,* 250–257.

Johnson, M. K., & Raye, C. L. (1981). Reality monitoring. *Psychological Review, 88,* 67–85.

Johnson, M. K., Raye, C. L., Foley, H. J., & Foley, M. A. (1981). Cognitive operations and decision bias in reality monitoring. *American Journal of Psychology, 94,* 37–64.

Jones, T. C., & Jacoby, L. L. (2001). Feature and conjunction errors in recognition memory: Evidence for dual-process theory. *Journal of Memory & Language, 45,* 82–102.

Jou, J., Matus, Y. E., Aldridge, J. W., Rogers, D. M., & Zimmerman, R. L. (2004). How similar is false recognition to veridical recognition objectively and subjectively? *Memory & Cognition, 32,* 824–840.

Kausler, D. H. (1974). *Psychology of verbal learning and memory.* New York, NY: Academic Press.

Kausler, D. H., & Settle, A. V. (1973). Associative relatedness vs. synonymity in the false-recognition effect. *Bulletin of the Psychonomic Society, 2,* 129–131.

Kawasaki-Miyaji, Y., Inoue, T., & Yama, H. (2003). Cross-linguistic false recognition: How do Japanese-dominant bilinguals process two languages: Japanese and English? *Psychologia, 46,* 255–267.

Kawasaki-Miyaji, Y., & Yama, H. (in press). The difference between implicit and explicit associative processes at study to create false memory in the DRM paradigm. *Memory.*

Kellogg, R. T. (2001). Presentation modality and mode of recall in verbal false memory. *Journal of Experimental Psychology: Learning, Memory, & Cognition, 27,* 913–919.

Kensinger, E. A., & Corkin, S. (2004). The effects of emotional content and aging on false memories. *Cognitive, Affective, & Behavioral Neuroscience, 4,* 1–9.

Kensinger, E. A., & Schacter, D. L. (1999). When true memories suppress false memories: Effects of ageing. *Cognitive Neuropsychology, 16,* 399–415.

Kihlstrom, J. F. (2004). An unbalanced balancing act: Blocked, recovered, and false memories in the laboratory and clinic. *Clinical Psychology: Science & Practice, 11,* 34–41.

Kim, N. S., & Ahn, W. (2002). Clinical psychologists' theory-based representations of mental disorders predict their diagnostic reasoning and memory. *Journal of Experimental Psychology: General, 131,* 451–476.

Kimball, D. R., & Bjork, R. A. (2002). Influences of intentional and unintentional forgetting on false memories. *Journal of Experimental Psychology: General, 131,* 116–130.

Kintsch, W. (1970). Models for free recall and recognition. In D. A. Norman (Ed.), *Models of human memory.* New York, NY: Academic Press.

Kirkpatrick, E. A. (1894). An experimental study in memory. *Psychological Review, 1,* 602–609.

Koriat, A., & Goldsmith, M. (1996). Monitoring and control processes in the strategic regulation of memory accuracy. *Psychological Review, 103,* 490–517.

Koutstaal, W., & Schacter, D. L. (1997). Gist-based false recognition of pictures in older and younger adults. *Journal of Memory & Language, 37,* 555–583.

Koutstaal, W., Schacter, D. L., & Brenner, C. (2001a). Dual task demands and gist-based false recognition of pictures in younger and older adults. *Journal of Memory & Language, 44,* 399–426.

Koutstaal, W., Schacter, D. L., Galluccio, L., & Stofer, K. A. (1999a). Reducing gist-based false recognition in older adults: Encoding and retrieval manipulations. *Psychology & Aging, 14,* 220–237.

Koutstaal, W., Schacter, D. L., Verfaellie, M., Brenner, C., & Jackson, E. M. (1999b). Perceptually based false recognition of novel objects in amnesia: Effects of category size and similarity to category prototypes. *Cognitive Neuropsychology, 16,* 317–341.

Koutstaal, W., Verfaellie, M., & Schacter, D. L. (2001b). Recognizing identical versus similar categorically related common objects: Further evidence for degraded gist representations in amnesia. *Neuropsychology, 15,* 268–289.

Lacey, J. I., & Smith, R. L. (1954). Conditioning and generalization of unconscious anxiety. *Science, 120,* 1045–1052.

Lampinen, J. M., Leding, J. K., Reed, K. & Odegard, T.N. (Unpublished, 2006). Global gist extraction in children and adults.

Lampinen, J. M., Meier, C., Arnal, J.A., & Leding, J.K. (2005). Compelling untruths: Content borrowing and vivid false memories. *Journal of Experimental Psychology: Learning, Memory & Cognition, 31,* 954–963.

Lampinen, J. M., Neuschatz, J. S., & Payne, D. G. (1998). Memory illusions and consciousness: Examining the phenomenology of true and false memories. *Current Psychology: Developmental, Learning, Personality, Social, 16,* 181–224.

Lampinen, J. M., Neuschatz, J. S., & Payne, D. G. (1999). Source attributions and false memories: A test of the demand characteristics account. *Psychonomic Bulletin & Review, 6,* 130–135.

Lampinen, J. M., Odegard, T. N., Blackshear, E., & Toglia, M. P. (in press). Phantom ROC. In F. Columbus (Ed.), *Progress in experimental psychology research.* Hauppauge, NY: Nova.

Lampinen, J. M., Odegard, T. N., & Neuschatz, J. S. (2004). Robust recollection rejection in the memory conjunction paradigm. *Journal of Experimental Psychology: Learning, Memory, & Cognition, 30,* 332–342.

Lampinen, J. M., & Schwartz, R. M. (2000). The impersistence of false memory persistence. *Memory, 8,* 393–400.

LaVoie, D. J., & Faulkner, K. (2000). Age differences in false recognition using a forced choice paradigm. *Experimental Aging Research, 26,* 367–381.

Laws, K. R., & Bhatt, R. (2005). False memories and delusional ideation in normal healthy subjects. *Personality and Individual Differences, 39,* 775–781.

Lee, Y. S., & Chang, S. C. (2004). Effects of criterion shift on false memory. *Psychologia: An International Journal of Psychology in the Orient, 47,* 191–202.

Lenton, A. P., Blair, I. V., & Hastie, R. (2001). Illusions of gender: Stereotypes evoke false memories. *Journal of Experimental Social Psychology, 37,* 3–14.

Libby, L. K., & Neisser, U. (2001). Structure and strategy in the associative false memory paradigm. *Memory, 9,* 145–163.

Light, L. L., Prull, M. P., La Voie, D. J., & Healy, M. R. (2000). Dual-process theories of memory in old age. In T. J. Perfect & E. A. Maylor (Eds.), *Models of cognitive aging* (pp. 238–300). New York, NY: Oxford University Press.

Lindauer, B. K., & Paris, S. G. (1976). Problems with a false recognition paradigm for developmental memory research. *Journal of Experimental Child Psychology, 22,* 319–330.

Lindsay, D. S., & Johnson, M. K. (1989). The eyewitness suggestibility effect and memory for source. *Memory & Cognition, 17,* 349–358.

Lindsay, D. S., & Read, J. D. (1994). Psychotherapy and memories of childhood sexual abuse: A cognitive perspective. *Applied Cognitive Psychology, 8,* 281–338.

Lockhart, R. S., & Craik, F. I. M. (1990). Levels of processing: A retrospective commentary on a framework for memory research. *Canadian Journal of Psychology, 44,* 87–112.

Loftus, E. F. (1991). Made in memory: Distortions in recollection after misleading information. In G. H. Bower (Ed.), *The psychology of learning and motivation: Advances in research and theory* (Vol. 27, pp. 187–215). San Diego, CA: Academic Press.

Loftus, E. F., Miller, D. G., & Burns, H. J. (1978). Semantic integration of verbal information into a visual memory. *Journal of Experimental Psychology: Human Learning & Memory, 4,* 19–31.

Lövdén, M. (2003). The episodic memory and inhibition accounts of age-related increases in false memories: A consistency check. *Journal of Memory & Language, 49,* 268–283.

Lövdén, M., & Johansson, M. (2003). Are covert verbal responses mediating false implicit memory? *Psychonomic Bulletin & Review, 10,* 724–729.

Lövdén, M., & Wahlin, Å. (2005). The sensory-cognition association in adulthood: Different magnitudes for processing speed, inhibition, episodic memory, and false memory? *Scandanadian Journal of Psychology, 46,* 253–262.

MacLeod, C. M. (1998). Directed forgetting. In J. M. Golding & C. M. MacLeod (Eds.), *Intentional forgetting: Interdisciplinary approaches* (pp. 1–57). Mahwah, NJ: Lawrence Erlbaum Associates, Inc.

MacLeod, C. M., & Nelson, T. O. (1976). An nonmonotonic lag function for false alarms to associates. *American Journal of Psychology, 89,* 127–135.

Madigan, S., & Neuse, J. (2004). False recognition and word length: A reanalysis of Roediger, Watson, McDermott, and Gallo (2001) and some new data. *Psychonomic Bulletin & Review, 11,* 567–573.

Marche, T. A., Brainerd, C. J., Lane, D. G., & Loehr, J. D. (2005). Item method directed forgetting diminishes false memory. *Memory, 13,* 749–758.

Marsh, E. J., & Bower, G. H. (2004). The role of rehearsal and generation in false memory creation. *Memory, 12,* 748–761.

Marsh, E. J., McDermott, K. B., & Roediger, H. L. III. (2004). Does test-induced priming play a role in the creation of false memories? *Memory, 12,* 44–55.

Marsh, R. L., & Hicks, J. L. (1998). Test formats change source-monitoring decision processes. *Journal of Experimental Psychology: Learning, Memory, & Cognition, 24,* 1137–1151.

Marsh, R. L., & Hicks, J. L. (2001). Output monitoring tests reveal false memories of memories that never existed. *Memory, 9,* 39–51.

Mather, M., Henkel, L. A., & Johnson, M. K. (1997). Evaluating characteristics of false memories: Remember/know judgments and memory characteristics questionnaire compared. *Memory & Cognition, 25,* 826–837.

Maylor, E. A., & Mo, A. (1999). Effects of study-test modality on false recognition. *British Journal of Psychology, 90,* 477–493.

McCabe, D. P., Presmanes, A. G., Robertson, C. L., & Smith, A. D. (2004). Item-specific processing reduces false memories. *Psychonomic Bulletin & Review, 11,* 1074–1079.

McCabe, D. P., & Smith, A. D. (2002). The effect of warnings on false memories in young and older adults. *Memory & Cognition, 30,* 1065–1077.

McClelland, J. L., & Rumelhart, D. E. (1986). *Parallel distributed processing: Explorations in the microstructure of cognition.* Cambridge, MA: MIT Press.

McDermott, K. B. (1996). The persistence of false memories in list recall. *Journal of Memory & Language, 35,* 212–230.

McDermott, K. B. (1997). Priming on perceptual implicit memory tests can be achieved through presentation of associates. *Psychonomic Bulletin & Review, 4,* 582–586.

McDermott, K. B, & Roediger, H. L. III. (1998). Attempting to avoid illusory memories: Robust false recognition of associates persists under conditions of explicit warnings and immediate testing. *Journal of Memory & Language, 39,* 508–520.

McDermott, K. B., & Watson, J. M. (2001). The rise and fall of false recall: The impact of presentation duration. *Journal of Memory & Language, 45*, 160–176.

McEvoy, C. L., Nelson, D. L., & Komatsu, T. (1999). What is the connection between true and false memories? The differential roles of interitem associations in recall and recognition. *Journal of Experimental Psychology: Learning, Memory, & Cognition, 25*, 1177–1194.

McGeoch, J. A. (1942). *The psychology of human learning.* New York, NY: Longmans, Green and Co.

McGeoch, J. A., & Irion, A. L. (1952). *The psychology of human learning* (2nd ed.). New York, NY: Longmans, Green and Co.

McKelvie, S. J. (1999). Effect of retrieval instructions on false recall. *Perceptual & Motor Skills, 88*, 876–878.

McKelvie, S. J. (2001). Effects of free and forced retrieval instructions on false recall and recognition. *Journal of General Psychology, 128*, 261–278.

McKelvie, S. J. (2003). False recall with the DRMRS ("drummers") procedure: A quantitative summary and review. *Perceptual & Motor Skills, 97*, 1011–1030.

McKelvie, S. J. (2004). False recognition with the Deese-Roediger-McDermott-Reid-Solso procedure: A quantitative summary. *Perceptual & Motor Skills, 98*, 1387–1408.

McKhann, G., Drachman, D., Folstein, M., Katzman, R., Price, D., & Stadlan, E. M. (1984). Clinical diagnosis of Alzheimer's disease: Report of the NINCDS-ADRDA work group under the auspices of the Department of Health and Human Services Task Force on Alzheimer's disease. *Neurology, 34*, 934–939.

McKone, E. (2004). Distinguishing true from false memories via lexical decision as a perceptual implicit test. *Australian Journal of Psychology, 56*, 42–49.

McKone, E., & Murphy, B. (2000). Implicit false memory: Effects of modality and multiple study presentations on long-lived semantic priming. *Journal of Memory & Language, 43*, 89–109.

McNally, R. J. (2003). *Remembering trauma.* Cambridge: Harvard University Press.

Meade, M. L., & Roediger, H. L. III. (2002). Explorations in the social contagion of memory. *Memory & Cognition, 30*, 995–1009.

Meade, M. L., & Roediger, H. L. III. (in press). The effect of forced recall on illusory recollection in younger and older adults. *American Journal of Psychology.*

Melo, B., Winocur, G., & Moscovitch, M. (1999). False recall and false recognition: An examination of the effects of selective and combined lesions to the medial temporal lobe/diencephalon and frontal lobe structures. *Cognitive Neuropsychology, 16*, 343–359.

Merritt, P. S., & DeLosh, E. L. (Unpublished, 2003). *Modality specific contributions to true and false recognition: An ERP study.* Colorado State University, Fort Collins, CO.

Metcalfe, J., Funnell, M., & Gazzaniga, M. (1995). Right-hemisphere memory superiority: Studies of a split-brain patient. *Psychological Science, 6*, 157–164.

Milani, R., & Curran, H. V. (2000). Effects of a low dose of alcohol on recollective experience of illusory memory. *Psychopharmacology, 147*, 397–402.

Miller, A. R., Baratta, C., Wynveen, C., & Rosenfeld, J. P. (2001). P300 latency, but not amplitude or topography, distinguishes between true and false recognition. *Journal of Experimental Psychology: Learning, Memory, & Cognition, 27*, 354–361.

Miller, M. B., & Wolford, G. L. (1999). Theoretical commentary: The role of criterion shift in false memory. *Psychological Review, 106*, 398–405.

Mintzer, M. Z., & Griffiths, R. R. (2000). Acute effects of triazolam on false recognition. *Memory & Cognition, 28*, 1357–1365.

Mintzer, M. Z., & Griffiths, R. R. (2001a). Acute dose-effects of scopolamine on false recognition. *Psychopharmacology, 153*, 425–433.

Mintzer, M. Z., & Griffiths, R. R. (2001b). Alcohol and false recognition: A dose-effect study. *Psychopharmacology, 159*, 51–57.

Mintzer, M. Z., & Griffiths, R. R. (2001c). False recognition in triazolam-induced amnesia. *Journal of Memory & Language, 44,* 475–492.

Mintzer, M. Z., & Snodgrass, J. G. (1999). The picture superiority effect: Support for the distinctiveness model. *American Journal of Psychology, 112,* 113–146.

Mitchell, K. J., & Johnson, M. K. (2000). Source monitoring: Attributing mental experiences. In E. Tulving & F. I. M. Craik (Eds.), *The Oxford handbook of memory* (pp. 179–195). Oxford, England: Oxford University Press.

Morgan, R. L., & Underwood, B. J. (1950). Proactive inhibition as a function of response similarity. *Journal of Experimental Psychology, 40,* 592–603.

Moritz, S., Gläscher, J., & Brassen, S. (2005). Investigation of mood-congruent false and true memory recognition in depression. *Depression and Anxiety, 21,* 9–17.

Moritz, S., Woodward, T. S., Cuttler, C., Whitman, J. C., & Watson, J. M. (2004). False memories in schizophrenia. *Neuropsychology, 18,* 276–283.

Morris, C. D., Bransford, J. D., & Franks, J. J. (1977). Levels of processing versus transfer appropriate processing. *Journal of Verbal Learning & Verbal Behavior, 16,* 519–533.

Moscovitch, M. (1995). Confabulation. In D. L. Schacter, J. T. Coyle, G. D. Fischbach, M. M. Mesulam, & L. E. Sullivan (Eds.), *Memory distortion: How minds, brains, and societies reconstruct the past* (pp. 226–254). Cambridge, MA: Harvard University Press.

Mukai, A. (2005). Awareness of the false memory manipulation and false recall for people's names as critical lrues in the Deese-Roediger-McDermott paradigm. *Perceptual & Motor Skills, 101,* 546–560.

Multhaup, K. S., & Conner, C. A. (2002). The effects of considering nonlist sources on the Deese-Roediger-McDermott memory illusion. *Journal of Memory & Language, 47,* 214–228.

Murdock, B. B. (1962). The serial position effect of free recall. *Journal of Experimental Psychology, 64,* 482–488.

Nadel, L., Payne, J. D., & Jacobs, W. J. (2002). The relationship between episodic memory and context: Clues from memory errors made while under stress. *Physiological Research, 51,* S3–S11.

Nebes, R. D. (1989). Semantic memory in Alzheimer's disease. *Psychological Bulletin, 106,* 377–394.

Neely, J. H. (1991). Semantic priming effects in visual word recognition: A selective review of current findings and theories. In D. Besner & G. Humphreys (Eds.), *Basic processes in reading: Visual word recognition* (pp. 264–336). Hillsdale, NJ: Lawrence Erlbaum Associates, Inc.

Neisser, U. (1967). *Cognitive psychology.* New York, NY: Appleton-Century-Crofts.

Nelson, D. L., McEvoy, C. L., & Pointer, L. (2003). Spreading activation or spooky action at a distance? *Journal of Experimental Psychology: Learning, Memory, & Cognition, 29,* 42–51.

Nelson, D. L., McEvoy, C. L., & Schreiber, T. A. (1998a). The University of South Florida word association, rhyme, and word fragment norms. http://www.usf.edu/FreeAssociation/

Nelson, D. L., McKinney, V. M., Gee, N. R., & Janczura, G. A. (1998b). Interpreting the influence of implicitly activated memories on recall and recognition. *Psychological Review, 105,* 299–324.

Nessler, D., & Mecklinger, A. (2003). ERP correlates of true and false recognition after different retention delays: Stimulus- and response-related processes. *Psychophysiology, 40,* 146–159.

Nessler, D., Mecklinger, A., & Penney, T. B. (2001). Event related brain potentials and illusory memories: The effects of differential encoding. *Cognitive Brain Research, 10,* 283–301.

Neuschatz, J. S., Benoit, G. E., & Payne, D. G. (2003). Effective warnings in the Deese-Roediger-McDermott false-memory paradigm: The role of identifiability. *Journal of Experimental Psychology: Learning, Memory, & Cognition, 29,* 35–40.

Neuschatz, J. S., Lampinen, J. M., Preston, E. L., Hawkins, E. R., & Toglia, M. P. (2002). The effect of memory schemata on memory and the phenomenological experience of naturalistic situations. *Applied Cognitive Psychology, 16,* 687–708.

Neuschatz, J. S., Payne, D. G., Lampinen, J. M., & Toglia, M. P. (2001). Assessing the effectiveness of warnings and the phenomenological characteristics of false memories. *Memory, 9,* 53–71.

Newstead, B. A., & Newstead, S. E. (1998). False recall and false memory: The effects of instructions on memory errors. *Applied Cognitive Psychology, 12,* 67–79.

Norman, K. A., & Schacter, D. L. (1997). False recognition in younger and older adults: Exploring the characteristics of illusory memories. *Memory & Cognition, 25,* 838–848.

Nosofsky, R. M. (1991). Tests of an exemplar model for relating perceptual classification and recognition memory. *Journal of Experimental Psychology: Human Perception & Performance, 17,* 3–27.

Odegard, T. N., & Lampinen, J. M. (2004). Memory conjunction errors for autobiographical events: More than just familiarity. *Memory, 12,* 288–300.

Paivio, A. (1971). *Imagery and verbal processes.* New York, NY: Holt, Rinehart, & Winston.

Park, L., Shobe, K. K., & Kihlstrom, J. F. (2005). Associative and categorical relations in the associative memory illusion. *Psychological Science, 16,* 792–797.

Parkin, A. J. (1983). The relationship between orienting tasks and the structure of memory traces: Evidence from false recognition. *British Journal of Psychology, 74,* 61–69.

Parkin, A. J., Bindschaedler, C., Harsent, L., & Metzler, C. (1996). Pathological false alarm rates following damage to the left frontal cortex. *Brain & Cognition, 32,* 14–27.

Paul, L. M. (1979). Two models of recognition memory: A test. *Journal of Experimental Psychology: Human Learning & Memory, 5,* 45–51.

Payne, D. G., Elie, C. J., Blackwell, J. M., & Neuschatz, J. S. (1996). Memory illusions: Recalling, recognizing, and recollecting events that never occurred. *Journal of Memory & Language, 35,* 261–285.

Payne, J. D., Nadel, L., Allen, J. J. B., Thomas, K. G. F., & Jacobs, W. J. (2002). The effects of experimentally induced stress on false recognition. *Memory, 10,* 1–6.

Peiffer, L. C., & Trull, T. J. (2000). Predictors of suggestibility and false-memory production in young adult women. *Journal of Personality Assessment, 74,* 384–399.

Pérez-Mata, M. N., Read, J. D., & Diges, M. (2002). Effects of divided attention and word concreteness on correct recall and false memory reports. *Memory, 10,* 161–177.

Pesta, B. J., Murphy, M. D., & Sanders, R. E. (2001). Are emotionally charged lures immune to false memory? *Journal of Experimental Psychology: Learning, Memory, & Cognition, 27,* 328–338.

Petersen, S. E., Fox, P. T., Posner, M. I., Mintun, M. A., & Raichle, M. E. (1989). Positron emission tomographic studies of the processing of single words. *Journal of Cognitive Neuroscience, 1,* 153–170.

Pierce, B. H., Gallo, D. A., Weiss, J. A., & Schacter, D. L. (2005a). The modality effect in false recognition: Evidence for test-based monitoring. *Memory & Cognition, 33,* 1407–1413.

Pierce, B. H., Simons, J. S., & Schacter, D. L. (2004). Aging and the seven sins of memory. *Advances in Cell Aging and Gerentology, 15,* 1–40.

Pierce, B. H., Sullivan, A. L., Schacter, D. L., & Budson, A. E. (2005b). Comparing source-based and gist-based false recognition in aging and Alzheimer's disease. *Neuropsychology, 19,* 411–419.

Platt, R. D., Lacey, S. C., Iobst, A. D., & Finkelman, D. (1998). Absorption, dissociation, and fantasy-proneness as predictors of memory distortion in autobiographical and laboratory-generated memories. *Applied Cognitive Psychology, 12,* S77–S89.

Pohl, R. F. (Ed.). (2004). *Cognitive illusions: A handbook on fallacies and biases in thinking, judgment and memory*. Hove, England: Psychology Press.

Pope, K. S. (1996). Memory, abuse, and science: Questioning claims about the false memory syndrome epidemic. *American Psychologist, 51*, 957–974.

Posner, M. I., & Keele, S. W. (1968). On the genesis of abstract ideas. *Journal of Experimental Psychology, 77*, 353–363.

Posner, M. I., & Keele, S. W. (1970). Retention of abstract ideas. *Journal of Experimental Psychology, 83*, 304–308.

Raaijmakers, J. G. W., & Zeelenberg, R. (2004). Evaluating the evidence for nonconscious processes in producing false memories. *Consciousness & Cognition, 13*, 169–172.

Rajaram, S. (1993). Remembering and knowing: Two means of access to the personal past. *Memory & Cognition, 21*, 89–102.

Read, J. D. (1996). From a passing thought to a false memory in 2 minutes: Confusing real and illusory events. *Psychonomic Bulletin & Review, 3*, 105–111.

Reich, R. R., Goldman, M. S., & Noll, J. A. (2004). Using the false memory paradigm to test two key elements of alcohol expectancy theory. *Experimental & Clinical Psychopharmacology, 12*, 102–110.

Reyna, V. F. (1995). Interference effects in memory and reasoning: A fuzzy-trace theory analysis. In F. N. Dempster & C. J. Brainerd (Eds.), *Interference and inhibition in cognition* (pp. 29–59). San Diego, CA: Academic Press.

Reyna, V. F. (1998). Fuzzy-trace theory and false memory. In M. Intons-Peterson & D. Best (Eds.), *Memory distortions and their prevention* (pp. 15–27). Mahwah, NJ: Lawrence Erlbaum Associates, Inc.

Reyna, V. F., & Brainerd, C. J. (1995). Fuzzy-trace theory: An interim synthesis. *Learning and Individual Differences, 7*, 1–75.

Reyna, V. F. & Kiernan, B. (1994). The development of gist versus verbatim memory in sentence recognition: Effects of lexical familiarity, semantic content, encoding instruction, and retention interval. *Developmental Psychology, 30*, 178–191.

Reyna, V. F., & Kiernan, B. (1995). Children's memory and interpretation of psychological metaphors. *Metaphor and Symbolic Activity, 10*, 309–331.

Reyna, V. F., & Lloyd, F. (1997). Theories of false memory in children and adults. *Learning & Individual Differences, 9*, 95–123.

Reyna, V. F., Mills, B., Estrada, S., & Brainerd, C. J. (in press). False memory in children: Data, theory, and legal implications. In M. Toglia & D. Read (Eds.), *Handbook of eyewitness psychology* (Vol. 1). Mahwah, NJ: Lawrence Erlbaum Associates, Inc.

Reyna, V. F., & Titcomb, A. L. (1996). Constraints on the suggestibility of eyewitness testimony: A fuzzy-trace theory analysis. In D. G. Payne & F. G. Conrad (Eds.), *Intersections in basic and applied memory research* (pp. 27–55). Mahwah, NJ: Lawrence Erlbaum Associates, Inc.

Reysen, M. B., & Nairne, J. S. (2002). Part-set cuing of false memories. *Psychonomic Bulletin & Review, 9*, 389–393.

Rhodes, M. G., & Anastasi, J. S. (2000). The effects of a levels-of-processing manipulation on false recall. *Psychonomic Bulletin & Review, 7*, 158–162.

Robinson, K. J., & Roediger, H. L. III. (1997). Associative processes in false recall and false recognition. *Psychological Science, 8*, 231–237.

Roediger, H. L. III. (1974). Inhibiting effects of recall. *Memory & Cognition, 2*, 261–269.

Roediger, H. L. III. (1990). Implicit memory: Retention without remembering. *American Psychologist, 45*, 1043–1056.

Roediger, H. L. III. (1996). Memory illusions. *Journal of Memory & Language, 35*, 76–100.

Roediger, H. L. III, Balota, D. A., & Watson, J. M. (2001a). Spreading activation and the arousal of false memories. In H. L. Roediger III, J. S. Nairne, I. Neath, & A. M. Surprenant (Eds.), *The nature of remembering: Essays in honor of Robert G. Crowder* (pp. 95–115). Washington, DC: American Psychological Association.

Roediger, H. L. III, & Gallo, D. A. (2001). Levels of processing: Some unanswered questions. In M. Naveh-Benjamin, M. Moscovitch, & H. L. Roediger (Eds.), *Perspectives on human memory and cognitive aging: Essays in honour of Fergus Craik.* New York, NY: Psychology Press.

Roediger, H. L. III, & McDermott, K. B. (1995). Creating false memories: Remembering words not presented in lists. *Journal of Experimental Psychology: Learning, Memory, & Cognition, 21,* 803–814.

Roediger, H. L. III, & McDermott, K. B. (1996). False perceptions of false memories. *Journal of Experimental Psychology: Learning, Memory, & Cognition, 22,* 814–816.

Roediger, H. L. III, & McDermott, K. B. (1999). False alarms and false memories. *Psychological Review, 106,* 406–410.

Roediger, H. L. III, & McDermott, K. B. (2000). Tricks of memory. *Current Directions in Psychological Science, 9,* 123–127.

Roediger, H. L. III, McDermott, K. B., Pisoni, D. B., & Gallo, D. A. (2004). Illusory recollection of voices. *Memory, 12,* 586–602.

Roediger, H. L. III, McDermott, K. B., & Robinson, K. J. (1998). The role of associative processes in creating false memories. In M. A. Conway, S. E. Gathercole, & C. Cornoldi (Eds.), *Theories of memory II* (pp. 187–245). Hove, England: Psychology Press.

Roediger, H. L. III, Meade, M. L., & Bergman, E. T. (2001b). Social contagion of memory. *Psychonomic Bulletin & Review, 8,* 365–371.

Roediger, H. L. III, Meade, M. L., Wong, A., Olson, K. R., & Gallo, D. A. (Unpublished, 2003). *The social transmission of false memories: Comparing Bartlett's (1932) repeated and serial reproduction techniques.* Washington University, St. Louis, MO.

Roediger, H. L. III, & Neely, J. H. (1982). Retrieval blocks in episodic and semantic memory. *Canadian Journal of Psychology, 36,* 213–242.

Roediger, H. L. III, & Payne, D. G. (1982). Hypermnesia: The role of repeated testing. *Journal of Experimental Psychology: Learning, Memory, & Cognition, 8,* 66–72.

Roediger, H. L. III, Watson, J. M., McDermott, K. B., & Gallo, D. A. (2001c). Factors that determine false recall: A multiple regression analysis. *Psychonomic Bulletin & Review, 8,* 385–407.

Rotello, C. M., Macmillan, N. A., & Van Tassel, G. (2000). Recall-to-reject in recognition: Evidence from ROC curves. *Journal of Memory & Language, 43,* 67–88.

Rugg, M. D., & Allan, K. (2000). Memory retrieval: An electrophysiological persepective. In M. S. Gazzaniga (Ed.), *The new cognitive neurosciences* (pp. 805–816). Cambridge, MA: MIT Press.

Russell, W. A., & Jenkins, J. J. (1954). *The complete Minnesota norms for responses to 100 words from the Kent-Rosanoff Word Association Test* (Technical Report No. 11, Contract N8 ONR 66216, Office of Naval Research). University of Minnesota.

Rybash, J. M., & Colilla, J. L. (1994). Source memory deficits and frontal lobe functioning in children. *Developmental Neuropsychology, 10,* 67–73.

Rybash, J. M., & Hrubi-Bopp, K. L. (2000). Source monitoring and false recollection: A life span developmental perspective. *Experimental Aging Research, 26,* 75–87.

Saegert, J. (1971). Retention interval and false recognition of implicit associative responses. *Journal of Verbal Learning & Verbal Behavior, 10,* 511–515.

Schacter, D. L. (1995). Memory distortion: History and current status. In D. L. Schacter, J. T. Coyle, G. D. Fischbach, M. M. Mesulam, & L. E. Sullivan (Eds.), *Memory distortions: How minds, brains, and societies reconstruct the past* (pp. 1–43). Cambridge, MA: Harvard University Press.

Schacter, D. L. (1999). The seven sins of memory: Insights from psychology and cognitive neuroscience. *American Psychologist, 54,* 182–203.

Schacter, D. L., Buckner, R. L., Koutstaal, W., Dale, A. M., & Rosen, B. R. (1997a). Late onset of anterior prefrontal activity during true and false recognition: An event-related fMRI study. *Neuroimage, 6,* 259–269.

Schacter, D. L., Cendan, D. L., Dodson, C. S., & Clifford, E. R. (2001). Retrieval conditions and false recognition: Testing the distinctiveness heuristic. *Psychonomic Bulletin & Review, 8*, 827–833.

Schacter, D. L., Curran, T., Gallucio, L., Millberg, W. P., & Bates, J. F. (1996a). False recognition and the right frontal lobe: A case study. *Neuropsychologia, 34*, 793–808.

Schacter, D. L., Israel, L., & Racine, C. (1999). Suppressing false recognition in younger and older adults: The distinctiveness heuristic. *Journal of Memory & Language, 40*, 1–24.

Schacter, D. L., Norman, K. A., & Koutstaal, W. (1998a). The cognitive neuroscience of constructive memory. *Annual Review of Psychology, 49*, 289–318.

Schacter, D. L., Reiman, E., Curran, T., Yun, L. S., Bandy, D., McDermott, K. B., & Roediger, H. L. III. (1996b). Neuroanatomical correlates of veridical and illusory recognition memory: Evidence from positron emission tomography. *Neuron, 17*, 267–274.

Schacter, D. L., & Slotnick, S. D. (2004). The cognitive neuroscience of memory distortion. *Neuron, 44*, 149–160.

Schacter, D. L., Verfaellie, M., & Anes, M. D. (1997b). Illusory memories in amnesic patients: Conceptual and perceptual false recognition. *Neuropsychology, 11*, 331–342.

Schacter, D. L., Verfaellie, M., Anes, M. D., & Racine, C. (1998b). When true recognition suppresses false recognition: Evidence from amnesic patients. *Journal of Cognitive Neuroscience, 10*, 668–679.

Schacter, D. L., Verfaellie, M., & Pradere, D. (1996c). Neuropsychology of memory illusions: False recall and recognition in amnesic patients. *Journal of Memory & Language, 35*, 319–334.

Schooler, J. W., Bendiksen, M. A., & Ambadar, Z. (1997). Taking the middle line: Can we accommodate both fabricated and recovered memories of sexual abuse? In M. Conway (Ed.), *Recovered and false memories* (pp. 251–292). Oxford, England: Oxford University Press.

Schooler, J. W., & Loftus, E. F. (1993). Multiple mechanisms mediate individual differences in eyewitness accuracy and suggestibility. In J. M. Puckett & H. W. Reese (Eds.), *Mechanisms of everyday cognition* (pp. 177–204). Hillsdale, NJ: Lawrence Erlbaum Associates, Inc.

Seamon, J. G., Berko, J. R., Sahlin, B., Yu, Y., Colker, J. M., & Gottfried, D. H. (in press). Can false memories spontaneously recover? *Memory*.

Seamon, J. G., Goodkind, M. S., Dumey, A. D., Dick, E., Aufseeser, M. S., Strickland, S. E., Woulfin, J. R., & Fung, N. S. (2003). "If I didn't write it, why would I remember it?" Effects of encoding, attention, and practice on accurate and false memory. *Memory & Cognition, 31*, 445–457.

Seamon, J. G., Guerry, J. D., Marsh, G. P., & Tracy, M. C. (2002a). Accurate and false recall in the Deese/Roediger and McDermott procedure: A methodological note on sex of participant. *Psychological Reports, 91*, 423–427.

Seamon, J. G., Lee, I. A., Toner, S. K., Wheeler, R. H., Goodkind, M. S., & Birch, A. D. (2002b). Thinking of critical words during study is unnecessary for false memory in the Deese, Roediger, and McDermott procedure. *Psychological Science, 13*, 526–531.

Seamon, J. G., Luo, C. R., & Gallo, D. A. (1998). Creating false memories of words with or without recognition of list items: Evidence for nonconscious processes. *Psychological Science, 9*, 20–26.

Seamon, J. G., Luo, C. R., Kopecky, J. J., Price, C. A., Rothschild, L., Fung, N. S., & Schwartz, M. A. (2002c). Are false memories more difficult to forget than accurate memories? The effect of retention interval on recall and recognition. *Memory & Cognition, 30*, 1054–1064.

Seamon, J. G., Luo, C. R., Schlegel, S. E., Greene, S. E., & Goldenberg, A. B. (2000). False memory for categorized pictures and words: The category associates procedure for studying memory errors in children and adults. *Journal of Memory & Language, 42*, 120–146.

Seamon, J. G., Luo, C. R., Schwartz, M. A., Jones, K. J., Lee, D. M., & Jones, S. J. (2002d). Repetition can have similar or different effects on accurate and false recognition. *Journal of Memory & Language, 46*, 323–340.

Seamon, J. G., Luo, C. R., Shulman, E. P., Toner, S. K., & Caglar, S. (2002e). False memories are hard to inhibit: Differential effects of directed forgetting on accurate and false recall in the DRM procedure. *Memory, 10*, 225–238.

Shiffrin, R. M., Huber, D. E., & Marinelli, K. (1995). Effects of category length and strength on familiarity in recognition. *Journal of Experimental Psychology: Learning, Memory, & Cognition, 21*, 267–287.

Simons, J. S., Lee, A. C. H., Graham, K. S., Verfaellie, M., Koutstaal, W., Hodges, J. R., Schacter, D. L., & Budson, A. E. (2005). Failing to get the gist: Reduced false recognition of semantic associates in semantic dementia. *Neuropsychology, 19*, 353–361.

Slamecka, N. J. (1968). An examination of trace storage in free recall. *Journal of Experimental Psychology, 76*, 504–513.

Slamecka, N. J., & Graf, P. (1978). The generation effect: Delineation of a phenomenon. *Journal of Experimental Psychology: Human Learning & Memory, 4*, 592–604.

Slotnick, S. D., & Schacter, D. L. (2004). A sensory signature that distinguishes true from false memories. *Nature Neuroscience, 7*, 664–672.

Smith, R. E., & Hunt, R. R. (1998). Presentation modality affects false memory. *Psychonomic Bulletin & Review, 5*, 710–715.

Smith, R. E., Lozito, J. P., & Bayen, U. (2005). Adult age differences in distinctive processing: The modality effect on false recall. *Psychology & Aging, 20*, 486–492.

Smith, S. M., Gerkens, D. R., Pierce, B. H., & Choi, H. (2002). The roles of associative responses at study and semantically guided recollection at test in false memory: The Kirkpatrick and Deese hypotheses. *Journal of Memory & Language, 47*, 436–447.

Smith, S. M., Tindell, D. R., Pierce, B. H., Gilliland, T. R., & Gerkens, D. R. (2001). The use of source memory to identify one's own episodic confusion errors. *Journal of Experimental Psychology: Learning, Memory, & Cognition, 27*, 362–374.

Smith, S. M., Ward, T. B., Tindell, D. R., Sifonis, C. M., & Wilkenfeld, M. J. (2000). Category structure and created memories. *Memory & Cognition, 28*, 386–395.

Snodgrass, J. G., & Corwin, J. (1988). Pragmatics of measuring recognition memory: Applications to dementia and amnesia. *Journal of Experimental Psychology: General, 117*, 34–50.

Solso, R. L., & McCarthy, J. E. (1981). Prototype formation of faces: A case of pseudo-memory. *British Journal of Psychology, 72*, 499–503.

Sommers, M. S., & Huff, L. M. (2003). The effects of age and dementia of the Alzheimer's type on phonological false memories. *Psychology & Aging, 18*, 791–806.

Sommers, M. S., & Lewis, B. P. (1999). Who really lives next door: Creating false memories with phonological neighbors. *Journal of Memory & Language, 40*, 83–108.

Soraci, S. A., Carlin, M. T., Toglia, M. P., Chechile, R. A., & Neuschatz, J. S. (2003). Generative processing and false memories: When there is no cost. *Journal of Experimental Psychology: Learning, Memory, & Cognition, 29*, 511–523.

Stadler, M. A., Roediger, H. L. III, & McDermot, K. B. (1999). Norms for word lists that create false memories. *Memory & Cognition, 27*, 494–500.

Starns, J. J., & Hicks, J. L. (2004). Episodic generation can cause semantic forgetting: Retrieval-induced forgetting of false memories. *Memory & Cognition, 32*, 602–609.

Storbeck, J., & Clore, G. L. (2005). With sadness comes accuracy; with happiness, false memory. *Psychological Science, 16*, 785–791.

Sulin, R. A., & Dooling, D. J. (1974). Intrusion of a thematic idea in retention of prose. *Journal of Experimental Psychology, 103*, 255–262.

Summerfield, C., & Mangels, J. A. (2005). Functional coupling between frontal and parietal lobes during recognition memory. *NeuroReport, 16*, 117–122.

Tajika, H., Neumann, E., Hamajima, H., & Iwahara, A. (2005). Eliciting false memories on implicit and explicit memory tests after incidental learning. *Japanese Psychological Research, 47*, 31–39.

Thapar, A., & McDermot, K. B. (2001). False recall and false recognition induced by presentation of associated words: Effects of retention interval and level of processing. *Memory & Cognition, 29*, 424–432.

Thomas, A. K., & Sommers, M. S. (2005). Attention to item-specific processing eliminates age effects in false memories. *Journal of Memory & Language, 52*, 71–86.

Thomson, D. M., & Tulving, E. (1970). Associative encoding and retrieval: Weak and strong cues. *Journal of Experimental Psychology, 86*, 255–262.

Toglia, M. P., Neuschatz, J. S., & Goodwin, K. A. (1999). Recall accuracy and illusory memories: When more is less. *Memory, 7*, 233–256.

Treisman, A., & Schmidt, H. (1982). Illusory conjunctions in the perception of objects. *Cognitive Psychology, 14*, 107–141.

Tse, C., & Neely, J. H. (2005). Assesing activation without source monitoring in the DRM false memory paradigm. *Journal of Memory & Language, 53*, 532–550.

Tulving, E. (1968). Theoretical issues in free recall. In T. R. Dixon & D. L. Horton (Eds.), *Verbal behavior and general behavior theory* (pp. 2–36). Englewood Cliffs, NJ: Prentice-Hall.

Tulving, E. (1972). Episodic and semantic memory. In E. Tulving & W. Donaldson (Eds.), *Organization of memory* (pp. 381–403). New York, NY: Academic Press.

Tulving, E. (1983). *Elements of episodic memory*. Oxford, England: Clarendon Press.

Tulving, E. (1985). Memory and consciousness. *Canadian Psychologist, 26*, 1–12.

Tulving, E., & Bower, G. H. (1974). The logic of memory representations. In G. H. Bower (Ed.), *The psychology of learning and motivation* (Vol. 8, pp. 265–301). San Diego, CA: Academic Press.

Tulving, E., & Madigan, S. A. (1970). Memory and verbal learning. *Annual Review of Psychology, 21*, 437–484.

Tulving, E., & Thomson, D. M. (1973). Encoding specificity and retrieval processes in episodic memory. *Psychological Review, 80*, 359–380.

Tun, P. A., Wingfield, A., Rosen, M. J., & Blanchard, L. (1998). Response latencies for false memories: Gist-based processes in normal aging. *Psychology & Aging, 13*, 230–241.

Tussing, A. A., & Greene, R. L. (1997). False recognition of associates: How robust is the effect? *Psychonomic Bulletin & Review, 4*, 572–576.

Tussing, A. A., & Greene, R. L. (1999). Differential effects of repetition on true and false recognition. *Journal of Memory & Language, 40*, 520–533.

Umeda, S., Akine, Y., & Kato, M. (2001). False recognition in patients with ventromedial prefrontal lesions. *Brain & Cognition, 47*, 362–365.

Umeda, S., Akine, Y., Kato, M., Muramatsu, T., Mimura, M., Kandatsu, S., Tanada, S., Obata, T., Ikehira, H., & Suhara, T. (2005). Functional network in the prefrontal cortex during episodic memory retrieval. *NeuroImage, 26*, 932–940.

Underwood, B. J. (1965). False recognition produced by implicit verbal responses. *Journal of Experimental Psychology, 70*, 122–129.

Underwood, B. J. (1974). The role of the association in recognition memory. *Journal of Experimental Psychology, 102*, 917–939.

Underwood, B. J., Kapelak, S. M., & Malmi, R. A. (1976). Integration of discrete verbal units in recognition memory. *Journal of Experimental Psychology: Human Learning & Memory, 2*, 293–300.

Urbach, T. P., Windmann, S. S., Payne, D. G., & Kutas, M. (2005). Mistaking memories: Neural precursors of memory illusions in electrical brain activity. *Psychological Science, 16*, 19–24.

Verfaellie, M., Page, K., Orlando, F., & Schacter, D. L. (2005). Impaired implicit memory for gist information in amnesia. *Neuropsychology, 19*, 760–769.

Verfaellie, M., Rapcsak, S. Z., Keane, M. M., & Alexander, M. P. (2004). Elevated false recognition in patients with frontal lobe damage is neither a general nor a unitary phenomenon. *Neuropsychology, 18*, 94–103.

Verfaellie, M., Schacter, D. L., & Cook, S. P. (2002). The effects of retrieval instructions on false recognition: Exploring the nature of the gist memory impairment in amnesia. *Neuropsychologia, 40*, 2360–2368.

Vogt, J., & Kimble, G. A. (1973). False recognition as a function of associative proximity. *Journal of Experimental Psychology, 99*, 143–145.

Volkmar, F. R., Klin, A., Schultz, R., Bronen, R., Marans, W. D., Sparrow, S., & Cohen, D. J. (1996). Asperger's syndrome. *Journal of the American Academy of Child & Adolescent Psychiatry, 35*, 118–123.

Wagner, A. D, Gabrieli, J. D. E., & Verfaellie, M. (1997). Dissociations between familiarity processes in explicit recognition and implicit perceptual memory. *Journal of Experimental Psychology: Learning, Memory, & Cognition, 23*, 305–323.

Waldie, B. D., & Kwong See, S. T. (2003). Remembering words never presented: False memory effects in dementia of the Alzheimer type. *Aging, Neuropsychology, & Cognition, 10*, 281–297.

Wallace, W. P. (1967). False recognition produced by laboratory-established associative responses. *Psychonomic Science, 7*, 139–140.

Wallace, W. P. (1968). Incidental learning: The influence of associative similarity and formal similarity in producing false recognition. *Journal of Verbal Learning & Verbal Behavior, 7*, 50–54.

Wallace, W. P., Malone, C. P., Swiergosz, M. J., & Amberg, M. D. (2000). On the generality of false recognition reversal. *Journal of Memory & Language, 43*, 561–575.

Watson, J. M., Balota, D. A., & Roediger, H. L. III. (2003). Creating false memories with hybrid lists of semantic and phonological associates: Over-additive false memories produced by converging associative networks. *Journal of Memory & Language, 49*, 95–118.

Watson, J. M., Balota, D. A., & Sergent-Marshall, S. D. (2001). Semantic, phonological, and hybrid veridical and false memories in healthy older adults and in individuals with dementia of the Alzheimer type. *Neuropsychology, 15*, 254–268.

Watson, J. M., Bunting, M. F., Poole, B. J., & Conway, A. R. A. (2005). Individual differences in susceptibility to false memory in the Deese-Roediger-McDermott paradigm. *Journal of Experimental Psychology: Learning, Memory, & Cognition, 31*, 76–85.

Watson, J. M., McDermott, K. B., & Balota, D. A. (2004). Attempting to avoid false memories in the Deese/Roediger-McDermott paradigm: Assessing the combined influence of practice and warnings in young and old adults. *Memory & Cognition, 32*, 135–141.

Weiss, A. P., Dodson, C. S., Goff, D. C., Schacter, D. L., & Heckers, S. (2002). Intact suppression of increased false recognition in schizophrenia. *American Journal of Psychiatry, 159*, 1506–1513.

Wenzel, A., Jostad, C., Brendle, J. R., Ferraro, F. R., & Lystad, C. M. (2004). An investigation of false memories in anxious and fearful individuals. *Behavioral & Cognitive Psychotherapy, 32*, 257–274.

Westerberg, C. E., & Marsolek, C. J. (2003a). Hemispheric asymmetries in memory processes as measured in a false recognition paradigm. *Cortex, 39*, 627–642.

Westerberg, C. E., & Marsolek, C. J. (2003b). Sensitivity reductions in false recognition: A measure of false memories with stronger theoretical implications. *Journal of Experimental Psychology: Learning, Memory, & Cognition, 29*, 747–759.

Wheeler, M. E., Petersen, S. E., & Buckner, R. L. (2000). Memory's echo: Vivid remembering reactivates sensory-specific cortex. *Proceedings of the National Academy of Sciences, 97*, 11125–11129.

Whittlesea, B. W. A. (2002). False memory and the discrepancy-attribution hypothesis: The prototype-familiarity illusion. *Journal of Experimental Psychology: General, 131*, 96–115.

Whittlesea, B. W., Masson, M. E. J., & Hughes, A. D. (2005). False memory following rapidly presented lists: The element of surprise. *Psychological Research, 69*, 420–430.

Whittlesea, B. W. A., & Williams, L. D. (1998). Why do strangers feel familiar, but friends don't? A discrepancy-attribution account of feelings of familiarity. *Acta Psychologica, 98*, 141–165.

Wickens, T. D., & Hirshman, E. (2000). False memories and statistical decision theory: Comment on Miller and Wolford (1999) and Roediger and McDermott (1999). *Psychological Review, 107*, 377–383.

Wilding, E. L. (1999). Separating retrieval strategies from retrieval success: An event-related potential study of source memory. *Neuropsychologia, 37*, 441–454.

Wilkinson, C., & Hyman, I. E. Jr. (1998). Individual differences related to two types of memory errors: Word lists may not generalize to autobiographical memory. *Applied Cognitive Psychology, 12*, S29–S46.

Winograd, E. (1968). List differentiation as a function of frequency and retention interval. *Journal of Experimental Psychology, 76*, 1–18.

Winograd, E., Peluso, J. P., & Glover, T. A. (1998). Individual differences in susceptibility to memory illusions. *Applied Cognitive Psychology, 12*, S5–S27.

Wixted, J. T. (2004). The psychology and neuroscience of forgetting. *Annual Review of Psychology, 55*, 235–269.

Wixted, J. T., & Stretch, V. (2000). The case against a criterion-shift account of false memory. *Psychological Review, 107*, 368–376.

Wright, D. B., Mathews, S. A., & Skagerberg, E. M. (2005a). Social recognition memory: The effect of other people's responses for previously seen and unseen items. *Journal of Experimental Psychology: Applied, 11*, 200–209.

Wright, D. B., Startup, H. M., & Mathews, S. A. (2005b). Mood, dissociation and false memories using the Deese-Roediger-McDermott procedure. *British Journal of Psychology, 96*, 283–293.

Yonelinas, A. P. (1997). Recognition memory ROCs for item and associative information: The contribution of recollection and familiarity. *Memory & Cognition, 25*, 747–763.

Yonelinas, A. P. (2001). Consciousness, control, and confidence: The three Cs of recognition memory. *Journal of Experimental Psychology: General, 130*, 361–379.

Yonelinas, A. P. (2002). The nature of recollection and familiarity: A review of 30 years of research. *Journal of Memory & Language, 46*, 441–517.

Zaki, S. R., Nosofsky, R. M., Stanton, R. D., & Cohen, A. L. (2003). Prototype and exemplar accounts of category learning and attentional allocation: A reassessment. *Journal of Experimental Psychology: Learning, Memory, & Cognition, 29*, 1160–1173.

Zeelenberg, R., Boot, I., & Peecher, D. (2005). Activating the critical lure during study is unnecessary for false recognition. *Consciousness & Cognition, 14*, 316–326.

Zeelenberg, R., & Pecher, D. (2002). False memories and lexical decision: Even twelve primes do not cause long-term semantic priming. *Acta Psychologica, 109*, 269–284.

Zeelenberg, R., Plomp, G., Raaijmakers, J. G. W. (2003). Can false memories be created through nonconscious processes? *Consciousness & Cognition, 12*, 403–412.

Zoellner, L. A., Foa, E. B., Brigidi, B. D., & Przeworski, A. (2000). Are trauma victims susceptible to "false memories"? *Journal of Abnormal Psychology, 109*, 517–524.

Author Index

Subject Index

A

absorption, 166
abuse, 160, 165–170, 172
activation-monitoring framework, 23, 98
aging effects, 116, 124, 160, 177, 184–202, 213, 217–218, 224, 248–250
alcohol effects, *see* drug effects
alcohol expectancies, 174–176
alcoholics, 203, 220, *see also* Korsakoff's syndrome, alcohol expectancies
alien abduction, 100, 160, 170–172
Alzheimer's disease, 124, 203, 212–220, 247–248, 250
amnesia, 203–219, 222–225, 247–248, *see also* medial temporal lobe patients, drug induced amnesia
anxiety, 141, 166, 168, 222
Asperger's syndrome, 203, 221
autism, *see* Asperger's syndrome
autobiographical memory, 82, 159, 161–162, 164, 245, 248, 250
association norms, 19–28, 57, 181
associative activation, 10, 14, 21, 39, 50–73, 80, 91–98, 131–137, 142–143, 207, 244, 247
associative recognition, 15, 99, 104

associative strength, 10, 19–20, 51–52, 57–61, 70–72, 94–95, 131, 153, 155, 179–180, 247
attributional framework, 5, 93–97, 105, 127–129, 250, *see also* source monitoring

B

backward associative strength, 19–20, 57–61, *see also* associative strength
behaviorism, 7–12, *see also* S→R psychology
blocking effects, *see* study blocking effects, test blocking effects
brain hemisphere effects, 203, 231–232, 242–243

C

categorization, 35, 53–56, 134, *see also* categorized lists
categorized lists, 59–60, 69, 82, 95, 100–103, 116, 153–154, 181, 191, 199–201, 208, 211, 217, 228, 233–235, 237
circadian rhythms, 189
collaborative recall, 154–155
concreteness, 40, 58, 105, 119–120, 134, 140

285